Teaching Language Online

Practical and accessible, this book comprehensively covers everything you need to know to design, develop, and deliver successful online, blended, and flipped language courses. Grounded in the principles of instructional design and communicative language teaching, this book serves as a compendium of best practices, research, and strategies for creating learner-centered online language instruction that builds students' proficiency within meaningful cultural contexts. This book addresses important topics such as finding and optimizing online resources and materials, learner engagement, teacher and student satisfaction and connectedness, professional development, and online language assessment.

Teaching Language Online features:

- A step-by-step guide aligned with the American Council on the Teaching of Foreign Languages (ACTFL), the Common European Framework of Reference (CEFR) for Languages: Learning, Teaching and Assessment, and the World-Class Instructional Design and Assessment (WIDA) standards
- Research-based best practices and tools to implement effective communicative language teaching (CLT) online
- Strategies and practices that apply equally to world languages and ESL/EFL contexts
- Key takeaway summaries, discussion questions, and suggestions for further reading in every chapter
- Free, downloadable eResources with further readings and more materials available at www.routledge.com/9781138387003

As the demand for language courses in online or blended formats grows, K-16 instructors urgently need resources to effectively transition their teaching online. Designed to help world language instructors, professors, and K-12 language educators regardless of their level of experience with online learning, this book walks through the steps to move from the traditional classroom format to effective, successful online teaching environments.

Victoria Russell is Professor of Spanish and Foreign Language Education and Coordinator of Online Programs in the Department of Modern and Classical Languages at Valdosta State University, USA.

Kathryn Murphy-Judy is Associate Professor of French and Coordinator of Languages in the School of World Studies at Virginia Commonwealth University (VCU), USA. She also directs the Liberal Studies for Early and Elementary Education Program in the VCU College of Humanities and Sciences.

Teaching Language Online

A Guide for Designing, Developing, and Delivering Online, Blended, and Flipped Language Courses

VICTORIA RUSSELL AND KATHRYN MURPHY-JUDY

Routledge
Taylor & Francis Group

NEW YORK AND LONDON

First published 2021
by Routledge
52 Vanderbilt Avenue, New York, NY 10017

and by Routledge
2 Park Square, Milton Park, Abingdon, Oxon, OX14 4RN

Routledge is an imprint of the Taylor & Francis Group, an informa business

© 2021 Taylor & Francis

The right of Victoria Russell and Kathryn Murphy-Judy to be identified as authors of this work has been asserted by them in accordance with sections 77 and 78 of the Copyright, Designs and Patents Act 1988.

Library of Congress Cataloging-in-Publication Data
Names: Russell, Victoria, author. | Murphy-Judy,
Kathryn, author.
Title: Teaching language online : A guide for designing, developing, and delivering online, blended, and flipped language courses / Victoria Russell and Kathryn Murphy-Judy.
Description: New York : Routledge, 2020. | Includes bibliographical references and index.
Identifiers: LCCN 2020010729 (print) | LCCN 2020010730 (ebook) | ISBN 9781138386983 (hardback) | ISBN 9781138387003 (paperback) | ISBN 9780429426483 (ebook)
Subjects: LCSH: Language and languages--Computer-assisted instruction. | Language and languages--Study and teaching--Computer network resources.
Classification: LCC P53.28 .R87 2020 (print) | LCC P53.28 (ebook) | DDC 418.0071--dc23
LC record available at https://lccn.loc.gov/2020010729
LC ebook record available at https://lccn.loc.gov/2020010730

ISBN: 9781138386983 (hbk)
ISBN: 9781138387003 (pbk)
ISBN: 9780429426483 (ebk)

Typeset in Bembo and Gill Sans
by Cenveo® Publisher Services

Visit the eResources: www.routledge.com/9781138387003

This book is dedicated to our families and friends who have supported us throughout this project and to our colleagues in the ACTFL Distance Learning SIG, CALICO, the NFLRC, CARLA, CASLS, and COERLL, among so many others, and of course, to our online students, without whom none of this would be possible.

Brief Contents

Contents

List of Figures

List of Tables

eResources

We have included with this book many references to organizations, programs, and websites that provide supplemental support and useful resources for effective online language teaching, from inception to implementation. We have gathered the links to these helpful resources in a single place, accessible on the book's product page. Whenever a site is available as an eResource, the eResource logo will appear next to where it is mentioned in the text.

You can access these links by visiting the book product page on our website: www.routledge.com/9781138387003. Click on the tab that says "Support Material," and select the document. The document with links is organized by chapter.

Chapter I Links

Learning Management Systems (LMS):

A list of over 400 Learning Management Systems and distance learning platforms can be found here with a filter for mobile or desktop deployment: https://elearningindustry.com/directory/software-categories/learning-management-systems

Specific Providers:
Blackboard: https://www.blackboard.com/ (institutional Blackboard sites will have their own address)

The open Blackboard LMS: https://www.blackboard.com/blackboard-open-lms.

Canvas: https://www.instructure.com/canvas/ (Note the mother company is called Instructure)

CourseSites (part of the Blackboard brand): https://coursesites.com/

D2L Brightspace: https://www.d2l.com/products/ (institutional D2L sites will have their own address)

Edmodo: https://new.edmodo.com/

Google Classroom: https://edu.google.com/products/classroom/

Course Builder: https://edu.google.com/openonline/course-builder/index.html

G Suite for Education: https://edu.google.com/products/gsuite-for-education

Google Course Kit: https://edu.google.com/assignments/ (an add-on for assignments)

Moodle: https://moodle.com/

Sakai: https://www.sakailms.org/ (institutional Sakai sites will have their own address)

Schoology: https://www.schoology.com/ (for K12)

MOOC Platforms:

The LangMOOC report on language MOOCs in Europe: https://www.langmooc.com/wp-content/uploads/2016/03/REPORT-LangMOOCs-O2-_V3.pdf

A list of MOOCs: https://www.mooc-list.com/initiatives-and-categories

MOOC Aggregators:
Class central: https://www.class-central.com/

EMMA: http://platform.europeanmoocs.eu/

Federica/EMMA ITALY: http://www.federica.eu/mooc

MOOCs.co: http://www.moocs.co/

My education path: http://myeducationpath.com/courses/

OERU: http://oeru.org/how-it-works/

OpenCourseWare Consortium: http://www.ocwconsortium.org/courses

OpenupEd: http://www.openuped.eu/

Specific MOOC Providers of Language or Language Related Courses
Alison IRELAND: https://www.alison.com

Canvas: https://www.canvas.net/?query=foreign%20languages

Class-central: https://www.class-central.com/subject/foreign-language

Coursera: https://www.coursera.org/browse/language-learning/other-languages
COURSEsites Open Education Platform USA: https://www.coursesites.com/
Education Portal=Study.com USA: https://study.com/academy/subj/foreign-language.html
ED-X: https://www.edx.org/learn/language
FUN Mooc: https://www.fun-mooc.fr/
Future learn (Open University): https://www.futurelearn.com/subjects/language-courses
FutureLearn UK: https://www.futurelearn.com/subjects/language-courses
Iversity GERMANY: https://iversity.org/
Miriada X: https://miriadax.net/home (offers Latin, Spanish, English, Portuguese)
The Mixxer USA: http://www.language-exchanges.org/node/106803
MOOC.org: https://www.edx.org/course/?subject=Language
Of Course: https://www.ofcourse.co.uk/category/languages
OpenClassrooms: https://openclassrooms.com/ (offers technical and professional learning in English, French, and Spanish)
Open EdX—Lagunita USA: https://www.edx.org/course/subject/language
Open Initiative (OLI) Learning US: https://oli.cmu.edu/product-category/language/
Open2Study/class central AUSTRALIA: https://www.open.edu.au/online-courses/subjects?keyword=languages
Saylor.org USA: http://www.saylor.org/
Shayam in India: https://swayam.gov.in/
TandemMOOC SPAIN: http://mooc.speakapps.org
Udemy.com USA: https://www.udemy.com
Xuetangx in China: https://next.xuetangx.com/

Standards, Protocols, Checklists for Quality Online Courses and Modules:

University of Geneva instructional design methods: http://edutechwiki.unige.ch/en/Instructional_design_method
California State University, Chico—Rubric for Online Instruction: http://www.csun.edu/sites/default/files/QOLT_Flyer.pdf
COIL Checklist for Online Interactive Learning: http://www.westga.edu/~distance/ojdla/summer72/tobin72.html
Connect Thinking Checklist: https://connectthinking.com.au/wp-content/uploads/2018/01/ELearning_quality_checklist_ConnectThinking2013.pdf

Going Hybrid: A How-To Manual (University of Colorado, Boulder): https://tinyurl.com/goinghybridatcu

Illinois Online (click the Instructional Design arrow for the full list): http://www.ion.uillinois.edu/initiatives/qoci/webrubric/webexample.asp

iNACOL (now called the Aurora Institute): https://aurora-institute.org/wp-content/uploads/national-standards-for-quality-online-courses-v2.pdf

Minnesota State University: https://www.mnstate.edu/uploadedFiles/Level_2/Content/Instructional_Technology_Services/Teaching-Learning/Online CourseDesignChecklist.pdf

MOILLE: Table 5. MOILLE based Questionnaire: https://www.langmooc.com/wp-content/uploads/2016/03/REPORT-LangMOOCs-O2-_V3.pdf

Quality Matters: https://www.qualitymatters.org/sites/default/files/PDFs/StandardsfromtheQMHigherEducationRubric.pdf

SREB (a checklist for evaluating online courses): http://publications.sreb.org/2006/06T06_Checklist_for_Evaluating-Online-Courses.pdf

University of Hawai'i , Mānoa, Center for Language and Technology—Quality Guidelines: http://clt.manoa.hawaii.edu/wp-content/uploads/2013/12/QualityGuidelines20131217.pdf

Mixed QM & UDL standards checklist: https://cpb-us-west-2-juc1ugur1qwqqqo4.stackpathdns.com/wp.towson.edu/dist/0/521/files/2018/03/UDLQMChecklist-13dmvza.pdf

Survey of several online learning delivery systems (MOOCS, Podcasts, Online courses, etc.): https://tech.ed.gov/wp-content/uploads/2014/11/Section-5-Online-Professional-Learning-Quality-Checklist-FINAL.pdf

Regulatory Bodies for Online Educational Delivery:

C-RAC—Council of Regional Accrediting Commissions (handbook): https://www2.ed.gov/admins/finaid/accred/accreditation-handbook.pdf

NC-SARA—National Council for State Authorization Reciprocity Agreements. Student questionnaire: https://www.nc-sara.org/student-questions

Western Interstate Commission for Higher Education offers its Online Course Exchange at: https://www.wiche.edu/ice/about/stakeholders/administrators

Creation Tools and Add-Ons:

List of 10 platforms with descriptions: https://www.techradar.com/news/best-online-learning-platform

Atomic Curriculum Tools add-on for Canvas LMS: https://products.ato
micjolt.com/atomic-apps-canvas/atomic-curriculum-tools/
DesignPLUS product from CIDI Labs: https://cidilabs.com/landing/design-
tools/
eLearning Industry: https://elearningindustry.com/directory/software-catego
ries/learning-management-systems
Google Open Online: https://edu.google.com/openonline/
LearnDash: https://www.learndash.com/
Ted-Ed: https://ed.ted.com/videos

Accessibility, Usability, Inclusivity, and UDL:

Accessibility Tool Kit: https://assets.techsmith.com/docs/Accessibility-
Assessment-Toolkit.pdf
ADA Compliance for online courses from EDUCAUSE: https://www
.washington.edu/doit/20-tips-teaching-accessible-online-course
Blackboard Ally: https://www.blackboard.com/teaching-learning/accessibility-
universal-design/blackboard-ally-lms
CIDI Labs DesignPLUS: https://cidilabs.com/landing/design-tools/
Universal Design for Learning Guidelines: http://udlguidelines.cast.org
University of Washington tips for accessibility: https://www.washington.edu/
doit/20-tips-teaching-accessible-online-course
WCAG web content accessibility: https://www.w3.org/WAI/standards-guid
elines/wcag/
WCAG 2.1 quick reference guide here: https://www.w3.org/WAI/WCA
G21/quickref/

Proctoring:

Examity: https://examity.com
Honorlock: https://honorlock.com
Pearson Vue: https://home.pearsonvue.com
ProctorU: https://www.proctoru.com includes ProctorU Auto
Proctorio: https://proctorio.com

Major Institutional Online Language Programs:

Arizona State University "Ocourses": https://go.asuonline.asu.edu/
Arizona State University on-campus major with some online courses: https://
asuonline.asu.edu/online-degree-programs/

Athabasca University (Canada) for English, French, and Spanish programs and courses: https://www.athabascau.ca/course/course-listings.php?/undergraduate/humanities/all
California University of Pennsylvania program in Arabic: https://www.calu.edu/academics/undergraduate/bachelors/arabic-language-and-culture/index.aspx
Carnegie Mellon University's Open Learning Initiative: https://oli.cmu.edu/
Languages: https://oli.cmu.edu/product-category/language/
The Open University, online language program and courses: http://www.openuniversity.edu/iswcourses/programmes/subjects/language-degrees
Oregon State University with programs in French, German, & Spanish and minors that include Chinese, Japanese, Korean, Italian and ASL: https://ecampus.oregonstate.edu/online-degrees/undergraduate/foreign-languages/
University of Maryland University College online language programs and courses: https://www.umgc.edu/academic-programs/liberal-arts-and-communications/foreign-languages.cfm
Valdosta State University, French and Spanish with two tracks each: https://www.valdosta.edu/programs/a/humanities-and-communication-studies/
William Woods University program in American Sign Language: https://www.williamwoods.edu/academics/online/transfer/asl_degree.html

Online K-12 Schools in the United States:

ACCESS Distance Learning (Alabama): https://accessdl.state.al.us/
Virtual Arkansas: https://virtualarkansas.org/
Florida Virtual School (FLVS): https://www.flvs.net/
Georgia Virtual School (GAVS) : https://gavirtualschool.org/
Kentucky Virtual Campus for K-12: http://www.kyvc4k12.org/
Louisiana Course Choice: http://www.louisianacoursechoice.net/
Maryland Virtual Learning Opportunities Program: https://sites.google.com/site/mdvirtuallearningopportunities/
Mississippi Virtual Public School (MVPS): https://www.connectionsacademy.com/mississippi-school
North Carolina Virtual Public School (NCVPS): http://www.ncvps.org/
South Carolina Virtual School Program (SCVSP): https://virtualsc.org/
Texas Virtual School Network (TxVSN): https://www.txvsn.org/
Virtual Virginia: https://www.virtualvirginia.org/
West Virginia Virtual School (WVVS): http://wvde.state.wv.us/vschool/

Resources for Training On Tools, Apps, and Software (for Students and Instructors):

General:
Hoonuit (formerly Atomic Learning and Versifit Technologies): https://hoonuit.com/atomic-learning-versifit-technologies-are-now-hoonuit/
LinkedIn Learning (formerly Lynda.com): https://www.lynda.com/subject/all

For Various Apps and Online Services:
Boomalang: https://www.boomalang.co/blog/my-boomalang-experience-from-a-nervous-student-to-a-confident-speaker-guest
Extempore: https://extemporeapp.com/extempore-user-guides-and-instructional-videos/
FlipGrid: https://static.flipgrid.com/docs/Flipgrid_foreign_language.pdf
GoReact: https://help.goreact.com/hc/en-us/articles/360003174051
Padlet: https://jn.padlet.com/category/6-posting (post of what online students do)
TalkAbroad: https://support.talkabroad.com/article/6-student-instruction-manual
VoiceThread: https://rutgers.instructure.com/courses/35/pages/voicethread?module_item_id=4877 (a nicely illustrated how-to from Rutgers University)
Zoom: https://support.zoom.us/hc/en-us/articles/201362193-Joining-a-Meeting

Other Sites and Utilities Mentioned:

CARLA Programs and Research on Assessment: https://carla.umn.edu/assessment/vac/CreateUnit/p_1.html
ACTFL Performance Descriptors for Language Learners: https://cms.azed.gov/home/GetDocumentFile?id=5748a47daadebe04c0b66e64
CASLS Guide to LinguaFolio Online: https://lfonetwork.uoregon.edu/wp-content/uploads/sites/5/2019/01/Teacher-Welcome-Packet-4.zip

Chapter 2 Links

Basic Tools for Online Course Design, Development, and Delivery:

Kent State University: https://www.kent.edu/onlineteaching/resources
Yale University:https://cls.yale.edu/faculty/resources/online-teaching-tools-and-resources

Valdosta State University: https://www.valdosta.edu/celt/resources.php
Virginia Commonwealth University:https://ctle.vcu.edu/resources/teaching-guides/
7 Tips to create effective visual communication for elearning: https://www.flearningstudio.com/effective-visual-communication-in-elearning/
The TED-Ed simple platform for creating and sharing online lessons: https://ed.ted.com
Course development checklist from Minnesota State University: https://www.mnstate.edu/uploadedFiles/Level_2/Content/Instructional_Technology_Services/Teaching-Learning/OnlineCourseDesignChecklist.pdf

Approaches:

CASLS Blended unit planner: https://lfonetwork.uoregon.edu/wp-content/uploads/sites/5/2015/09/Blended-unit-planner-final-1.0.pdf
Digital Storytelling (see more in Chapter 3): https://www.emergingedtech.com/2017/04/digital-storytelling-for-the-language-learning classroom/ and https://www.scribd.com/doc/79101242/10-Digital-Storytelling-Projects
Project Based Language Learning: http://nflrc.hawaii.edu/projects/view/2014A/
Question Formulation Technique: https://rightquestion.org/what-is-the-qft/
Webquests: http://zunal.com/process.php?w=21401

Finding Resources and Authentic Materials:

Museums, Libraries, Archives for Locating Authentic Materials and Ready-Made Lessons:
Bibliothèque Nationale: https://www.bnf.fr/fr
Google Arts & Culture: https://artsandculture.google.com/
J. Paul Getty Museum: https://www.getty.edu/education/teachers/classroom_resources/
Le Louvre: https://www.louvre.fr/en/visites-en-ligne
National Gallery of Art: https://www.nga.gov/education/learningresources.html
Ohio State University Spanish Dialects Archive: http://dialectos.osu.edu
Rijks Museum: https://artsandculture.google.com/partner/rijksmuseum
San Francisco Museum of Art: https://www.sfmoma.org/teacher-resources/
Uffizi Gallery: https://artsandculture.google.com/partner/uffizi-gallery
VMFA: http://vmfa-resources.org/

Media Outlets with Language Learning Facilities:
Asia Society (https://asiasociety.org/): https://asiasociety.org/china-learning-initiatives/teq-instructional-videos-chinese-language-teaching

BBC language education:
  http://www.bbc.co.uk/languages/french/
  http://www.bbc.co.uk/languages/german/
  http://www.bbc.co.uk/languages/spanish/
  http://www.bbc.co.uk/languages/chinese/
  http://www.bbc.co.uk/languages/italian/
  http://www.bbc.co.uk/languages/portuguese/
  http://www.bbc.co.uk/languages/greek/
  http://www.bbc.co.uk/languages/polish/
  http://www.bbc.co.uk/languages/other/quickfix/arabic.shtml
  32 other LCTLs: http://www.bbc.co.uk/languages/other/quickfix/
Canadian government site: https://www.noslangues-ourlanguages.gc.ca/
en/index
Deutsche Welle:
  French lessons:
  https://www.dw.com/en/learn-german/mission-paris-episodes/s-9836
  German lessons:
  https://www.dw.com/en/learn-german/s-2469
  https://twitter.com/dw_learngerman
  https://www.dw.com/en/learn-german/deutsch-interaktiv/s-9572
  https://www.dw.com/en/learn-german/mission-europe/s-9831
Language Portal of Canada: http://www.noslangues-ourlanguages.gc.ca/
Radio France Internationale (RFI): https://savoirs.rfi.fr/en/apprendre-enseigner
TED talks (in target languages and/or with TL transcripts): https://www
.ted.com/
TV5 (France): https://langue-francaise.tv5monde.com/decouvrir

Screencapturing and Screencasting:

Adobe Captivate: https://www.adobe.com/products/captivate.html
Camtasia: https://www.techsmith.com/video-editor.html
Grab (Apple): pre-OS Catalina https://support.apple.com/guide/grab/
welcome/mac
Jing: https://www.techsmith.com/jing-tool.html
QuickTime: support.apple.com › quicktime
Screencast-o-matic: https://screencast-o-matic.com
Screenshot (Apple): (OS Catalina 10.15+) https://support.apple.com/en-us/
HT201361
SnagIt: https://www.techsmith.com/screen-capture.html
Windows (simple screenshot): Ctrl + Print Screen (Print Scrn)

Tools for Interaction:

Various tools: https://designingoutcomes.com/assets/PadWheelV4/PadWheel_Poster_V4.pdf
Google Forms plus Flubaroo: http://www.flubaroo.com/hc/quizzes-in-google-forms
Hot Potatoes: https://hotpot.uvic.ca/
H5P: https://h5p.org/
Jane Hart's Center for Learning & Performance: http://c4lpt.co.uk/
Mentimeter: https://www.mentimeter.com/
NearPod: https://nearpod.com/
NFLRC PLN: https://clt.manoa.hawaii.edu/pln
SoftChalk: https://softchalk.com/
Twine: https://twinery.org/

Virtual Exchanges:

Tandem exchanges:
COIL: http://coil.suny.edu/
Class2Class: https://class2class.com/
The MiXXer: https://www.language-exchanges.org/
Soliya: https://www.soliya.net/
UniCollaboration: https://www.unicollaboration.org/
WeSpeke: https://www.linkedin.com/company/wespeke

Conversation services (paid):
Boomalang: https://www.boomalang.co/
LinguaMeeting: https://www.linguameeting.com/
Linkr Education: https://www.linkreducation.com/en/
Talk Abroad: https://talkabroad.com/

VoIP tools and services (to set up exchanges after identifying partner):
Google Meet: https://tools.google.com/dlpage/hangoutplugin
Google Voice: https://voice.google.com/u/0/calls
Skype: https://www.skype.com/en/
Viber: https://www.viber.com/
WeChat: https://www.wechat.com/en/
Whatsapp: https://www.whatsapp.com

Other exchange tools (phone apps, chat services, gaming):
Augmented Reality and Interactive Storytelling (ARIS): https://fielddaylab .org/make/aris/
FlipGrid: https://info.flipgrid.com/
HelloTalk: https://www.hellotalk.com/?lang=en
Minecraft: https://www.minecraft.net/en-us/
Paris Occupé: https://sites.google.com/site/occupiedparisprofs/
Polar FLE with Inspector Roger Duflair: http://www.polarfle.com/
Second Life: https://secondlife.com/

Video Resources:

Video servers worldwide:
List of video sites like YouTube: http://l-lists.com/en/lists/r5l5dj.html
Aparat (Iranian): https://www.aparat.com/
Daily Motion: https://www.dailymotion.com/us
Globo (Brazil): https://globoplay.globo.com/
Instagram: https://www.instagram.com/
Internet Archive (choose by language): https://archive.org/details/movies
Iqiyi (China): https://www.iqiyi.com/
Kakao (Korean): https://tv.kakao.com/
Kanopy Film streaming services (institutional account): https://www.kanopy .com/
Lumière project (U.C. Berkeley): https://lumiere.berkeley.edu/
Myspace: https://myspace.com/
Nico Douga (Japanese): http://www.nicovideo.jp/
Open Video Project: https://open-video.org/
RuTube (Russian): https://rutube.ru/
TeacherTube (safe videos for K-12): https://www.teachertube.com/
Veblr (Indian): https://veblr.com/
Vidivodo (Turkish): http://www.vidivodo.com/
Vimeo: https://vimeo.com/
Vkontakte (Russian video and social network): https://vk.com/
Vimeo: https://vimeo.com
YinYueTai (Chinese music videos): http://www.yinyuetai.com/
Youku (Chinese): http://www.youku.com/
YouTube: https://www.youtube.com/

Video Conferencing/Virtual Classrooms:
Adobe Connect: https://www.adobe.com/products/adobeconnect.html
Blackboard Collaborate: https://www.blackboard.com/teaching-learning/colla
boration-web-conferencing/blackboard-collaborate
Google Meet: https://gsuite.google.com/products/chat/
Go-to-Meeting: https://www.gotomeeting.com/l
WebEx: https://cart.webex.com/
Zoom: https://zoom.us/

Video Production and Commentary:
Animoto: https://animoto.com/
Annotation Studio: https://www.annotationstudio.org/
Flixtime: https://www.videomaker.com/
Masher: https://www.masher.com/
WeVideo: https://www.wevideo.com/
Muvee: https://www.muvee.com/
Veo: https://www.veo.co/
Kaltura: https://videos.kaltura.com/
Panopto: https://www.panopto.com/
Camtasia: https://www.techsmith.com/video-editor.html
Video Review: https://www.techsmith.com/video-review.html
Adobe Rush (mobile): https://www.adobe.com/products/premiere-rush.
html

Other Tools for Interaction (Writing, Assessment, and Social reading)

Writing:
Adobe Spark: https://spark.adobe.com/
ARIS (Augmented Reality and Interactive Storytelling): https://fielddaylab
.org/make/aris/

Digital storytelling:
https://www.schrockguide.net/digital-storytelling.html

Assessment:
Extempore: https://extemporeapp.com/
Go React: https://get.goreact.com/

Kahoot: https://kahoot.com/
Mentimeter: https://www.mentimeter.com/
Poll Everywhere: https://www.polleverywhere.com/
Quizlet: https://quizlet.com/
Socrative: https://socrative.com/

Social Reading:
Annotator: http://annotatorjs.org/
Annotation Studio (MIT): https://www.annotationstudio.org/
Classroom Salon: http://www.corporatesalon.com/
eComma: https://ecomma.coerll.utexas.edu/about-ecomma/
eMargin: http://emargin.bcu.ac.uk/
Genius: https://genius.com/
Google Docs: https://www.google.com/docs/about/
Hypothes.is: https://web.hypothes.is/
Lacuna: https://www.lacunastories.com/
Marginalia: http://webmarginalia.net/
NowComment: https://nowcomment.com/
Perusall: https://perusall.com/
Ponder (browser add-on and iOS app): https://www.ponder.co/
Vialogues (video annotation): https://vialogues.com/

Chapter 3 Links

Authentic Video Resources:

This is Language (TIL): https://www.thisislanguage.com/
Yabla: https://www.yabla.com/

Can-Do Statements/Descriptors:

NCSSFL-ACTFL (2017) Can-Do Statements:
https://www.actfl.org/resources/ncssfl-actfl-can-do-statements
NCSSFL-ACTFL (2017) Intercultural Communication Novice-Distinguished
Can-Do Statements:
link:https://www.actfl.org/sites/default/files/can-dos/Intercultural%20
Can-Do_Statements.pdf
NCSSFL-ACTFL (2017) Intercultural Reflection Tool: https://www.actfl.org/
sites/default/files/can-dos/Intercultural%20Can-Dos_Reflections%20Scenarios
.pdf

WIDA (2016) K-12 Can Do Descriptors, Key Uses Edition: https://wida .wisc.edu/teach/can-do/descriptors

Conversation Platforms:

En Vivo: https://www.wiley.com/college/sc/envivo/
LinguaMeeting: https://www.linguameeting.com/
Speaky: https://www.speaky.com/
TalkAbroad: www.Talkabroad.com
WeSpeke: http://en-us.wespeke.com/index.html

Digital Storytelling:

Digital storytelling examples (CARLA): https://carla.umn.edu/technology/ modules/storytelling/examples.html
How to create a digital story (CARLA): https://carla.umn.edu/technology/ modules/storytelling/create.html
Digital Storytelling preparation activities (CARLA): https://carla.umn.edu/ technology/modules/storytelling/activities.html
How to assess a digital story: https://carla.umn.edu/technology/modules/ storytelling/discussion.html
PhotoStory 3 Download: https://www.microsoft.com/en-us/download/details .aspx?id=11132

Language Exchange Resources:

Italki: https://www.italki.com/partners
Language Exchange: https://en.language.exchange/
The Mixxer: https://www.language-exchanges.org/
14 Free Language Exchange Websites: https://www.lifewire.com/free- language-exchange-websites-1357059

Language Learning Resources and Materials:

CARLA Materials: http://carla.umn.edu/
COERLL Materials: http://coerll.utexas.edu/coerll/materials
LangMedia: https://langmedia.fivecolleges.edu/
MERLOT: https://www.merlot.org/merlot/index.htm
Today's Front Pages: http://www.newseum.org/todaysfrontpages/

Language Learning Standards, Performance Descriptors, and Proficiency Guidelines:

ACTFL 2012 Proficiency Guidelines: https://www.actfl.org/resources/actfl-proficiency-guidelines-2012
ACTFL 2015 Performance Descriptors for Language Learners: https://cms.azed.gov/home/GetDocumentFile?id=5748a47daadebe04c0b66e64
ACTFL & CAEP 2015 Program Standards for the Preparation of Foreign Language Teachers: https://www.actfl.org/sites/default/files/caep/ACTFLCAEPStandards2013_v2015.pdf
Council of Europe Common European Framework of Reference for Languages: Learning, Teaching, Assessment: https://rm.coe.int/CoERMPublicCommonSearchServices/DisplayDCTMContent?documentId=0900001680459f97
National Standards Collaborative Board World-Readiness Standards for Learning Languages (4th ed.): https://www.actfl.org/sites/default/files/publications/standards/World-ReadinessStandardsforLearningLanguages.pdf
NCSSFL-ACTFL 2017 Can Do Statements: https://www.actfl.org/resources/ncssfl-actfl-can-do-statements
WIDA 2012 Amplification of the English Language Development Standards Kindergarten–Grade 12: https://wida.wisc.edu/sites/default/files/resource/2012-ELD-Standards.pdf
WIDA 2018 Performance definitions: Listening and Reading grades K–12: https://wida.wisc.edu/sites/default/files/resource/Performance-Definitions-Receptive-Domains.pdf
WIDA 2018 Performance definitions: Speaking and Writing grades K–12: https://wida.wisc.edu/sites/default/files/resource/Performance-Definitions-Expressive-Domains.pdf

Online Collaboration Tools:

Lino: http://en.linoit.com/
Padlet: https://padlet.com/
Google Docs: https://www.google.com/docs/about/

Online Rubric Makers:

Annenberg Learner (Custom): http://www.learner.org/workshops/hswriting/interactives/rubric/
iRubric (Custom): https://www.rcampus.com/indexrubric.cfm?
RubiStar (Custom): http://rubistar.4teachers.org/index.php

Teachnology (Premade and Custom): https://www.teach-nology.com/web_tools/rubrics/
RubricMaker (Custom): https://rubric-maker.com/

Pragmatics-Focused Instruction:

CARLA (Methods): http://www.carla.umn.edu/speechacts/
CARLA (Japanese): http://www.carla.umn.edu/speechacts/japanese/introtospeechacts/index.htm
CARLA (Spanish): http://carla.umn.edu/speechacts/sp_pragmatics/home.html
COERLL (Methods): https://coerll.utexas.edu/methods/modules/pragmatics/
J. César Félix-Brasdefer (Spanish): http://www.indiana.edu/~discprag/index.html

Proficiency Testing:

Language Testing International (LTI): https://www.languagetesting.com/

Screen Capturing and/or Editing Tools:

Camtasia: https://www.techsmith.com/video-editor.html
Filmora: https://filmora.wondershare.com/
Jing: https://jing.en.softonic.com/?ex=REG-60.1
Screencast-O-Matic: https://screencast-o-matic.com/home
Snagit: https://www.techsmith.com/screen-capture.html

Student Curation:

Cool Tools for School: https://cooltoolsforschool.net/curation-tools/
WordPress: https://linkinglearning.wordpress.com/2015/03/06/digital-content-curation-a-vital-strategy-for-education/
Wakelet: https://wakelet.com/

Text Chat Platforms:

Bilingua: https://bilingua.io/
HelloTalk: https://www.hellotalk.com/#en
HiNative: https://hinative.com/
Tandem: https://www.tandem.net/

Voice Boards:

VoiceThread Home: https://voicethread.com/
VoiceThread Higher Education: https://voicethread.com/products/highered
VoiceThread K-12: https://voicethread.com/products/k12

Voice Recording Tools:

Audacity: https://www.audacityteam.org/
Online Voice Recorder: https://online-voice-recorder.com/
Vocaroo: https://vocaroo.com/

Chapter 4 Links

Basic Online Language Design and Delivery Collaboratory:

Home Page: https://sites.google.com/site/bolddcollaboratory/home
Workshops: https://sites.google.com/site/bolddcollaboratory/home/colla
boratory-panels-presentations

Center for Advanced Research on Language Acquisition (CARLA) at the University of Minnesota:

CARLA's Home Page: https://carla.umn.edu/
CARLA's Summer Institutes: https://carla.umn.edu/institutes/index.html
CARLA's Onsite Workshops: https://carla.umn.edu/presentations/index.html
CoBaLTT (CARLA): https://carla.umn.edu/cobaltt/index.html
CARLA's Wiki: http://carlatech.pbworks.com/w/page/15065374/FrontPage

Center for Language & Technology (CLT) at the University of Hawai'i at Mānoa:

Designing, Developing, and Teaching Online and Hybrid Technology Intensive Courses: https://clt.manoa.hawaii.edu/designing-developing-teaching-online-hti-course-resources/
Online Teaching Resources: https://clt.manoa.hawaii.edu/online-teaching-resources/
Projects: https://clt.manoa.hawaii.edu/project-listing/#current-projects

Center for Open Educational Resources and Language Learning (COERLL) at the University of Texas at Austin:

COERLL's Home Page: https://www.coerll.utexas.edu/coerll/
COERLL's Language Learning Resources: https://www.coerll.utexas.edu/coerll/materials/language-learning-materials
COERLL's Teaching Methods Resources: https://www.coerll.utexas.edu/coerll/materials/teaching-methods
COERLL's Open Education Resources: https://www.coerll.utexas.edu/coerll/materials/open-education

Computer-Assisted Language Instruction Consortium (CALICO):

Home Page: https://calico.org/
Conference: https://calico.org/calico-conference/
SIGs: https://calico.org/sigs/
CALICO Journal: https://journals.equinoxpub.com/index.php/CALICO
CALICO's Edited Book Series: https://calico.org/book-series/

EDUCAUSE:

Home Page: https://www.educause.edu/
Core Data Service Tool: https://www.educause.edu/research-and-publications/research/core-data-service

European Association of Computer-Assisted Language Learning:

Home page: http://www.eurocall-languages.org/
Conference: http://www.eurocall-languages.org/conference-homepage
The EuroCALL Review: https://polipapers.upv.es/index.php/eurocall/index
ReCall Journal: http://www.eurocall-languages.org/publications/recall-journal

International Association for Language Learning Technology (IALLT):

Home Page: https://iallt.org/about/
Regional Groups: https://iallt.org/about/regional-groups/
Conference: https://iallt.org/conferences/
IALLT Journal: https://journal.iallt.org/
FLTMAG: https://fltmag.com/

Mentoring Program for Online Language Teachers:

Application for ACTFL Mentoring Program: https://www.actfl.org/learn/
mentoring-program
ACTFL DL SIG / NFLRC Mentoring Program for Online Language Teachers:
http://nflrc.hawaii.edu/events/view/106/
Resources for the ACTFL DL SIG / NFLRC Mentoring Program for Online
Language Teachers: http://nflrc.hawaii.edu/events/view/105/

Multimedia Educational Resource for Learning and Online Teaching (MERLOT):

Home Page: https://www.merlot.org/merlot/
World Language Community: https://www.merlot.org/merlot/WorldLangu
ages.htm

National Foreign Language Resource Center (NFLRC) at the University of Hawai'i at Mānoa:

NFLRC Home Page: http://nflrc.hawaii.edu/
NFLRC Projects: http://nflrc.hawaii.edu/projects/
NFLRC Online Professional Development: http://nflrc.hawaii.edu/projects/
view/2014D/
NFLRC PEBBLES (Project-Based Language Learning Repository): http://
nflrc.hawaii.edu/projects/view/2014G/
NFLRC Project-Based Language Learning: http://nflrc.hawaii.edu/projects/
view/2014A/

North Carolina Virtual Public School (NCVPS):

Home Page: https://ncvps.org/

Online Learning Consortium (OLC):

Home Page: https://onlinelearningconsortium.org/
Online Teaching Certificate Programs: https://onlinelearningconsortium.org/
learn/teaching-certificates/

Other U.S. National Language Resource Centers:

Center for Advanced Language Proficiency Education and Research (CALPER): http://calper.la.psu.edu/

Center for Applied Second Language Studies (CASLS): https://casls.uoregon.edu/

Center for Educational Resources in Culture, Language, and Literacy (CERCLL): http://cercll.arizona.edu

Center for Languages of the Central Asian Region (CELCAR): https://celcar.indiana.edu/

Center for Urban Language Teaching and Research (CULTR): https://cultr.gsu.edu/

National African Language Resource Center (NALRC): https://nalrc.indiana.edu/

National East Asian Languages Resource Center (NEALRC): https://nealrc.osu.edu/

National Heritage Language Resource Center (NHLRC): https://nhlrc.ucla.edu/NHLRC/home

The Assessment and Evaluation Language Resource Center (AELRC): https://aelrc.georgetown.edu/

The Center for Slavic, Eurasian and East European Studies (CSEEES): https://slaviccenters.duke.edu/

The National Resource Center for Asian Languages (NRCAL): http://www.fullerton.edu/nrcal/

The Open Language Resource Center (OLRC): http://olrc.ku.edu/

Professionals in Education Advancing Research and Language Learning (PEARLL): http://www.pearll.nflc.umd.edu/

Second Language Teaching and Research Center (L2TReC): https://l2trec.utah.edu/

STARTALK:

Home Page: https://startalk.umd.edu/public/about

STARTALK Grant Application Information: https://startalk.umd.edu/sophie/#/app/home

Telecollaboration:

Telecollaboration Readings (CARLA): https://carla.umn.edu/technology/modules/cmc/readings.html

Telecollaboration Examples (CARLA): https://carla.umn.edu/technology/modules/cmc/examples.html
How to Create a Telecollaboration (CARLA): https://carla.umn.edu/technology/modules/cmc/create.html
Telecollaboration Resources (CARLA): https://carla.umn.edu/technology/modules/cmc/resources.html

WebQuests:

Overview of Webquests: https://webquest.org/
Search for Webquests: http://www.webquest.org/search/index.php
Information on Webquests: https://www.teachingenglish.org.uk/article/web quests
How to Create a Webquest (CARLA): https://carla.umn.edu/technology/modules/webquests/create.html

Chapter 5 Links:

ACTFL Performance Descriptors for Language Learners:

https://cms.azed.gov/home/GetDocumentFile?id=5748a47daadebe04c0b 66e64

CARLA's Integrated Performance Assessments (IPAs):

https://carla.umn.edu/assessment/vac/CreateUnit/p_2.html

Community of Inquiry:

Community of Inquiry (CoI) Website: https://coi.athabascau.ca/
Community of Inquiry (CoI) Survey: https://coi.athabascau.ca/coi-model/coi-survey/

Linguafolio Digital Portfolios:

Linguafolio: https://linguafolio.uoregon.edu/site/landing-page

NCSSFL-ACTFL Can-Do Statements:

https://www.actfl.org/resources/ncssfl-actfl-can-do-statements

Online Student Connectedness Survey (OSCS), available in the article below:

http://www.irrodl.org/index.php/irrodl/article/view/1171

Stock Photos and Videos:

Pexels Website: https://www.pexels.com/
Pexels' Licensing Agreement: https://www.pexels.com/photo-license/

Survey Tools:

Google Forms: https://www.google.com/forms/about/
SurveyMonkey: https://www.surveymonkey.com/

Word-Class Instructional Design and Assessment (WIDA) Resources:

WIDA K-12 Can Do Descriptors, Key Uses Edition: https://wida.wisc.edu/teach/can-do/descriptors
WIDA Performance Definitions for Speaking and Writing: https://wida.wisc.edu/sites/default/files/resource/Performance-Definitions-Expressive-Domains.pdf
WIDA Performance Definitions for Listening and Reading: https://wida.wisc.edu/sites/default/files/resource/Performance-Definitions-Receptive-Domains.pdf

Author Biographies

Victoria Russell, Ph.D., is a Professor of Spanish and Foreign Language Education at Valdosta State University (VSU). She has been a language educator for the past 30 years. Victoria earned a doctorate in Second Language Acquisition & Instructional Technology in 2009 after spending many years teaching at the middle, high school, and community college levels both in the United States and abroad. She began teaching Spanish online in 2007 and she currently serves as the Coordinator of Online Programs for the Department of Modern and Classical Languages at VSU, where she helped create fully online degree and certificate programs in Spanish, French, and TESOL, as well as online MAT programs in Foreign Language Education and English for Speakers of Other Languages. She has published in the areas of online language teaching and learning, world language teacher education, and Spanish pragmatics. She led the effort, with Dr. Kathryn Murphy-Judy and Dr. Julio C. Rodríguez, to create a national mentoring program for online language educators, she served as Chair of the American Council on the Teaching of Foreign Languages (ACTFL) Distance Learning Special Interest Group from 2015–2018, and she has given numerous national and international workshops and presentations on online language course design, development, and delivery.

Kathryn Murphy-Judy, Ph.D., has been teaching French for over 45 years. She has been working with computer-assisted language learning (CALL) since 1983. In 1997, she started teaching language online. She created first- and second-year online French courses at Virginia Commonwealth University in 2010–2011. She co-created the Basic Online Language Design and Delivery Collaboratory with colleagues from the Computer-Assisted Language Instruction Consortium (CALICO) and ACTFL in 2012. Dr. Murphy-Judy has given numerous workshops for teachers on the design and delivery of online language teaching and learning since 2012 in the United States, Canada, China, Colombia, Mexico, and Taiwan. She helped create the ACTFL Distance Learning Special Interest Group/National Foreign Language Resource Center (NFLRC) Mentoring Program for Online Language Teachers with Dr. Russell and Dr. Rodríguez of the NFLRC. She has also edited two volumes on CALL in the CALICO Monograph Series and has written many articles and chapters on her online and digital work.

Introduction

If you have opened this guidebook, you are likely looking for guidance in designing, developing, and delivering online language teaching. Even if you're a veteran classroom language teacher, you may not have had exposure to teaching in an online environment. And even if you do have experience integrating instructional technologies in your classroom, you may not know where or exactly how to start creating and delivering online learning for students of your language. Or, you may have some experience teaching online, but you want to learn new techniques that will improve your students' outcomes and experiences. Whichever your specific need for implementing language instruction online, you've come to the right place. It is important to note that this book will be helpful for teachers of all world languages, including those who teach English as a second or foreign language. Although we work in higher education in the United States, we have made every effort to be global in our exploration of practices and resources. We have also included plenty of resources and content for those who work in K-12 settings.

As the authors of this guide, we have many years of experience creating, teaching, researching, and giving hands-on workshops in the field of online language education. We are two markedly different educators/technologists with a healthy mix of knowledge, experiences, and styles that complement one another. We are similar in that we are both language teachers, language teacher educators, and we both have designed, developed, and delivered countless online language courses. Moreover, we are both grounded in the standards-based communicative language teaching principles and practices that underpin this guidebook. We have discovered through years of working together, first in the Basic Online Language Design and Delivery (BOLDD) Collaboratory, then in the American Council of Teachers of Foreign Languages (ACTFL) Distance Learning Special Interest Group (DL SIG), and now on this book, that our differing strengths and perspectives push us to rethink and reexamine our preexisting notions regarding online language education. Therefore, in this book we have managed to assemble a wealth of models, practices, and research that are expanded and enriched by our differences. Still, we have melded them into a single voice with a common mission: to share the best of what we know and what we do in language teaching online with you, our fellow language educators. We acknowledge the influence from the ideas of and collaborations with experts in computer-assisted language learning (CALL) whom we have met through BOLDD, ACTFL, the Computer-Assisted Language Instruction Consortium (CALICO), the International Association for Language Learning and Technology (IALLT), several of the national language resource centers (LRC), as well as our colleagues who are language educators from across the world. This guide is a compendium, then, of the research, strategies, practices, and materials that we have gathered over many years of working in this field. Throughout the writing process, we found ourselves having recourse to some of the very strategies and media for collaboration that we describe in these pages. We value multilingualism and interculturality, and the suggestions that we offer in this book will help you create a meaningful cultural context for language instruction, whether the delivery model is fully online, blended, or flipped. Our primary aim here is to respond to your needs for guidance by sharing what we know and do—teaching languages online.

A few definitions are in order. Online language pedagogy refers to knowledge of the pedagogy and the appropriate technologies to teach language online. At times, "te(a)chnologies" is used to describe the harmonious blend of sound language teaching and appropriate technologies that promote student learning. Sometimes we will refer to online teaching and learning as "eLearning," "distance learning," and "virtual learning," which are all occasionally used, although distance learning encompasses more delivery options than are covered here, like two-way live video instruction. We also address a variety of learning environments and delivery modes: "online," "hybrid" or "blended," "classroom," and "flipped." We use the Online Learning Consortium (OLC) definitions by Mayadas, Miller, and Sener (2015) who assert that "Online" or "eLearning" refers to: "[a]ll course activity … done online [with] no require-ments for on-campus activity" (p. 0). A blended or hybrid course—the two terms used synonymously in this guide—indicates "[o]nline activity [that] is mixed with classroom meetings, replacing a significant percentage, but not all required face-to-face instructional activities" (p. 0). A classroom course is one where "[c]ourse activity is organized around scheduled class meetings held onsite at an institution or another location" (p. 0). We also use the terms "tra-ditional," "brick-and-mortar," and "face-to-face" for campus-based classrooms. For flipped learning, we prefer the Flipped Learning Network (2014) defi-nition, which is "a pedagogical approach" that creates "a dynamic, interactive [group] learning environment" for learners to explore and apply concepts cre-atively with their teacher (p. 1). The teacher acts as a "guide on the side" for group sessions, all the while providing direct instruction for the learners in their individual learning spaces online (Flipped Learning Network, 2014, p. 1). As we explain and show various kinds of eLearning, we refer to them variously as "programs," "courses," "modules," and "lessons." Some of us design, develop, and deliver an entire program, which may include more than one course and may span various levels of instruction. Others create a single course composed of several modules. We use the generally accepted term "module" to refer to the units or blocks of instruction within a course that are based on an organizing set of learning objectives. For the smaller chunks of a unit of instruction, we use words like "lesson" or refer to them more generally as learning materials, activ-ities, or opportunities. Within individual chapters of this guide, terminologies specific to its content will be defined. When we teach language in an instruc-tional setting, most often there are at least two languages operating. We call the language of the school and its surrounding linguistic community the "L1" for "first language." Sometimes, we will call it the "home" or "native" language. For the language we teach, we generally write "L2," for "second language," but we may also call it the "target language." We occasionally use the term "affordance" in line with Hoven's (2007) definition "to refer to the character-istics and potential uses that individual learners felt that different software tools had to offer them" (p. 136). Other technological and pedagogical terms are defined as they come up. Don't be afraid of this book being too technical or jargonistic. All of the technical and pedagogical terms are defined within the chapters and we provide clear examples that illustrate their meaning and usage.

How should you use this book? Its structure is simple and straightforward. We expect you, our readers, to have widely varying backgrounds, and therefore, a range of needs. Each chapter stands alone and can be consulted for its individual guidance. To get a better idea of the content that is covered, this introduction contains a summary of each of the chapters and their major sections. The first chapter begins by setting up the basic structure for the design, development, and delivery of an online language learning project. The frame is a time-tested, process-model called ADDIE, which stands for analysis, design, delivery, implementation, and evaluation. Based on that model, Chapter 1 explores the analysis (A) and design (D) phases in depth. The section on analysis uses a question-answer format to tease out the most important considerations that need to be investigated before beginning to plan and build a successful design. It prompts readers to think about the context, the technologies and media, the learners, the course content, and the instructional staffing that is required for building an online lesson, module, course, and/or program. Armed with the answers to these questions, readers can move on to the next section, which covers the design phase. The design model detailed here is called backward design or learning by design. By beginning with the end in mind—that is, the desired learning goals—designers next determine what kinds of evidence the learners must produce through assessments to show that they have reached their learning outcomes. Only after articulating the goals and their assessments does the designer take up the task of creating the learning materials and opportunities that will lead learners toward the targeted knowledge and skills. Those of you not tasked with designing a new program or revising an old one may opt to skip all or parts of this chapter. Still, the information on how to create teaching, social, and cognitive presence is applicable beyond just designing online projects. Knowing how an online project has been conceptualized and organized, too, is a good background for teaching online. The information in Chapter 1 may also help online instructors better scaffold student learning needs that may arise along the way.

Chapter 2 proceeds to the second D of ADDIE, development. During the development phase, all the materials from course content to user guides are laid out. Yet, in this guide, we start with developing the most important element in the learning puzzle: the learner. Developing an online learner to be successful in the language, to learn how to learn a language, to learn how to learn online, and to become an autonomous, lifelong learner is perhaps the most critical task of course development. Developing the learner integrates into all of the other facets of development, from setting up the learning platform and creating the orientation and support documentation to using video to reach today's visual learners. Interactions, too, are foundational to developing learners' communication skills and cultural knowledge. Interactivity is a key to engaging learners and moving new knowledge from short- to long-term memory. The three kinds of interactions that learners engage in—with the teacher, with other learners, and with the content—are examined through the lens of online language pedagogy along with a host of technologies that optimize online language teaching and learning. The ins and outs of assessment are spelled out next, with ideas for creating them as well as other resources and ancillaries that will help differentiate learning for all students. The last section of this chapter takes a walk on the wild side. With the explosion in technologies, artificial intelligence, robotics, and social reconfigurations that promise radical changes yet to come, it suggests ways to keep ahead of the shockwave.

Chapter 3 is, in every sense, the heart of this book. We are language educators and this chapter looks at how and why we do what we do from the vantage of online delivery. By exploring what makes teaching language online special, we come to more fully understand our core practices, not only online and in blended and flipped environments, but in every language class we may ever teach. The theories, approaches, practices, and pedagogies that are presented in this chapter make our teaching special across the board. The chapter begins with a deep look at the competencies that underpin mastery of online language pedagogy, which is foundational for all online language educators. The authors also demonstrate, with guidelines and clear examples, how to implement communicative language teaching (CLT) and core practices—also known as high leverage teaching practices—in online, blended, or flipped learning environments. Of course, throughout this chapter, the real focus is on what the learners will be able to do as a result of our instruction; therefore, Chapter 3 is all about integration (or teaching), which is the "I" of the ADDIE model. This chapter includes building learners' pragmatic, intercultural, and communicative competence; creating standards-based lessons that are appropriate for learner proficiency level; and assessing students holistically to promote CLT, to name a few of the topics that are covered. Some readers may opt to start with this chapter to reaffirm their grasp of CLT and to learn how to enact it online. This chapter will also help readers prepare themselves for the exciting transition to online delivery. Nowadays, there is no escaping eLearning, and as this chapter clearly shows, we wouldn't want to!

In Chapter 4, the authors stress the importance of seeking professional development (PD) to improve our skills and create our toolbox for teaching online. It is a short but meaty chapter that is filled to the brim with a full range of PD, including how to plug into an online community of practitioners— whether through participating in an online mentoring program, attending a summer institute, or participating in webinars. This chapter describes many ways to connect with others who teach language online. The authors also show readers where to locate online professional development materials in online language pedagogy and how to become involved in professional organizations that offer conferences, webinars, and workshops for online language educators. Included in this chapter are many open educational resources provided by Language Resource Centers (LRCs) that are located around the United States. Several LRCs are highlighted in the chapter, with many others listed in the book's eResources. All of the LRCs offer valuable materials, resources, and activities for those who teach language in online and blended environments, including resources for those who teach less commonly taught languages. This is a go-to chapter for both new and veteran language faculty.

Chapter 5 rounds up the core content of the guidebook. This chapter on relevant research in online language teaching reviews studies on learner and teacher satisfaction, online class size, language learner anxiety, and best practices, all of which are topics that are fundamental to online course delivery. It also examines studies on social presence, connectedness, and assessment, which are often more difficult for instructors to enact in the online environment. The research is presented in a way that is clear and free of jargon; and most importantly, the authors provide many practical implications from the research findings that readers can apply to their own instructional contexts. In other words, readers learn about what works and why in online, blended, and flipped language classrooms. After an online teaching project launches, studies like those presented in Chapter 5 ask important questions about the effectiveness and the outcomes of an eLearning intervention. From collecting data and conducting research, we learn what works and what doesn't. Each study reviewed is followed by pedagogical implications and practical examples for improving our online practices. In the ADDIE model, the evaluation phase is not an end, but rather the beginning of new and better practices based on evaluation data and an examination of the research.

The concluding chapter brings this journey into online teaching and learning to an end. But just as this book begins with the end in mind, the end opens up to new beginnings. Details on recent and current growth across the globe remind us how timely our endeavors are to design, develop, and deliver online language teaching. Moreover, the conclusion throws the doors of language education wide open to see our future. All we need to do is walk confidently through, armed with the knowledge, skills, and practices of effective online language educators.

You may be asking, "Why this book now"? All around us, increasingly, our fellow language professionals are being asked to design, develop, and teach online or blended language courses, all too often without the necessary professional development and tools. While we are familiar with many excellent books, articles, and websites that touch on teaching languages online (and which are noted throughout this book), we found that the full scope—from design and development to delivery, framed by communicative language teaching, backed by studies on what is working and why, and bolstered by additional resources for professional development—simply hasn't been available in a single, practical location. So, our primary purpose has been to craft a book that delivers it all. While this may be the most immediate aim of the book, we have kept in mind that there are issues of great importance, not just to language teachers, but to all educators in the 21st century, such as responding to the increasing student demand for online learning.

We see enrollments increasing steadily online while the general college enrollments are decreasing (Lederman, 2018). We know in higher education in the United States that the number of students taking brick-and-mortar language classes and the number of programs offering languages are declining (Looney & Lusin, 2018). Last year, a loss of 651 language programs from 2016–2019 was reported (Johnson, 2019). Access to language learning is needed, especially in the United States. Online delivery may be able to counteract at least some of the loss in student numbers by opening access to non-traditional students (Clinefelter, Aslanian, & Magda, 2019). On the other side of the virtual desk, online education may help offset the critical shortage of teachers by opening doors to educators who cannot travel to onsite teaching locations. The conclusion of the book discusses the future of online language teaching as well as how new technologies may impact online language education.

Another reason to design and deliver quality online language programs is to increase digital literacy. Through carefully planned and scaffolded lessons, students are led to engage with the communication devices they will need professionally and personally for their future. Intentionally crafted activities and interactions promote their collaborative skills, also needed in their 21st century toolbox. The Organisation for Economic Co-operation and Development (2013) is making important strides at the national level to prepare students for 21st century skills, such as the ability to use, access, and manipulate information creatively, the ability to adapt to change and complexity, and "broadly, the capacity to appreciate diversity, disorder and ambiguity" (Bangou & Vasilopoulos, 2018, p. 146). While traditional classrooms can and do realize some of these goals, online teaching and learning pushes students to their limits in these areas.

For language educators transitioning to the online environment, we offer this volume. Some of us read better in print, others want electronic books. This one is offered in both formats. The website companion to the book on the Routledge Taylor & Francis website includes a tab for eResources to connect you with a wealth of further readings, materials, images, videos, and more to expand your thinking and practices beyond the limits of this book. The beauty of education is that it is a never-ending quest for knowledge. We are glad that you have chosen to pursue yours with us through this guidebook, thereby joining us in the thrilling new frontiers of online language education. The cyber-sky's the limit.

References

Bangou, F., & Vasilopoulos, G. (2018). Disrupting course design in online CALL teacher education: An experimentation. *E-Learning and Digital Media, 15*(3), 146–163. https://doi.org/10.1177/2042753018773765

Clinefelter, D. L., Aslanian, C. B., & Magda, A. J. (2019). *Online college students 2019: Comprehensive data on demands and preferences*. Louisville, KY: Wiley edu, LLC.

Flipped Learning Network (FLN). (2014). *The four pillars of F-L-I-P™*. Retrieved from https://flippedlearning.org/wp-content/uploads/2016/07/FLIP_handout_FNL_Web.pdf

Hoven, D. (2007). The affordances of technology for student teachers to shape their teacher education experience. In M. A. Kassen, R. Z. Lavine, K. Murphy-Judy, & M. Peters (Eds.), *Preparing and developing technology-proficient L2 teachers* (pp. 133–163). San Marcos, TX: CALICO.

Johnson, S. (2019, January). Colleges lose a 'stunning' 651 foreign language programs in 3 years, *Chronicle of Higher Education*. Retrieved from https://www.chronicle.com/article/Colleges-Lose-a-Stunning-/245526/

Lederman, D. (2018, December). Online enrollments grow, but pace slows. *Inside Higher Education*. Retrieved from https://www.insidehighered.com/digital-learning/article/2019/12/11/more-students-study-online-rate-growth-slowed-2018

Looney, D., & Lusin, N. (2018, February). *Enrollments in languages other than English in United States institutions of higher education, Summer 2016 and Fall 2016: Preliminary report*. Retrieved from https://www.mla.org/content/download/83540/ 2197676/2016-Enrollments-Short-Report.pdf

Mayadas, F., Miller, G., & Sener, J. (2015, April). *Definitions of e-learning courses and programs, version 2.0*. OLC Insights [weblog]. Retrieved from https://onlinelearningconsortium.org/updated-e-learning-definitions-2/

Organisation for Economic Co-operation and Development (OECD). (2013). *Innovative learning environments*. Paris, France: Educational Research and Innovation, OECD Publishing. DOI: http://dx.doi.org/10.1787/9789264203488-en

Chapter 1

What Are the Basics of Online Course Design?

Introduction

What do you need to know to design a quality online language course? Before accepting the challenge to create an online language program, course, or module, the educators who initiate and shepherd the project should ask themselves, "Why are we doing this?" The answer should be, "To increase learner proficiency in language and intercultural communication and to include the 21st century skills of digital literacy and autonomous learning." Those are key elements that should be included in the resulting statement of purpose. For content courses (e.g., literature, civilization, language for business, etc.), one includes the appropriate knowledge and skills as goals. Armed with a clear vision of what students will be able to do by the end of the program, course, or module, the project team gathers models, tools, materials, and resources to realize its goals. This chapter focuses on what a project team or designer should consider for completely online courses as well as for the online modules of blended and flipped courses. Often, language faculty with little to no formal training in instructional design and even less in instructional design for online teaching and learning are called upon to create online language courses and programs, according to data from the Basic Online Language

Design and Delivery Collaboratory (BOLDD) Survey of Online Language Education (Murphy-Judy & Johnshoy, 2017). This chapter offers theories and research and models in instructional design, distance and online instructional design, and computer-assisted language learning (CALL). It also culls from the effective practices of veteran online language educators. The authors primarily address secondary and postsecondary educational settings and adult and young adult learners; yet, corporate, military, and government educators may also benefit from this content. While the design principles covered in this chapter apply to secondary education, they do not specifically address state or district standards, parental oversight, privacy issues for minors, and the like. Such issues should arise during the analysis phase of the design process by K-12 design teams. Still, good instructional design, standards-based programs, and proficiency-based communicative teaching and learning are foundational across settings, languages, levels of instruction, and modes of delivery in world languages. See Chapter 3 for a deeper explanation of the importance of professional standards and proficiency-based courses and programs.

Not all online educators design their own online programs, courses, or modules, so some readers may opt to skim this chapter, but knowledge of how online programs are built from the ground up may prove useful. This chapter will help those facing the daunting task of designing or redesigning an online second- or foreign-language program or course. The chapter begins with an explanation of the *Analysis-Design-Development-Integration-Evaluation* (ADDIE) process of instructional design, since this is the foundation of good design. Next, the analysis (A) and design (D) phases of ADDIE are described in further detail and with particular regard to the field of online language education. The design model used is that of backward design, which shifts the emphasis from content coverage as the objective to what learners will be able to do as a result of instruction (Wiggins & McTighe, 2005). Finally, given the centrality of evaluation (E) in the ADDIE model, both the analysis and design sections of this chapter each end with a checklist, which will ensure that designers have planned for and included all of the relevant elements.

The ADDIE Model

ADDIE is an industry standard for the instructional design process (Clark, 2015; Dick & Carey, 2014; Gustafson & Branch, 2002; Magliaro & Shambaugh, 2006). In this chapter and the next, it serves as an organizing principle. A visual representation of this model is presented in Figure 1.1. Each step of the

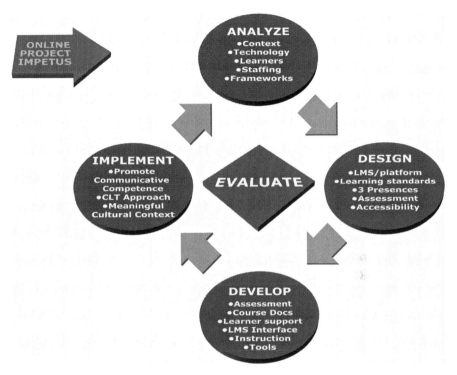

Figure 1.1 An ADDIE model for online language design, development, and delivery, graphic created by Kathryn Murphy-Judy.

CC BY SA 4.0.

ADDIE process is defined in line with Figure 1.1. After the short definitions, there is an in-depth discussion of the analysis and design phases.

In Chapter 1, the authors focus on the analysis and design aspects of ADDIE. Chapter 2 covers the development phase of ADDIE, and the authors show examples of how technology tools and applications are used to develop an online language class. In Chapter 3, the authors focus on different aspects of integration (teaching) and how to teach online communicatively, while Chapter 4 provides information on online professional development and open educational resources for online language educators. Chapter 5 examines the research on online language teaching and learning and the authors provide examples of how to incorporate research and best practices into online language courses. The evaluation piece of ADDIE is interwoven through all of the chapters.

Instructional design is a systematic and systemic approach to creating effective, efficient, and engaging instructional experiences. It follows methodical and logical progression, such that its various elements interact in dynamic and interdependent ways, leading to the creation of entirely online, blended, flipped, or traditional, brick-and-mortar instruction (Hromalik, 2016). ADDIE stems from a cognitive or behavioral instructional theory of learning (Skinner, 1974/2017), where learning is assumed to progress through a step-by-step process. Later learning theories, like constructivism, (Vygotsky, 1980) constructionism (Harel & Papert, 1991), and connectivism (Downes, 2005; Siemens, 2005) recognize that learning is much "messier" and thus, offer options for more student-centered and differentiated teaching and learning. The ADDIE approach offers a systematic process to help designers organize and execute an effective workflow, regardless of the theory of learning.

The "A" in the ADDIE model stands for careful, comprehensive analysis. This step serves to explore key questions: who is initiating, supporting, and driving the project and what are the broader institutional parameters (learning management system and technology infrastructure, administrative mandates and policies, instructional staffing); which technologies and media will drive and support the design, development, integration, and evaluation of the program; who are the learners in relation to the targeted instruction; and, what are learning goals, philosophies, approaches, and strategies for realizing the desired learning outcomes.

Analysis is followed by Design. Design provides a coherent structure and framework from which units, modules, tasks, assignments, and assessments, as well as support documents, resources, and support mechanisms eventually emerge. To engage in effective action, whether in life or instruction, according to Stephen Covey (1989) one should always "begin with the end in mind" (p. 98). It is the design mantra for this chapter.

For the Development phase, or the second D in ADDIE, the designer must begin with the learning goals that are based on professional standards, which are then broken down into unit or module objectives. The developer will then create the summative assessments, which will match up with the overall learning goals and objectives and lesson or module formative assessments that are tied to the course objectives (this is known as backward design). By starting with the creation of the summative assessments, all of the lesson materials, tasks, activities, and formative assessments will follow; however, they must be sequenced logically. This process is the foundation of a sound design framework that is based on clear learning goals, objectives, and professional standards. In the ADDIE process, the course creators revisit each of the previous stages as needed. For example, during development, they may revisit the analysis and design phases.

After doing a trial run of a new course with colleagues (alpha testing) or a small set of students (beta testing), the real work begins. The rubber hits the road with Integration. Although discussed briefly in this chapter, it is the stuff of Chapter 3, which shows readers how to deliver online language instruction communicatively.

And, finally the "E" of Evaluation, which has already been discussed in the Introduction, explores processes of evaluation that are integral to each of the ADDIE phases. It is not the end of the road, but rather a feedback mechanism to inform and improve the entire project continuously. It ensures the maintenance of the quality and sustainability of the program. The ADDIE model, as clearly visualized in Figure 1.1, emphasizes the centrality of evaluation, such that, at every juncture in its creation, development, and deployment, there is reflection, critique, and possibly revision. Since evaluation charts progress toward the "end in mind" of each step as well as that of the entire project, it is addressed at the end of each step in the design process. When one begins with the end in mind, evaluation can and should take place at the end of each stage of the process.

Analysis

This section is intended for faculty tasked with designing an online language program or course but who have little or no access to instructional design support staff and are not sure where to start. In most institutions, the curricular goals—what students should be able to do, know, and understand as a result of a program or course—are usually pre-defined. Still, an in-depth analysis may well lead to revising, refining, or improving the targeted outcomes as they evolve within the online context. A wide-scale analysis stage may be less important for the design of modules in hybrid and flipped courses, where faculty have a different rapport with their students as well as having recourse to face-to-face sessions.

Analysis is critical to the creation of effective online learning environments. According to Shearer (2003), analysis must include, "the audience characteristics, geographic dispersion of the audience, the technologies available to the audience, the goals of the learners, the goals and missions of the learning organization, the costs that must be recovered, the costs of delivery, the political environment at the time for the learning organization, the faculty compensation, and the market competition" (p. 275). Analysis, then, includes the obvious and even the political and financial reasons for launching an online language initiative. It explores and appraises the institutional setting as well as the human element, such as instructional designers (if there are any), faculty, students, and staff. Moreover, other institutionally specific factors must be recognized before actual design concepts begin to take shape. Analysis should include the learning theories (cognitive, constructivist, constructionist, and/or connectivist) and pedagogies (communicative, task-based, content-based, etc.) that will frame the project (see Chapter 3). It accounts for institutional (or departmental) curriculum, learning goals, and anticipated learning outcomes in the projected online environment. Therefore Analysis is a highly detailed section of the present chapter because the resulting comprehensive information about the context, the means, the people, and the content will pave the way to a robust, success-oriented design, which will reduce costs, delays, and problems. It allows the project team or designer to start identifying, locating, and gathering the people, tools, and materials that the project will need. It will provide the information needed to plot out the trajectories and time frames for a timely, successful launch. Moreover, analysis persists throughout the life of the project, even after its launch, since ongoing evaluation may indicate that new or revised analyses are warranted.

Analysis involves a mega-view of the whole context of the instructional project. In this phase of ADDIE, an overarching pre-appraisal of all the reasons for creating an online program or course helps the designer(s), developer(s), and faculty not only to frame the project but also to sustain it throughout its development and deployment phases. Broadly posed, these questions include: What is the primary motivation for this initiative: student demand; administrative cost cutting or revenue generation; better ways to deliver language instruction; a commercial venture with the expectation of marketability (a growing concern for academic entities); or a "techie" interest in applying cool new tools, data mining, gaming, virtual reality, or other new emerging technologies and innovative approaches and practices for language learning? Which levels of administration, management, and faculty are most supportive of the initiative and what will keep them on board (and what might alienate them)? Knowing the vested interest(s) lying behind the impetus to create an online language program or course is vital to designing for success, navigating successfully through the various phases, and maintaining rapport with and support of the major stakeholders. Moreover, the Association of Departments of Foreign Languages (ADFL) has stated:

> Many language departments across the country teach hybrid and online courses. The decision to implement such courses should be one that is fully supported by the language department concerned. The addition of hybrid or online language courses does not save time or money and is not a cost-saving measure. Rather, adding hybrid or online language courses

requires the use of more resources than the traditional course and requires additional funding and time on the part of all involved. The process must include input from all stakeholders (e.g., administrators, technical support, instructors, students), and administrators must make a long-term commitment to providing the resources to sustain such courses.

(ADFL, 2014)

The questions detailed below systematically probe the institutional and administrative context, technological and distance media concerns, the learner population, the content, and finally, instruction and instructional staffing. They are the questions that should ground an online language project *before* any actual design choices are made.

Context Analysis

In this segment, questions are raised relating to the overarching institutional and administrative motivations, structures, infrastructures, support units, as well as budgetary and financial issues. These questions will help the reader understand what is involved in context analysis.

What or Who Is Driving the Creation of This Online Language Program?

Most educators would prefer that the impetus for any learning environment or new program would arise organically from a teaching and learning dynamic. Realistically, other forces often lie behind the creation of an online program or the conversion of a traditional, brick-and-mortar venue to hybrid or online delivery. Still, a push in the direction of online instruction may be what is needed to urge traditional faculty to embrace digital media or to revamp an "old school" curriculum into something more suitable for 21st century learning. As Clayton Christensen of Harvard has warned, students are opting with their keyboards and their feet to pursue education outside brick-and-mortar institutions. He has predicted that over half of all American colleges and universities will close or go bankrupt by 2030 (Christensen, 2011). For language programs, the downward trend in postsecondary enrollments highlighted by Looney and Lusin (2019) in the Modern Language Association (MLA) report on 2016 enrollments may in part stem from a lack of innovative, 21st century types of language learning approaches, in particular, online and mobile delivery, that stimulate and maintain student interest and provide the anytime, anywhere learning that students today want. Ours is an economy of badge credentialing,

24/7 access to knowledge and training, and modularized and open learning (e.g., Git-hub and YouTube). If someone wants to learn a new skill, they choose one or more media options that break down the process, skipping those they already know or don't find useful. Choice and flexibility can often be a strong factor in learner enticement and engagement in online learning.

Other drivers for online language programs may arise from administrative concerns to cut costs, increase revenue, address limited campus space issues, attract new students, and increase enrollments. Faculty may want to launch an online program to respond to student requests, to integrate new media, to exploit new technology, or to address personal needs of limited time and/or mobility, whether theirs, their students', or both. Whatever forces drive what will necessarily be a time-intensive and potentially costly endeavor, they must be faced honestly and openly. They also need to be kept in mind throughout the design, development, integration, and evaluation of the resulting program. Yet even if the rationale for an online language program at the executive level may not be driven entirely by learning needs or pedagogical issues, the designer or design team can still construct a successful online program that realizes excellence in teaching and learning. It requires negotiating the financial or administrative impetus with sound, standards-based courseware, to the mutual benefit of everyone involved: students, faculty, administration, and community. Valdosta State University (VSU), for example, has created two fully online bachelor's programs, in Spanish and in French, with the Spanish program having won national awards as the best online program and value for the money for students. These programs achieve both financial and pedagogical goals.

What Are the Institutional Parameters?

Online language learning may emerge from a wide array of providers: a college or university, a school district, an online school, a company, a government, or a military sector. It may take a variety of forms; the most frequently cited by Murphy-Judy and Johnshoy (2017) are: an entirely online program; online courses or sequences in a brick-and-mortar language department; a supplemental course in a given curriculum; developmental or remedial support modules meant to enhance traditional, brick-and-mortar learning; a course or several courses distributed across multiple campuses; a course or set of modules intended for a cohort in a less-commonly-taught language or in other content areas or disciplines (business, area studies, engineering, nursing, etc.); independent or self-paced study modules; lessons within a traditional, on-campus language course meant to increase or decrease class size or to individualize or differentiate learning; or a response to learner needs for time- and place-independent interactions (known as "asynchronous learning"). Increasingly, parts of a course are provided online, as in hybrid and flipped classrooms.

Given the immense range of possible configurations, each new design must be planned within its particular context. Arizona State University (ASU), for example, offers an entire Spanish degree online at ASU Online called "Ocourses"; yet, its brick-and-mortar campus also offers Spanish courses online, called "icourses" that are completely distinct from the ASU Online offerings. Such distinct programs, each with its own infrastructure and deployment, arise from the specificity of the institution, its needs, and those of the targeted learner populations. Another example is the University of Maryland Global Campus (UMGC), which offers many languages online and a major in East Asian Studies with corresponding Japanese and Chinese language courses also online. Since UMGC serves a large military and diplomatic student body in the United States, courses for those populations are mostly offered asynchronously for security and accessibility reasons. UMGC has adapted its time frames to student needs by offering eight-week fixed-session courses. All of their language offerings, except Korean, have online sections: Arabic, Chinese, French, German, Japanese, and Spanish. Institutions with smaller footprints than those of ASU and UMGC operate within their specific contexts. When Carnegie Mellon University undertook its Online Learning Initiative (OLI), its context included online course development in several disciplines funded by large foundational grants (Hewlett, Gates, Kresge, Lumina, NSF, Spencer, W.S. Johnson). Today, OLI language courses (French and Arabic) are used worldwide in face-to-face, hybrid, flipped, and completely online venues, like the online French program at Old Dominion University (ODU). North Carolina Virtual Public School (NCVPS), Virtual Virginia, and Florida Virtual School (FLVS), as K-12 providers, work within the public school systems of their states. Commercial enterprises (Rosetta Stone, Duolingo, Mango Languages, Busuu, FluentU, Babbel, etc.) and entities like the Defense Language Institute face their own set of issues with respect to the target population, security issues, revenue streams, as well as educational and state regulations and issues related to accreditation and federal student loan programs. Readers are encouraged to further explore the online language programs listed above to determine which model best meets the needs of their context and leaners. Links to VSU, ASU, UMGC, ODU, NCVPS, and FLVS are provided in the eResources section of this book.

Some online educational programs may set their sights on learners nationwide if not worldwide. Where a program admits students from all over the country, national governmental regulations for interstate educational delivery likely come into play. If the program targets international learners, supra-national issues of educational regulations and accreditation need to be taken into account. More information on these types of constraints are detailed below.

Where Is the Funding Coming From?

Closely related to the first question about institutional parameters is the question of funding. It is essential to know at the design phase who is footing the bill, how deep the pockets are, and what the criteria are for continued funding. If funding is external, is a prototype or pilot course expected to stimulate further funding? Designing for a prototype differs significantly from a completely new program launch. For external funding, part of the analysis phase includes researching, locating, and contacting funding sources (federal programs, foundations, special donors, go-fund-me operations, loans, venture capital, etc.). Obviously, the financial reality of a project determines many aspects in each phase of its creation. It also factors into its breadth and time constraints.

If funding is internal to an institution or company, the kinds and amounts of institutional support have to be analyzed and assessed. Will they be top-down from the president or provost, a dean, the school board, or the CEO or owner of a company? If so, will the project have to negotiate with each unit whose support and participation are needed (the information technology unit, faculty, public and alumni relations, the center for teaching excellence, the online learning office, etc.) or will a specific administrative unit pave the way and orchestrate all stakeholders? If the internal funding is bottom-up, arising from the hard work of one or more faculty, what are the chances of eventually getting additional financial support and continuation of the project? Will there be financial and administrative support to "convince" those less than favorable toward online education (administrators, other faculty, students, parents, etc.)? Who are the go-to people who can provide support or bring their influence to bear on the project?

Besides the funding for the analysis, design, and development phases, one must also consider how the program will be sustained. Will it be through tuition and fees? If it is a massive open online course (MOOC) or some other open educational platform, in other words, courses that are openly available for everyone in the community to use for free, will they be funded through advertising, subscription, or fees for credentialing or badging (an e-credential offered to those who successfully complete their training)? Is it a pay-as-you-go model? Financial sustainability over the long term is a critical factor in analysis.

There is a caveat in this section on analysis of funding and finances. In the beginning, online education was seen by some as a "cash cow": massive courses created once and deployed to droves of students, with little to no instructional staffing. Indeed, once the content was created by an expert, the course—or so it was imagined—could be handed off to teaching assistants or other "cost-effective" instructional staff who would handle 40–50 students per section or, at least, multiple sections with 10–20 students in each one. MOOCs, of course, emerged as the wild exaggeration of such a configuration with potentially hundreds, if not thousands, of students receiving little to no ongoing faculty oversight or input thanks to online materials, automated feedback, and student–student learning communities. As the ADFL (2014) statement quoted above warns, online teaching and learning is not a cost saving measure. See Chapter 5 for a review of the research on optimal online class size.

A major pitfall to avoid, then, is having cost savings or increased tuition revenue as the primary impetus for creating an online language program. If financial gains are the main goal, then there is a danger of engaging in practices that are not optimal for successful online delivery, such as using teaching assistants and adjunct faculty who have not received adequate professional development in online course delivery, instructional technologies, or both. There is also the temptation to use canned, one-size-fits-all courseware, which will not result in engaging, effective language learning.

Lastly, sometimes a single module may be created by a lone instructor as part of a face-to-face, hybrid/blended, or flipped classroom. Over time more modules may emerge until such time as all together they could be gathered into a whole course curriculum. Even if a program develops like this over time, the transition into an entirely online venue and the inclusion of all course elements to support learning at a distance would have to be identified through a thorough analysis.

 ## How Supportive Are the Administrators, Supervisors, and Colleagues?

Connected to the question of funding is that of philosophical and pedagogical support. When colleagues and supervisors work against an online project, their foot-dragging and roadblocks may end up scuttling a worthwhile endeavor, even once it has been created and is operational. At one institution, two nationally recognized online educators saw their online courses shut down because their immediate supervisors did not believe that first- and second-year language courses could be delivered online, despite funding and support from the provost and president. Elsewhere, the online programs and courses will die if other faculty are not ready to take over should the creator leave or be reassigned. Chapter 4 highlights professional development opportunities that can help sustain online language teaching and learning in this latter instance.

In addition to having a supportive environment, one must consider how realistic expectations are at various levels of administration. Will enough time, personnel, and general support be accorded for the course design, development, and delivery? In a series of responses to design questions over three years, the BOLDD Survey (Murphy-Judy & Johnshoy, 2017) has shown:

- most institutions expect an online course to be designed and developed in a three- to four-month period and be ready to deploy after only a summer or a semester of analysis, design, and development;
- often there is little to no remuneration for the program creator (if that person is faculty);
- the program creator is afforded little to no professional development for this work.

Across all three years of the survey, the picture of a significant lack of institutional support of the most elemental kind has become apparent. Part and parcel of the question of institutional support is the answer to the question, "What will be the professional benefits and rewards, if any, for an individual or team that creates and develops such a program?" If there are no benefits, if online course creation does not factor into annual evaluations, promotions, or raises, then most likely it is not really valued by the institution. Determining if the heavy workload and responsibilities involved in creating and deploying an online program provide a sufficient return on investment for designers and instructors is critical. If faculty members are asked to take on a challenging task, such as designing and developing an online program, course, or even a module, which is a section of an online course, then they should get the specifics of the compensation and the weight (in terms of course load, amount of time involved, etc.) in writing, lest the current winds change direction.

What Are the Organizational or Institutional Constraints and Time Factors?

Constraints take the form of time factors, institutional structures and strictures (e.g., learning management systems, technology support, faculty loads, reporting hierarchies, etc.), and accreditation. The time allotted to design and develop an online course should be counted as an institutional constraint. It should also be factored into the supervision and evaluation of the project team. Its members should propose realistic timelines, keeping firmly in mind that technology-dependent projects often take longer and cost more than expected.

Another critical time factor is that of the length or term of the course. Must it correspond to traditional, brick-and-mortar course time frames for logistical, academic, or other reasons? Will the online program be expected to set up one or more time frames? If so, a whole host of questions and issues will arise, most justifiably centered on the learner (see below). Will there be a single, fixed time frame; will it be self-paced; or will there be variability, such as the UMGC program that was discussed previously? Even if self-paced, students and faculty need a time constraint of some sort. Will the course offer rolling start and finish dates? How will the online course interface with traditional, brick-and-mortar language courses and programs for courses offered in both traditional and online formats in the same school or department? If a major impetus in the delineation and integration of an online curriculum is to improve and individualize language learning by implementing emerging technologies and innovative approaches and practices, now is the time to rethink and articulate a new pedagogy. The BOLDD Survey has shown, however, that most online providers are expected to adhere to the time constraints and curricula of existing on-campus language classes, rather than adopting time frames and learning opportunities afforded by online learning. For more information on considering time and time constraints for online, blended and traditional courses, see Bates (2019) in the recommended reading section at the end of this chapter. Further analysis of curricula and course content is addressed below, under "Content."

Institutional factors may include who is expected to design the course and who will teach it. Such issues arise in great measure from whomever oversees the project institutionally. If there is time and funding for instructional designers, technologists, and faculty to work together, chances are better that a robust, successful program will emerge. In a perfect world, all three would bring their expertise to the table. However, in the real world, faculty members who create such programs or courses are often expected to have the requisite instructional design and technology skills to build it entirely themselves. The OLI at Carnegie Mellon University, with significant outside funding, benefited from rich human resources. Few institutions responding to the BOLDD Survey, however, noted such resources and collaborative teams. Online language learning (OLL) tends to be initiated by a single faculty member who functions as designer, developer, and instructor.

Connected to the issue of human resources are the institutional expectations of the instructor in terms of number of students, number of classes, hours of student-teacher engagement, office hours, homework/correcting/grading time, contact with parents (if K-12), amount of responsibility for course revisions and updates, and the like. Online teaching is known to be time intensive in the language field (MLA, 2013). Unless the time to design, develop, and deliver is factored in, undue stress and discontent, if not failure, may ensue.

Personnel tasked with creating the online language program or course must be aware of the rules and regulations that will impact its design and delivery. Some schools will have departmental or college-level parameters for eLearning, others operate at a higher level, in the provost's office or through an office of online education. Various states in the United States have regulations for secondary and postsecondary online teaching and learning, but federal legislation implementation has once again been delayed (Downs, 2018). Since eLearning by its very nature crosses local, state, and national borders, the online education team must abide by the regulations that govern online education in their target markets. The UMGC case demonstrated this kind of forethought during the design phase by recognizing the requirements of its military and diplomatic student populations and thus creating asynchronous courses in response to their needs and constraints. At colleges and universities in the United States, accrediting bodies like the Southern Association of Colleges and Schools (SACS) (1997/2012; 2016), the Southern Region Education Board (SREB) (2012), the Council of Regional Accrediting Commissions (C-RAC) (2011), the Western Interstate Commission for Higher Education (WICHE) (2018), and the National Council of State Authorization Reciprocity Agreements (NC-SARA) (2019) also provide regulations for online course delivery. Accreditation for distance education in the United States is comprehensively addressed through the Distance Education Accreditating Commission (DEAC) (n.d.).

Finally, in this discussion of institutional constraints, one would be remiss not to address what may be seen as its opposite: openness. It is conceivable for online courses to be entirely free and open. Many institutions support the use of open educational resources (OER), which are materials and resources that may be shared, transformed, and/or redistributed without infringing on any copyright laws. The OER philosophy underlies the operations of many massively open online courses; however, few high-quality language MOOCs exist to date. Moreover, recently EdX, one of the largest and best-known MOOC providers, announced its conversion into a for-profit venture (McKenzie, 2018). Several others also charge for some courses, especially where course credit is involved. To date, few studies have examined MOOC effectiveness in language learning environments, and it is unclear whether MOOCs can provide the level of interaction that is necessary for successful language learning. Still, China has seen an extraordinary rise in its number of MOOCs. Some are state supported and must obey educational policies and regulations to gain national recognition. Notably, languages rank as the fifth largest subject area of the 3,000 nationally recognized courses in 2020 (Ma, 2019). India, too, has thousands of MOOCs. Its National Ministry of Education has accredited the Study Webs of Active-Learning for Young Aspiring Minds (SWAYAM) courses in French, German, Japanese, Russian, Sanskrit, and Spanish (Patra, 2019). Designing for openness adds another layer of questions and considerations to the analysis phase of the ADDIE process. If creating MOOCs for China or India, state regulations and registries will have to be navigated.

Who Else Is Offering Similar Online Education?

Recognizing the competition serves several functions: first, it is important to examine the cost, flexibility, reputation, accessibility, credentialing, etc. of competitor programs. Second, it provides a view of reasonable costs, time frames, standards, criteria, and the like in the current market. Third, it offers models and options for the developer or project team to consider. The authors always recommend that faculty looking to teach languages online first take one or more online language courses themselves; the same advice applies to project design and development teams.

Technology and Media Analysis

A learning management system is the software used for the administration, documentation, tracking, reporting, and delivery of educational content. It is where courses, whether online or traditional, house many, if not all, the learning documents for their learners. In an online venue, the learning management system (LMS) plays a central role for learners and faculty alike.

Which LMS or Other Base Will Serve as the Learning Platform?

Most educational enterprises use an LMS like Google Classroom, Blackboard, Moodle, D2L Brightspace, Canvas, or Edmodo. With the rise of MOOCs around 2010, consortia and proprietary systems emerged like Coursera, edX, FUN, FutureLearn, Miríada X, OpenClassrooms among the top providers. Choosing which platform to use may fall to the design team or it may be imposed by institutional decision makers. Some schools have selected a given platform (e.g., Moodle or Canvas) while the rest of campus uses another LMS like Blackboard. The decision of platform should optimally be determined during the analysis phase. Due to its pivotal role in the analysis phase, discussions and explorations with school leaders in instructional technology and more broadly with those in information technology at one's institution should be undertaken early in the process.

Which Technological Resources beyond the LMS Are Available to Designers, Instructors, and Learners?

Most LMSs offer a variety of add-on tools beneficial to language learning, such as tools that can allow a voice discussion board (e.g., VoiceThread) and tools that allow for online synchronous meetings (e.g., Zoom or Communicate®). See more about these tools in Chapters 2 and 3. Some institutions grant LMS access to Hoonuit (formerly Atomic Learning and Versifit Technologies) or LinkedIn Learning (formerly Lynda.com), two electronic warehouses for digital instruction, professional development, and skill enhancement. These resources are very valuable for online students who may need training on a particular tool or application and they can be linked into an online course to support student learning as needed.

Whoever designs a new online learning program needs to discover current apps and technologies as well as stay abreast of emerging ones that may prove to be powerful assets in 21st century language learning. This varies from language to language, especially where second language (L2) phonological and/or writing systems significantly differ from those of the first language (L1). Regardless of the funding source for tools, choosing the right ones is paramount. Online course developers can also consult with colleagues who are instructional technology experts, both on campus and in their communities of practice. With new technologies and media emerging constantly, one needs to stay abreast of exciting and effective new ways to provide language learning online (Blake, 2010, 2011). In addition, there may be constraints stemming from privacy and accessibility laws, institutional policies, and/or issues of availability, security, or learner access. The universal design for learning (UDL)—which ensures that students with exceptional needs, such as visual or hearing impairment—easily accommodates to the online venue (Rose, Meyer, Strangman, & Rappolt, 2002). One needs to discover the usability and constraints of all factors under consideration for the proposed program or course such as the LMS, social media, software packages, publisher materials, apps, etc. An important question is whether the organization creating the online language course abides by the

Web Content Accessibility Guidelines (WCAG). When followed during the design process, the WCAG ensure that the online course includes strategies, resources, and standards that make it accessible to people with disabilities.

To What Extent Will Mobile Access Be Important to the Course?

When BOLDD first started offering workshops on online language design and delivery, smartphones and tablets were just entering the educational scene. Now they are ubiquitous. Many learners today live by their smartphones. It is forecast that, "Mobile data traffic will grow at a compound annual growth rate (CAGR) of 47 percent from 2016 to 2021, reaching 49.0 exabytes per month by 2021" with an exabyte equaling one billion gigabytes (Cisco, 2019, p. 0). By 2021, there will be more mobile devices than people on the planet, although this does not mean everyone will own one. Any viable online program needs to consider the role of mobile delivery in response to the anytime, anywhere expectations of today's students. However, certain materials and resources for the course, such as some publisher-delivered ones, may require using a computer. The analysis questions below on learners, technologies, and content will expand on critical issues in mobile access and engagement.

Learner Analysis

Learners and their learning are the driving force behind teaching, whether face-to-face, hybrid, or online. In building a distance language learning course or entire program, designers consider student age, cognitive development, social and economic status, career aspirations, location, and reasons for taking languages online.

Who Will Be the Online Students?

In any given online course, there may be students from regular and home schools, community colleges, and other colleges and universities. The student body may include those studying or interning abroad, retirees, businesspeople, other faculty, even learners from other countries whose L1 is not that of the country in which the course originates. Learner access to the minimum technology requirements, such as access to a computer and the Internet, has to be taken into account. For students who lack access to the basic requirements, is there access in their community at times convenient to their schedules? For example, does their school or campus have a language lab or bank of computers? Do local libraries offer the needed computer facilities? It may seem ludicrous, but some students sign up for an online course lacking a computer and the ancillary components (headset, microphone, video camera, speakers, etc.). Some may have only a cell phone, which they expect to suffice for completing course assignments, assessments, and interactions. Indeed, Clinefelter, Aslanian, and Magda (2019) report that 66% of online students want to use their mobile devices to complete their work (p. 33). In addition to hardware, Internet access, too, is crucial; yet, some lower-income students may lack WIFI access at home or in their community. Students in rural areas may have no access to broadband connections or the available Internet providers have prohibitively expensive data plans and/or slow connectivity. Such potential limitations can be highly detrimental to student access and success so they must be considered.

Beyond financial and logistical issues, language learning online, especially at the lower levels, often attracts learners with novice skills in the target language and novice language learning strategies and know-how, often compounded by a novice level in online learning and in instructional technologies in general. A thoughtful, broad assessment of target population demographics, circumstances, and backgrounds will promote the design of a healthy, successful program and suggest pathways and resources to differentiate learing and support students with special needs. Despite the notion that the current generation of students is technologically savvy, while indeed they are with respect to some forms of social media, often they are not so in the kinds of digital media and computer-mediated communication of an educational environment. Moreover, Clinefelter et al. report that "One-third of online college students are first-generation college students, and 13% have no prior college experience" (2019, p. 18). If they enroll in an online language course, they may well be at the novice level in postsecondary education as well as in the language and in online learning. Finally, if the language course is a requirement, there may also be a lack of engagement with or motivation for learning a language. For this reason, the level of learner autonomy may start out quite low. Appraisal of prospective learners and learning profiles will lead to an appropriate design plan.

How Diverse Will the Online Learners Be?

The impact of race, gender, ethnicity, national origin, age, and/or disability may be lessened in that an online environment often reduces visible differences, but systemic inequities may still persist. Educators must recognize and value diversity to teach inclusively (Bonilla-Silva, 2006; Center for Applied Special Technology [CAST], 2018a, 2018b). Other critical factors in learner diversity include cultural background, proficiency level, study habits, and perseverance or grit. Learning paths should always be differentiated; yet, how best to do that and knowing which strategies in online learning will promote inclusive differentiation depends in part on knowing who the audience will be.

Access to the technologies, technology support, and tutoring support influence how best to bolster all learners, online and offline. It is especially important to consider the needs of students with disabilities, finding ways to assure Americans with Disabilities Act (ADA) compliance and to address other special learning and access needs. In the European Union, there is the European Accessibility Act (Official Journal of the European Union, 2019). The 20 tips for designing an accessible online course by Burgstahler (2018) will help in analysis and in the upcoming design phase. More on UDL and ADA compliance can be found in the discussion below on the design of compliant programs. Designers from countries outside the United States and the European Union should familiarize themselves with the regulations for their circumstances.

As part of the analysis of learner diversity, one should also probe when and where learners will engage in learning. Will they be on-campus, off-campus, at home, or at work? Will they encounter the course during set class hours, in the evening or on the weekend, or during some other time frame of their choosing? Will they access the course asynchronously, synchronously, or a mix of both modes? Course scheduling and pacing, whether semester-based, with rolling starts, or with flexible start and finish dates, must be examined with regard to the learner population to design effectively.

 ## Why Are Students Taking the Course?

Learner attitudes toward and motivations for taking an online course must be considered, together with the institution's mission, strategic planning, and issues of accreditation. Many learners want an educational opportunity that frees them from the space and time constraints of the brick-and-mortar classroom. Some may have disabilities that make online education a better fit. Others work full-time and are seeking a language course that fits their schedule.

A false reason that can hamper online learning, however, arises from learner misconceptions about online learning and the amount of learner autonomy it will require of them. Some students sign up for an online language course thinking incorrectly that it will entail only reading and writing, with minimal speaking and listening involved. By analyzing learners' reasons for taking the course online, the eventual design can create course descriptions and a robust learner orientation to foster good online learning habits and frames of mind to help dispel counterproductive ones.

What Kind of Community of Inquiry (COI) Will Be Best for the Targeted Learners?

Presence is extremely important in the online environment. Teaching and learning require human connectedness. Learners benefit from a sense of community with the teacher and fellow learners as they move toward shared learning goals. In the analysis phase, designers seek the best ways to foster a sense of community and belonging for their targeted population. For one set, it may revolve around the campus identity or a mascot. For another, it may be the prestige of the institution. Yet another may seek an adult, professional learning community through a local college. Or maybe the *esprit de corps* will center around common social concerns. A strong sense of connectedness to the content, to the teacher, and to their peers creates the type of COI needed for successful online learning (Boettcher & Conrad, 2016).

Content Analysis

Early online language programs were limited in their pedagogical approach by the LMS text-based interface. Today's digital multimedia allow online language educators to offer instruction across a full range of communicative and interactive modes.

 ## What Is the Philosophy, Standards, and Methodologies for the Proposed Program or Course?

In the United States, most language professionals adhere to the American Council on the Teaching of Foreign Languages (ACTFL) World-Readiness Standards, with its 5 Cs: Communication, Cultures, Connections, Comparisons, and Communities (National Standards Collaborative Board, 2015). In Europe and elsewhere the Common European Framework of Reference (CEFR) for Languages: Learning, Teaching, Assessment is used by language educators (Council of Europe, 2011). For English as a second language (ESL) in the United States, there are the national World-Class Instructional Design and Assessment (WIDA) English Language Development Standards (WIDA, 2012). Professional standards are addressed below under Design as well as in Chapter 3.

Another essential element to be analyzed is the main approach that will be used online. Communicative language teaching suits the online environment well. Strategies like project-based learning (PBL), active learning, and cooperative and collaborative learning can be successfully integrated into a communicative approach. Chapter 3 fleshes out ways to develop and integrate communicative language teaching and learning into the online, blended, or flipped environments.

What Is the Proficiency Level of the Content That Learners Will Learn?

Instruction is the interplay between learners, instructors, and content. To analyze issues surrounding this interplay that take place in the L2, the designer or the project team needs to roughly target the entry level of student proficiency. In the case of an upper-level or content-based language course, for example Advanced German Conversation or Chinese for Business, it will be the baseline incoming proficiency level students need to engage in the course content and activities. Language acquisition is not a lockstep, straight line, linear process. Learners start and continue their language learning paths while displaying a wide range of abilities, aptitudes, and experiences. Their starting levels may be determined by previous coursework and grades, by placement testing, or from standardized proficiency testing. How learner deficits in proficiency and remediation of language skills will be tackled should also be addressed from the very beginning. What kinds of scaffolding and differentiation will need to be deployed to address disparities? Such questions must be asked and answered whatever the mode of delivery. Yet, in the online venue, they may be harder to discover and their possible existence needs to be proactively prepared for. Eventually, the designer or team must also explore and decide at which degree of proficiency the final learning targets will be set.

Who Selects the Base Materials for Content Delivery?

With regard to teaching and learning materials, the designer or team scopes out the choice of the materials, that is, the textbook (if there will be one), online resources, such as workbooks and activities, the tools to support and scaffold language learning, and applications to engage learners in communicative interactivity. The institutional analysis will discover who ultimately has control over these choices: the administration or central office, the faculty, the online team, or outside consultants. It will be important to determine which materials will differ from corresponding on-campus course offerings. The BOLDD Survey shows most of the responding institutions use essentially the same course materials for online and traditional language courses even though the online environment could (and should!) promote innovative, connected learning opportunities. Yet, many language programs are sequenced so students can move between traditional and online courses seamlessly and not incur additional textbook costs. These decisions must be faced early in the process of creating an online program.

To What Extent Will the Online Course Articulate with Other Language Curricula?

Articulation with the traditional language curricula may determine several aspects of content and approach in the online program or course. If the project is to create modules for flipped or hybrid courses, the question is moot. At the course level, will the course stay in sync with on-campus courses so learners can move smoothly between one and the other? For some programs, the online program segregates its learners from traditional, brick-and-mortar language courses, as is the case of the ASU online courses mentioned above. Other programs keep their learners in lockstep, which enables the students to move fluidly between on-campus and online courses as suits their needs.

Instructional Staffing Analysis

Analysis of instructional staffing goes beyond identifying who will teach the course. While the answer is evident in the traditional, brick-and-mortar class, it is not as clear online.

Who Will Teach the Online Course Now and in the Future?

Many educators who design online courses also teach them. Yet, for the sake of sustainability, programs need to be built so that faculty with proper training in online instruction will be hired. Determining if current faculty have the background and experience is crucial to launching and sustaining the project. If there are qualified, local instructional staff, there is less concern. If, however, the teaching corps will consist of adjunct or contingent faculty, and/or graduate teaching assistants, then the analysis phase needs to explore the amount of training, preparation, and guidance needed well before the program or course launches.

How Will the Instructional Staff Get Selected, Trained, and Evaluated?

Often, the designer plays no part in who is selected. Ideally, instructors with technology training, or better yet, those with experience in computer-assisted language learning and knowledge of online language pedagogy would be hired (see Chapter 3). Faculty, tutors, or assistants without such qualifications will need training and/or mentoring. The analysis phase should indicate if a training program is called for and its time frame (see Chapter 4 for more on professional development). Job postings for online positions as well as end-of-course teacher evaluations must also be thought about. If the right questions about instructional staffing, selection, training, and evaluation are thoroughly discussed and asked, the design phase sets up appropriate response mechanisms. This is also when questions should arise about criteria for evaluation. Fortunately, a growing body of research and literature on teacher education for online language learning meets that need. See Chapter 5 for a review of the relevant research on online language teaching and learning.

 ## Who Besides the Teacher of Record Will Be Available as Instructional Staff and at What Cost?

The BOLDD survey data correlated learner success online with having more than one instructional staff member per course. In addition to the instructor of record, online programs ought to investigate tutors (local or online, native or non-native, paid or unpaid), peer conversation partners (e.g., international students on campus, upper-level students, teletandem exchange partners), graders, teaching assistants, or some combination of these. The design team needs to find out what staffing resources are available for their program. The cost of such instructional staffing also has to be calculated and included in the cost analysis. The less obvious cost—that of the instructional faculty's time and effort in the design, development, and delivery of the online course—should also figure into this analysis. Teaching online takes more time per student generally than traditional, on-campus courses (Kenny & Fluck, 2017; MLA, 2013). If the initiating faculty member is also expected to guide and support ancillary teaching staff (graders, mentors, coaches), that, too, must be accounted for in terms of faculty time and compensation.

Evaluation of the Analysis Phase

Given the complexity and variety of any online program or course creation, its analysis phase should reflect breadth and depth. The questions provided above probe the major functions and roles in the design, development, and deployment of an online language program. They are not, however, exhaustive. A question that should always be kept in mind throughout the analysis process is, "What else do we need to know, given our circumstances and situation and those of the learners?" Even the analysis phase warrants an evaluation of whether it has done its job. Moreover, as the rest of the ADDIE process unfolds, the project team may need to engage in further analysis or revisit given questions and responses should new circumstances warrant it. This is especially the case as new technologies and media emerge, as institutions make important changes, as faculty come and go, and, of course, as students evolve with the times.

Here is a checklist that covers the most important aspects to be analyzed:

☐ The initial impetus and sustaining reason(s) for offering this online language course or program (institutional and programmatic) are fully recognized.

☐ The person(s) or unit(s) that support or may impede the project have been identified.

☐ The funding source(s) to create and to sustain the course or program are clear.

☐ The target learner population (characteristics, geographic dispersion, technologies available to them, their goals) is defined.

☐ The place of the online course or program within other courses and programs is articulated.

☐ Technologies and resources available to the project team for project creation and delivery are listed.

☐ The timeframe for the project is clear and feasible.

☐ Staffing, including support and professional development for designers, instructors, assistants, and evaluators is arranged or if needed, is being planned.

☐ External constraints, including accessibility, professional standards, accreditation, and local/state/national regulations are recognized and shared with the whole project team.

Design

Analysis is followed by the "D" of design. All the parts of ADDIE are essential, but good design is the bedrock upon which the course rests. Based on answers and considerations spelled out during the analysis phase, the designer or design team sets to work. The design phase produces a coherent structure and framework within which units, modules, tasks, assignments, and assessments, as well as support documents, resources, and support mechanisms, will be developed. As already noted, effective action begins the end goal in mind (Covey, 1989). In the online language environment, the element of distance, with its impact on learners and learning, must remain central to planning. It helps to create a design map or wireframe for the whole course, adding in and showing connections between all the various components as they emerge during the design process. Such mapping helps the project team and any other stakeholders to see the big picture at all times. Moreover, a version of the mapping can be used, as will be explained below, as both an orientation and a navigation tool for the learners.

The distance factor weighs especially heavily in the online language course. Specific to language learning, learning goals and expected outcomes are generally articulated in proficiency terms (ACTFL, WIDA, or CEFR scales) and measured by performance indicators—what the learners can do—across the three modes of communication (interpretive, interpersonal, presentational) according to ACTFL and the National Council of State Supervisors for Foreign Languages (NCSSFL), across the four skills (reading, writing, listening, and speaking) for WIDA, and across the three activities (reception, production, interaction) according to Council of Europe's CEFR. Depending on the program or the course, there may be additional instructional goals (e.g., graduate reading proficiency; medical, legal, or business certification; digital literacy; civic or community engagement, etc.). Still, linguistic improvement and increased intercultural awareness always factor into the language curriculum. Goals are further divided into smaller learning objectives that, taken together, should move the learner along pathways toward the expected learning outcomes. The new Bloom's Digital Taxonomy provides a hierarchy of skill and knowledge development within a suite of cognitive processes and digital modalities across all disciplines (Anderson et al., 2001; Armstrong, 2016; Sneed, 2016). This new version is especially useful for thinking about and planning for digital learning. Moreover, the active verbs in the taxonomy integrate well with the NCSSFL-ACTFL Can-Do Statements (2017) and WIDA Can Do Descriptors (2016), thus helping guide proficiency goal setting. In language education, performance across the three modes of communication (for world languages) or across the four skills (for ESL) allows the instructional designer to focus on the interplay and integration of all three modes such that learners increase their proficiency in all four skills at the same time as their intercultural competency. Chapters 2 and 3 delve more deeply into these areas.

Learning Platform for Course Delivery

Most educational organizations already have an LMS platform like Blackboard, Canvas, D2L Brightspace, Moodle, Sakai, Angel, or Google Classroom for face-to-face, hybrid, and online teaching and learning. There are instances,

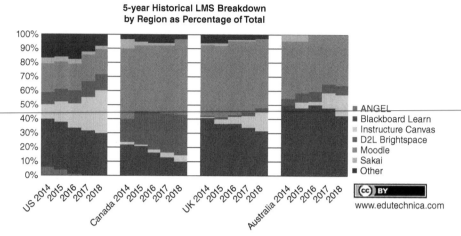

Figure 1.2 5-year historical LMS breakdown by region as percentage of total.

Graphic created by Edutechnica.com, 2018. CC BY SA 4.0.

however, where the online education division may adopt a different one. Besides the major platforms listed, other types of LMS solutions exist such as WordPress with a plugin like LearnDash to manage, coordinate, and develop the online learning site. Figure 1.2 shows the relative size of the market share from 2014–2018 in higher education institutions' LMSs in the United States, Canada, United Kingdom, and Australia. It is noteworthy that in 2019, Canvas has pulled ahead of Blackboard in the market share in higher education in the United States (Edutechnica, 2019).

   The online magazine, *eLearning Industry*, offers a directory of nearly 400 LMS options, with a host of institutional types, subscriptions, and various affordances, or ways that the LMS can be used. In addition, many LMSs offer free trials. Yet, some readers may plan to run their own online school, like the Rapp brothers' Spanish MOOC some ten years ago. In this instance, it will take time and effort to research and choose the best platform for the type of program or course that is anticipated. One other delivery platform to consider is an entirely mobile one. As discussed below, the demand for mobile eLearning is steadily increasing. There are even some LMSs that offer only a mobile platform.

In the less frequent instance, where the designer or team also chooses the learning platform, it should be noted that larger systems, like Blackboard and Canvas, are expensive and often the cost per student exceeds $1000. Even if one opts for Moodle, Edmodo, or WordPress (LearnDash), which offer ostensibly free open-source learning platforms, they will likely require a great deal of tailoring and setup, which are time-consuming. This is typically the work of information technology (IT) staff that usually exceeds the know-how of faculty and instructional designers. The Moodle site offers a list of support companies that—for a fee—provide such expertise. Moodle, Edmodo, Google, and LearnDash (the WordPress solution) also have pricing options for services beyond the free license. The other important factor in setting up one's own LMS is hosting, which would necessitate the purchase of a domain name and delivering online learning at scale, which precludes a basement server or an inexpensive cloud option.

Google's Open Online Education

Although relatively new, the Google Open Online Education platform has already made inroads into K-12 schools thanks to Google Classroom. It also attracts start-ups and do-it-yourselfers. It is open and free but can be custom tailored for a price.

Since this book on online language design, development, and delivery is global in context, it should be noted that Google is generally banned in China. Although it would be illegal, the ban can be circumvented through virtual private networks (VPN). For an online educational program, it would be ill-advised to do so. Chinese companies have created programs that replace most of the banned functions. Elsewhere, in Crimea, Cuba, Iran, North Korea, Sudan, and Syria, Google limits some of its offerings. Still, the Google reach is extensive and otherwise globally viable. The G Suite for Education houses its latest cloud-based and scalable educational services like Mail, Calendar, Drive (with Docs, Sheets, Slides, etc.), Sites, Forms, Meets, Jamboard, Vault, and Classroom. See Table 1.1 for more detail on selected Google apps and services useful in online language environments.

Mobile Platforms

Within the enormous growth in online education worldwide, a fair share comes from mobile learning. Clement (2020) in a Statistica report shows that already 51% of web page views in the world are via mobile devices other than tablets; the percentage rises to over 65% in Asia and just under 60% in Africa and by 2020, smartphone user numbers will increase to just under 3 billion people (p. 0). The study, "Online College Students 2019" (Clinefelter et al., 2019) underscores that a majority of online students (56%) use their mobile devices for learning and two-thirds expect their courses to be deliverable on those devices (p. 32). Moreover, the younger generation, those under 45, want their learning experience to look and feel like the apps they routinely use on their phones. Thus, an LMS or learning platform that ports well to mobile devices, especially smartphones, is optimal.

Table 1.1 Selected Google products for online language environments.

Google Arts and Culture	An online platform giving access to high-resolution reproductions of art from partner museums.
Google Drive apps (included in the G Suite for Education): Docs, Sheets, Slides	Applications that rival costly utilities and productivity tools from Microsoft, Adobe, Apple, and other companies for academic work in the 21st century.
Google Earth	A computer program that gives a 3D representation of Earth from satellite imagery that allows users to zoom in on locations. Information can be attached to locations. Many embedded lessons already exist like the Louvre and ancient Rome.
Google Expeditions	Over 900 AR and over 100 VR lessons. Through the Cardboard viewer (or other 3D goggles) and Cardboard Camera, classes can explore 360° views of people, places, and things.
Google Meet	A communication product like Skype or other video chat programs, with integrated messenger services and Google Talk.
Google Reader	Aggregating application and site to gather and annotate from the web.
Google Scholar	An open web search engine that scours the full text or metadata of scholarly publications.
Google Translate	A multilingual machine translation service that can be used as a website interface, as a mobile, or programmed as an application interface.
Google Voice	Voice telephone service over Internet protocol (VoIP) with a "real" phone number that takes messages and transfer calls to and from other phones.

Any number of learning platforms and apps either have a mobile interface or can operate entirely in a mobile mode. During the design phase, the importance of mobile delivery should be determined. During development, however, the important step is to try out various pages across different platforms: iOS, Android, Huawei's Hongmeng OS, and, of course, any new ones that will emerge on the market from here on out. It may be the case that only certain parts of a lesson can be ported over to a mobile device. Learners must be made aware, for example, that proctored testing cannot be conducted via their phones. Still, almost all other apps (VoiceThread, publisher supersites, videos, LMSs) are available in mobile versions. Some of the desktop/laptop bells and whistles may be lacking, but much is available. In fact, there are several mobile-first LMSs, like Edvance 360, Kannu, and It's Learning, which (as is increasingly a business practice) start with a cloud-based mobile version that later is adapted to a desktop version. A useful infographic from eLearning

Infographics (2019) on mobile eLearning is linked in the e-resources. If the project team plans to create a program or course that is primarily mobile, it will be important to review Stockwell and Hubbard's ten principles for mobile language learning (2013, pp. 8–10).

However, a smartphone alone rarely suffices for delivery of an entirely online language course. While students should be able to access many if not most materials on their mobile devices, where they cannot or will be limited in their learning, students should be notified in the course overview and in the specific module that mobile access and interactivity is limited or impossible. Social media on phones and tablets can, however, open up a wide range of interpretive, interpersonal, and even presentational opportunities to students, providing real-world engagement in the communities, connections, comparisons, and cultures of the L2. Still, mobile delivery of a language lesson needs to be accompanied by learner development: the students must be coached to pay attention to the lesson and interaction. Using a phone is perceived by learners as more personal than academic. Students may require scaffolding to allow optimal use of the technology as a tool of online language learning (Stockwell & Hubbard, 2013).

Finally, it is important to make sure that as the materials are produced, they can be viewed on desktops, laptops, tablets, and mobile phones, making sure that the interface is clear, navigable, and accessible across whichever devices will be allowed.

Design Issues Specific to Languages

Online language instruction faces special design issues because language is both the content and the means of instruction. Ninety percent of instruction should be delivered in the target language (ACTFL, 2017). Recent work in neuroscience shows that code switching between languages (L1–L2) may increase cognitive load, especially for novice and intermediate language learners. Nonetheless, short, targeted use of the L1 can free up valuable learning time for practicing and engaging in the target language. Cook (2001) proposes four viable reasons for using the L1 in language lessons: efficiency, learning, naturalness, and external reference. Developing video tutorials to explain the online learning interface is an example of efficiency. It may be faster and easier for learners to grasp how to use course interface if the instructions are in L1. Moreover, user guides may already exist in one's institution or be provided by a publisher or an app company, which would relieve the designers and developers from that task.

Learners already struggling with the "foreignness" of an L2 may find themselves also facing a "foreign" learning environment in the online venue. A faulty or confusing online lesson can be fixed, but a confusing overall design or one lacking a consistent interface with clear navigation is equally alienating for students. The on-campus classroom allows faculty to use all their senses in perceiving student reactions. Teachers can incorporate current events and campus happenings in the moment in a live class. This may happen less frequently in asynchronous online classes. Then again, instructors can use weekly communications to add in such immediacy and of course, faculty and students may interact occasionally synchronously to exchange news.

Specific to language learning in the current educational context in the United States, learning goals are determined and articulated in the World-Readiness Standards for Learning Languages (National Standards Collaborative Board, 2015) and by the ACTFL Proficiency Guidelines (ACTFL, 2012) for speaking, writing, listening, and reading for world languages and by the WIDA Amplification of the English Language Development Standards Kindergarten–Grade 12 (WIDA, 2012) for ESL. The following graphic from the Center for Advanced Research on Language Acquisition (CARLA), until recently one of the federally funded Language Resource Centers (LRCs), shows the constant interactions among standards, instructional goals, assessments, and learning activities (Figure 1.3). For those educators in the K-12 arena, it includes a slot for the Common Core standards from the United States.

Outside the United States, educators may opt to explore the Common European Framework of Reference (CEFR) Standards for Languages: Learning, Teaching, and Assessment and its European Language Portfolio (ELP). In this guide, however, the authors refer primarily to the ACTFL and WIDA guidelines.

Beginning as early as 2003, in line with research on the importance of learner portfolio assessment and reflection and with a successful model of the ELP, various members of NCSSFL started drafting their own version of a language learning portfolio, called LinguaFolio. An online version arose after five years of testing the pencil-and-paper version, thanks to the Center for Advanced Studies in Second Language Studies (CASLS) and the National Foreign Language Center (NFLC), both federally funded Language Resource Centers (LRCs). In 2017, NCSSFL and ACTFL revised the Can-Do Statements to include intercultural competencies. Currently, CASLS offers LinguaFolio Online (LFO) and a mobile version.

LinguaFolio organizes learning goals in line with three modes of communication:

- Interpretive: Learners understand, interpret, and analyze what is heard, read, or viewed on a variety of topics.
- Interpersonal: Learners interact and negotiate meaning in spoken, signed, or written conversations to share information, reactions, feelings, and opinions.

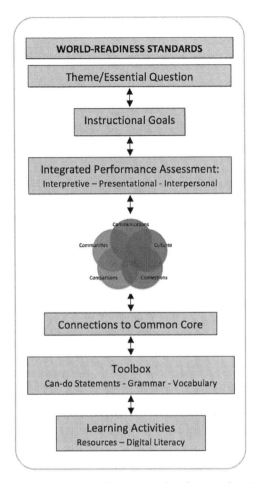

Figure 1.3 Flowchart for developing an IPA created for *Create a Standards-Based Integrated Performance Assessment Unit Step-by-Step* at the Center for Advanced Research on Language Acquisition (CARLA) at the University of Minnesota (Clementi, n.d.).

Graphic used with permission.

• Presentational: Learners present information, concepts, and ideas to inform, explain, persuade, and narrate on a variety of topics using appropriate media and adapting to various audiences of listeners, readers, or viewers (NCSSFL-ACTFL, 2017).

Through the ePortfolio system of LinguaFolio, curriculum designers and faculty are able to articulate nationally valid, level-appropriate learning goals and objectives for a unit or course. LinguaFolio allows educators to "design curriculum and units based on Benchmarks and Indicators and provide professional learning for educators on how to move learners up the proficiency levels. Educators collaborate to design end-of-unit or end-of-course assessments to provide evidence of learners independently and consistently demonstrating the targeted level of proficiency" (NCSSFL-ACTFL, 2017). The instructor's guide available on the CASLS LFO site details how to use backward design (see below) to plan a whole course as well as units within that course.

An essential feature of LinguaFolio involves assessment. In addition to offering its unit planning guide, it helps curriculum designers create the final course or unit assessment based on an essential concept or question, and then, with the end firmly in mind, backward engineer all the necessary learning targets along with their integrated performance assessments (a way of cycling through all three modes, assessing learner outcomes) toward realizing the proficiency goals, along with any scaffolding, practice, assignments, and homework needed to support, scaffold, and promote student learning. As a result, learners finish with a reflection on their own learning. Several studies have shown the power of such reflection on student autonomy and success (Hromalik & Koszalka, 2018; Reinders & White, 2016; Ribbe & Bezanilla, 2013; Zhong, 2018; Ziegler & Moeller, 2012). How the Can-Do Statements and proficiency goal setting aligns with communicative language teaching is fully detailed in Chapter 3.

Although it does not address language education, Bates' discussion of learning time frames does pertain to online language courses (2019). He states that rather than trying to equate the number of hours for an online course with a traditional classroom's contact and homework hours, the equivalence should arise from the work assigned to achieve the same "notional" learning, which in language circles is determined by what learners "Can-Do." By creating online, blended, and flipped courses that deliver the same notional-functional (i.e., proficiency-based learning) outcomes as brick-and-mortar courses, there will be no difference in the quality of the education. Nevertheless, the designers need to specify a target of total time to be spent on a course by an average student. The total study time for a lesson or module includes the structured learning of the course content plus the time for activities, interactions, and tasks to practice and assess the learning targets. The designer or design team should take care not to underestimate the amount of time it will take students to complete their lessons and modules online. Getting an outside perspective on the student workload, often part of the work of an instructional designer, can avoid overburdening students with excessive workloads (Bates, 2019).

Backward Design

The authors of this book subscribe to the backward design approach. It is also referred to in a more learner-centric fashion as "Understanding by Design" (UbD). It has three major steps: (1) begin by articulating the learning outcomes, that is, what learners will be able to do at the end of the learning experience in proficiency terms; (2) create learning assessments and assignments that will provide evidence of the level of attainment of the learning outcomes; and, (3) sequence and scaffold instructional materials, interactions, and activities to ensure successful progress toward being able to express what has been learned. OLL goals and expected learning outcomes are often determined by a language department or school system. They are balanced with the institutional realities discovered during the analysis phase. In particular, in the online language learning environment, the distance factor permeates all thinking and planning about the goals, the evidence of student learning, and the necessary steps to lead students to success (Wiggins et al., 2005). Figure 1.4 encapsulates the process:

The Backward Design Approach

Identify desired results.
What should the learners understand, know and be able to do by the end?

Determine assessment evidence.
How will the learners' understanding, knowledge and skills be checked?

Plan learning experiences and instruction.
What learning activities, interactions, and scaffolding do learners need to be successful?

Understanding by Design by Wiggins & McTighe, 2005.

Figure 1.4 The backward design process based on Wiggins & McTighe (2005).

Cognitive approaches in second language acquisition (SLA) describe the spiraling movement from novice-level proficiency through the highest, distinguished levels. Shrum and Glisan (2010) succinctly outline the pedagogical process as being a top-down or backward design approach that can be used for an entire program, a unit, or even a single lesson. They promote the use of authentic texts determined by the current and targeted proficiency levels. Goals are followed by organizing the learning objectives into a series of units or modules, each with its own set of unit or module objectives, which can also include Can-Do Statements for students to engage in goal setting and reflection. It is the nature of language acquisition that the learning goals should overlap and repeat. The 2001 Bloom's Taxonomy shown in Figure 1.5 provides an incremental framework for knowledge, skill, and/or attitude attainment within a suite of progressively developing cognitive processes (Anderson et al., 2001). Project designers using backward design should align learning objectives with expected learning outcomes and make sure that learners have adequate scaffolding to reach the targeted performance goals.

If world language educators choose to use the materials provided by the CASLS LinguaFolio team, a comprehensive approach to backward design is detailed in its teacher's guide. Its power arises from starting with a concept, and then elaborating performance goals across the three modes of communication (interpretive, interpersonal, and presentational). The Can-Do Statements help

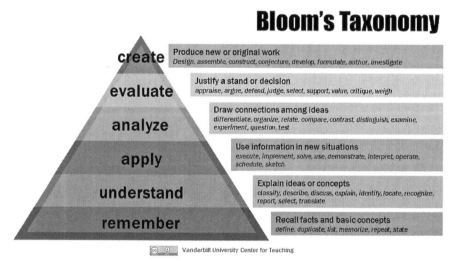

Figure 1.5   The new Bloom's Taxonomy.

Vanderbilt University Center for Teaching. CC BY 2.0, 2016.

learners set their own language learning goals, reflect on them, and think critically about the unit concept through the lens of the target language and culture (CASLS, 2017). Concepts like social justice, immigration, change, time, relationships, identity, and collaboration drive the acquisition of vocabulary, forms, and structures by having learners engage with the real world in the target language. The rest of the guide breaks down the steps of unit planning based on the overarching concept(s). Integration of the NCSSFL-ACTFL Can-Do Statements into formative assessments gives online course designers a solid, research-based structure for their instruc- tion (NCSSFL-ACTFL, 2017). CARLA also offers numerous resources for the backward design of units and their assessments. The graphic below (Figure 1.6) from the Ohio Department of Education describes the pro- cesses involved in world language backward design at the level of a the- matic unit, but it is equally valid at the program or course level and it can be easily adapted for ESL contexts.

Synchronous v. Asynchronous Models of Delivery

The type of delivery mode—synchronous, asynchronous, or a combination of both—will have been explored and decided at the analysis phase. Synchronous delivery occurs when the learners and instructor are co-present online at the same time. Asynchronous learning assumes that learner(s) need not be present simultaneously with any other persons in the learning environment. This is

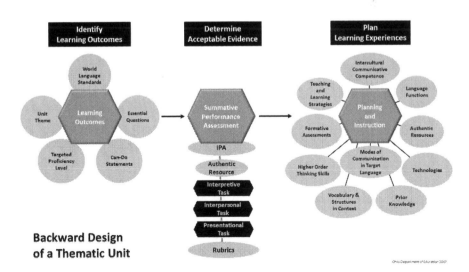

Figure 1.6 Backward design of a thematic unit created by the Ohio Department of Education (n.d.).

often referred to as anytime/anyplace instruction. Analysis of the institutional context and the learners will determine the best delivery mode. An effective approach to classroom learning today is that of the flipped classroom, where explicit instruction is offered asynchronously (e.g., as preparatory modules prior to brick-and-mortar class meetings). For example, before a session during which learners interact together in real time on a learning opportunity like a jigsaw task, they will have watched an interactive video that introduces and focuses their attention on the vocabulary and structures they will need to use in the class session in order to communicate and execute in-class tasks. If the module includes synchronous class meetings, they can be used to troubleshoot learner misconceptions and elicit learners' ways of conceptualizing new forms, processes, and understandings of prepared materials. Flipped learning also emphasizes learner-learner and/or learner-instructor activities that maximize communicative language learning (for more on communicative language teaching and flipped approaches, see Chapter 3). In the completely asynchronous setting, it may be much more difficult to orchestrate learner-learner or learner-instructor dialogue in real time, especially truly interpersonal oral interactions, during which learners negotiate meaning. Chapter 2 provides more guidance on how to develop modules with interactivity and Chapter 3 provides examples of online activities across all three modes of communication.

The Getting Started Module

Designing for learner success is critical to a good online course. Quality Matters (QM), a national leader in good design and development of online learning, makes the Getting Started module a requirement for effective online courses in every discipline. Online language learners may be new to the online learning environment and they may be unaware of strategies for successful online learning to take place. Media images of learning in bed, on the beach, surrounded by friends and pets—however great they are as marketing ploys—give learners a distorted view of online learning and, importantly, a skewed perspective of the focus, attention, planning, and persistence that it entails. Today's learners prefer clean, simple text, visuals, videos, and game-like instructions and task directions over dense text (Burns, 2019). Using visuals like screenshots, video clips, interactive exercises, and gaming options in the Getting Started module and orientation materials enhances students' ability and willingness to handle the distance factor. Moreover, it primes the pump for using visual and interactive course

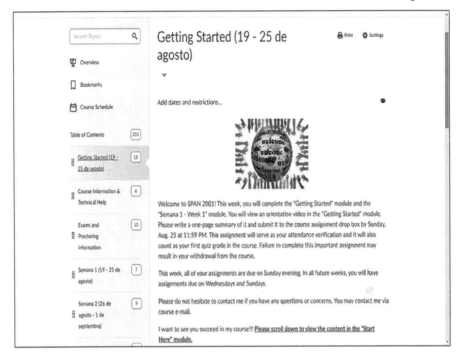

Figure 1.7 Screenshot of a getting started module for online Spanish on D2L's Brightspace platform.

D2L product screenshot reprinted with permission from D2L Corporation.

materials, which should also be as multimodal (engaging multiple senses), active, and as engaging as possible. See Figure 1.7 for an example of a Getting Started module that is clean and simple.

Online instruction should have redundancies with information located in more than one area or with links to click back to previous pages or windows. However, multiple or redundant links may confuse learners, especially those who are linear thinkers. The course design map, which was suggested earlier, can be re-used as a content map in the Getting Started module. If the LMS does not include such a mapping device, the designer/developer(s) can create a content map, carefully marking connections and redundancies for their own as much as for the learners' sakes. In addition, clearly listing and linking assignments, assessments, and interactions (e.g., discussions, paired work, etc.) is essential for online students. This information can appear both in the Getting Started module and/or in a Frequently Asked Questions (FAQ) folder.

The Getting Started module should contain models of successful online language learning for the proficiency level of the targeted audience. The more students see the traits and habits of successful learners, the more likely it will be that they will succeed in the course. Short profiles of successful students and clips of them engaging in best practices, for example, can be extremely instrumental. Integrating learning standards and proficiency targets into introductory materials helps direct the learners and their learning. The NCSSL-ACTFL Can-Do Statements are particularly helpful in this respect (Ziegler & Moeller, 2012). Furthermore, CASLS offers them in digital and mobile versions of LinguaFolio Online.

In addition to the basic information to orient the learner toward successful learning, the Getting Started module should list all the necessary hardware, software, and wetware (i.e., the human brain, which refers to the acumen needed to operate the hardware and software). Many online education providers offer a one-size-fits-all approach to orienting students to learning online. However, for online language learning, extra steps and training are critical. Students must be prepared to work on all four skills across the three modes of communication (interpretive reading or listening, interpersonal speaking or writing, and presentational speaking and/or writing) by means of tools for audio-visual recording and online collaboration and communication (see Chapter 2 for online tools that stimulate the three modes of communication).

Throughout the design and development phases, course creators should keep a running list of these applications and tools since user instructions are needed for each one. Some training may be generic, supplied by the product maker or training sites like Hoonuit and LinkedIn Learning. Design teams may be able to tailor the generic ones for language learning online through extra steps or non-standard uses. Some generic user instructions are even available in various languages, which is a great way of infusing authentic communication in the interpretive reading mode if the learners' proficiency level is high enough to understand this content in the target language. An example can be found in the PDF from FlipGrid for world languages. Again, demonstrating competent engagement with the technologies and instruction through short video clips or other graphic, audio, or multimedia imagery promotes success in online learning. The graphic below (Figure 1.8) is used to familiarize students with the course site for engaging in curation tasks in an Intermediate-level blended French course.

Teaching, Social, and Cognitive Presences

Transactional distance in online education was defined by Moore in 1991 as "a psychological and communication space to be crossed, a space of potential misunderstanding between the inputs of instructor and those of the learner"

Figure 1.8 Screenshot with callouts as activity instructions for a blended course on the French2@VCU curation site of rampages.us, 2017.

(Moore, 1991, p. 23). Three primary types of presence in distance learning have been posited by educators to reduce that distance: teaching, social, and cognitive (Moore, 1991; Zhang, 2003). Presence in online teaching and learning is a critical aspect of student engagement in secondary and postsecondary online education (Garrison 2006a, 2006b; Pascarella & Terenzini, 2005; Kuh, 2005; Chickering & Gamson, 1987). Garrison and other scholars have fleshed out the idea of a community of inquiry in online educational or distance settings. (Garrison, Anderson, & Archer, 2000). What follows details teaching, social, and cognitive presence in the online learning environment (Garrison, 2006a, 2006b).

Teaching Presence

Teaching presence emerges from a robust, thoughtful design of the materials, tasks, and their articulated steps, as well as their learning support mechanisms (Shea, 2006; Shea, Pickett, & Pelz, 2003). Teaching presence is designed intentionally into an online course to ensure an easy, logical passage through the flow of course materials and to help learners avoid a sense of alienation or isolation. Some proven techniques to create and promote teaching presence are a humanizing instructor introduction, easy navigation, accessible help and guides, and a clear course calendar with a list of all due dates.

A welcome e-mail or Start Here document should make students feel that they are part of a learning community with a very real, human teacher. This can be done in different ways, like an e-mail or welcome letter or by a personal introduction via audio or video clip. For advanced students, the introduction might be in the target language. Other instructors create a tab or folder on the LMS that includes instructional staff contact information, a personal video or photos, and other "snapshots" of a very human instructor. Some create a teaching persona or an avatar like those from gaming and virtual worlds. A friendly teaching avatar is quite appropriate in large institutional or commercial settings where instructional staff routinely rotate in and out of online courses and where a highly adaptable, changeable teaching presence is needed. The University of Texas at Austin, for its online French OER materials, has Tex, a teaching armadillo, to tap into state and school pride (see Figure 1.9 below). School spirit and a sense of belonging is important to many learners (Chickering & Gamson, 1987; Stephens, Fryberg, Markus, Johnson, & Covarrubias, 2012). There are myriad ways to personalize one's online presence from avatars to emoticons, from e-mails to announcements, from assessment feedback to encouraging notes. Anything that compensates for the lack of immediacy and humanness of the teacher in the online environment creates teaching presence.

Tex: Il faut que j'**appelle** Paw-Paw ce soir.

Tex: I have to call Paw-Paw tonight.

Tammy: D'accord. A quelle heure est-ce qu'il faut que nous **appelions** Paw-Paw?

Tammy: Okay. What time do we have to call Paw-Paw?

Tex explique les règles à ses étudiants:

Tex explains the rules to his students:

Il faut que vous **parliez** clairement; pas de chewing-gum!

You must speak clearly; no chewing gum!

Bien sûr, il faut qu'on **finisse** avant midi. Le déjeuner, c'est sacré!

Of course, we must end before meal times. Lunch is sacred!

Joe-Bob, il faut que tu **attendes** la fin du cours avant de dormir.

Joe-Bob, you must wait until the end of class before sleeping.

Et il faut que nous **sortions** ensemble après le cours de révision pour prendre un verre.

We must go out together after the review to have a drink.

texercises

Figure 1.9 The University of Texas avatar, Tex, the armadillo, from *Français Interactif* by the Department of French, University of Texas, Austin. (n.d.).

Policies for group and individual interactions with students through e-mail, the LMS learning platform(s), and apps should take students' lives, learning curves, and workloads into consideration. At the same time, faculty should not lose work-life balance nor be expected to be available 24/7 to respond to the open time frames of online learning. The online venue does mean, nevertheless, that learners are working at odd hours, perhaps in intense spurts. Overly long response times can frustrate students and lead to their disengagement. Well-designed policies and routines unburden the faculty workload as well as promote student success. Still, given the distance factor, the instructor does need to send out frequent, supportive, and timely announcements, reminders, and feedback. Designing standard messages and reminders with predetermined turnaround times figures into the design process.

The second part of the teaching presence is that of learner to content (i.e., the media and materials that provide the vehicle for learning). Since learners need to connect smoothly to the LMS and given that they may often interact with more than one interface (the LMS, a publisher website, YouTube videos, various apps, virtual exchange or tutoring sites, etc.), it becomes extremely important to avoid confusing or hard-to-locate resources. Some learners may prefer to read print copy over digital reading. Research shows comprehension is higher from print-based reading. Singer and Alexander (2016) state, "While there were no differences across mediums when students identified the main idea of the text, students recalled key points linked to the main idea and other relevant information better when engaged with print" (p. 155). Boettcher and Conrad (2016) argue for all digital content to the exclusion of print; yet, for the sake of accessibility and usability for all learners, especially older learners, print content should be also made available (Jabr, 2013; Singer & Alexander, 2016). Nonetheless, multimedia, linking, and digitally interactive content often scaffold learning and engage students better and may not lend themselves to print.

Some dimensions of face-to-face communication, such as touch and smell, turning to a peer for quick help, an immediate intervention by the instructor, or pairing off for a live scavenger hunt may seem hard to replicate online. Yet even in asynchronous online courses, in-the-moment reactivity, pop-up questions, links to additional resources, and nested videos can be created to compensate for the loss of the face-to-face immediacy and presence. Part of a module design might include a recorded synchronous session, the video of which is annotated and made interactive with embedded quizzes. If the basic design allows for synchronous learning sessions, the designer/instructor can indicate during the design process which activities are best suited to video delivery and interactions via Skype, Zoom, Collaborate, or other virtual meeting platforms such as GoReact, VoiceThread, or FlipGrid, which allow students and/or instructors to interact orally. See Chapters 2 and 3 for more information on these platforms.

Designing first-week, midterm, and final surveys that gauge students' sense of the teaching presence helps catch feelings of estrangement. Problems can be remediated by additional announcements, encouraging e-mails, more supportive feedback on work submitted, or a midterm video recounting the successes the class has achieved. Most educational institutions already encourage midterm grade reports, but the online arena is best served by even more frequent reporting and grade updates since the impetus of student performance in a traditional classroom and the immediacy of its scaffolding are less present and tend to convey less urgency in online learning environments (Kelly, 2014). High withdrawal and failure rates online often stem from a perceived lack of human interaction and attention (Hart, 2012). Successful programs manage to foster a healthy online teaching presence, with timely, consistent responses and encouragement (Bowers & Kumar, 2015).

At some larger institutions, design factors and materials to implement best practices in developing and delivering content are provided to faculty creating new courses. The State University of New York (SUNY) Learning Network offers a flexible online platform through its course management system along with instructional design staffing and support (Shea et al., 2003). A consistent design framework enables SUNY online students to successfully navigate online courses. As faculty develop courses, they customize the design framework and attend to their teaching presence by: a) setting the curriculum, b) establishing time parameters, c) utilizing the medium effectively, and d) establishing netiquette, which are the ground rules for civil communication online. Each step reinforces best practices in maintaining teaching presence.

Social Presence

Social presence is "the ability to project one's self and establish personal and purposeful relationships. The three main aspects of social presence … are effective communication, open communication and group cohesion" (Garrison, 2006b). In our field, where communication across many borders and media and its emphasis on cultural competencies to foster understanding and cohesion among disparate peoples are of paramount importance, social presence is doubly important. In the asynchronous online classroom, creating social presence reduces the alienating effects of the foreignness of the subject matter and the online venue. There are two types of social presence to establish: that of the class as a whole group, as well as that of individual learners as they interface with the teacher and classmates. Creating social presence fosters the identity formation of individual learners as language learners and increasingly competent intercultural agents. Garrison and Arbaugh (2007) warn that "groups do not naturally coalesce … particularly in situations where the task and challenge is to make sense of complex and disparate information" (p. 163). They advise direction and facilitation to achieve greater group development. In online language learning, students may find the learning environment doubly "foreign." They are entering a linguistic and cultural world unlike the physical one they inhabit as well as doing so in a "foreign" medium, where making group connections, providing mutual support, and sharing knowledge and skills are especially important.

For adolescent and young adult learners for whom personal and social identity formation is a work in progress, assuming a new and "foreign" facet to their "self" through the acquisition of a new language may feel destabilizing or even threatening, which could complicate already awkward social interactions in online spaces. Designing a space for peer exchange in the L1 for learners at lower levels of proficiency to discuss and reflect on language learning and foreign cultural experiences may help to enhance the collective experience. The Communities and Comparisons standards of the ACTFL World-Readiness Standards (National Standards Collaborative Board, 2015) can come into play. Learners can share where and how they can engage in intercultural experiences. They can then also build social presence with outside L2 communities, like international students and visitors on campus and beyond. Many cities have Sister City organizations, fellowship groups, language and cultural resource centers and associations, and Chambers of Commerce where the learner can increase social presence. The work of social presence is often the core of a language classroom. Warm-ups like those suggested under teaching presence help create social presence, where the learning community shares information about families and pets, likes and dislikes, and who they are as people. Questions and answers become exchanges of real information and not just vocabulary exercises. Nonetheless, the online classroom is an academic experience, not just an occasion for interpersonal bonding. The social presence in class needs to grow from group cohesion toward a group solidarity by working toward a common learning goal (Garrison, 2006a, p. 27).

Cognitive Presence

Garrison (2006b) define cognitive presence as the point in "a cycle of practical inquiry where participants move deliberately from understanding the problem or issue through to exploration, integration and application" (p. 65). It involves the upper reaches of Bloom's Taxonomy (Anderson et al., 2001). Moving beyond exploration to resolution is difficult to achieve online and depends heavily on the instructional role (Garrison, 2006b). Online teachers, through the materials and instructions they provide (the teaching presence), must construct a field of practical steps that lead learners to collaborate, process their learning together (social presence), and finally reflect upon it individually to resolve and consolidate the entire learning process (cognitive presence). These steps require more thought and preparation in a language learning environment, where 90% of instruction is delivered in the target language. At lower levels of language acquisition, it takes considerable planning and forethought to design online instruction and interactions in the target language for novice language students. Therefore, it is vital to employ images, circumlocutions, cognates, animations, and videos to facilitate students' comprehension in the target language. As Glisan and Donato (2017) write, "Using the [target language] TL in ways that foster comprehension requires more than showing pictures or making gestures to illustrate what is said.... [L]anguage learning is precisely about language and meaning; an overreliance on using pictures and gestures could prevent learners from engaging cognitively with the TL. Pictures and gestures ... should never entirely replace learners' attention to the meanings and functions that language forms convey" (p. 22). Online modules can support teaching in the target language with scaffolding resources that learners access as needed and that lead them precisely to working through the meanings and functions the language is conveying.

Paying careful attention to the three presences during each aspect of the instructional design process is of paramount importance for stimulating learner engagement in the course. Research findings on the three presences are presented in Chapter 5 and it should be noted here that the most difficult presence to foster in an online course or program is social presence.

Designing for Assessment of Student Learning

In backward design, once the learning outcomes are clearly stated, the designer or design team determines the evidence that will demonstrate what students should be able to do as a result of instruction. Based on the ACTFL standards that have guided the field of world language education in the United States for over three decades, the linguistic and cultural competencies, progressing from Novice through Distinguished proficiencies, describe what language users know and can do in the three modes of communication—interpretive,

Table 1.2 Table comparing proficiency levels in CEFR, ILR, and ACTFL scales

CEFR	ILR	ACTFL
0	0	Novice Low
0	0/0+	Mid
A1.1	0/0+	High
A1.2 /A2	1	Intermediate Low
A2/B1.1	1/1+	Mid
B1.1/B1.2	1+	High
B1.2/B2.1	1+/2	Advanced Low
B2.1/B2.2	2/2+	Mid
C1.1	3	High
C1.2	3/3+	Superior
C2	4/4+	Distinguished

Note. Wikipedia, n.d. Retrieved in part from: https://en.wikipedia.org/wiki/ILR_scale. CC BY SA 4.0.

interpersonal, and presentational—and their intercultural competence. The proficiency framework arose in part from recognition of the Interagency Language Roundtable (IRL) ratings that have guided United States federal agencies in assessing linguistic and cultural competencies of its staff and of other governmental stakeholders. They are similar to the CEFR standards and outcomes articulated by the Council of Europe in the 1970s and 1980s. The elaboration of the corresponding proficiency framework, known as the ACTFL Proficiency Guidelines, is harmonized with the ILR and CEFR levels in Table 1.2 (ACTFL, 2012; North, 2006).

The ACTFL ratings are set forth in five levels: Novice, Intermediate, Advanced, Superior, and Distinguished. The Novice through Advanced levels have three sublevels each: Low, Mid, High. The CEFR has only three levels on its scale: A, B, and C. Each of its levels contains two subscales: 1 and 2. Thus, one might have an A1 through C2 rating. The IRL Scales range from 0 (no proficiency), 1 (elementary), 2 (limited working), 3 (professional working), 4 (full professional), through 5 (native or bilingual), which is not listed on this table since it does not have a corresponding ACTLF or CEFR level. A full description of ACTFL, CEFR, and WIDA proficiency levels is presented in Chapter 3.

Given that some online language programs can enroll learners from around the world, the various standards and scales should figure into the learning outcomes and they should be used to determine the proficiency expected by the end of the course of instruction. In addition to the more general proficiency goals, the instructor, designer, or design team must also refer to the specific learning outcomes for content courses and professional certifications like legal or medical translation and interpretation. During the analysis phase, the minimum acceptable level of proficiency for entering and exiting the course is determined. Setting proficiency targets for an online course sets the stage to select precise standards and Can-Do Statements. Based on these, the instructor, designer, or design team chooses the scaffolding mechanisms, activities, and resources needed to achieve them. The types of evidence to be collected are chosen to demonstrate student performance at that level. The course designers should additionally be considering which ACTFL Performance Descriptors (ACTFL, 2015) or WIDA Performance Definitions (WIDA, 2018a, 2018b) align with summative unit and/or final course assessments.

Next, the instructional designers must choose the types of evidence and rubrics that will demonstrate the level of individual student learning and performance of communication tasks at the targeted proficiency level. Differentiating the types of evidence permits diverse learners to show what they can do on a given performance task. In UDL, the idea is to allow learners multiple means of expression (see Chapter 2 for a deeper discussion of UDL and multiple means of expression). Designers and instructors need to set up multiple ways for students to show their ability to perform on a given task or assessment. Hans Traxler's often-used cartoon in Figure 1.10 satirizes so-called

„Im Sinne einer gerechten Auslese lautet die Prüfungsfrage für Sie alle gleich: Klettern Sie auf den Baum!"

Figure 1.10 Cartoon showing the need for differentiated testing.

(Traxler, 1983) Permission to reprint granted.

equitable testing situations. The learners—a crow, a monkey, a pelican, an elephant, a fish, a seal, and a dog—are given a one-size-fits-all test: to climb a tree!

Differentiation has to be built into both instruction and assessment. Tasks, activities, and assessments should allow learner individuation as much as possible. For example, an online module or lesson might include a single text with three means of representation: written text, an audio reading of the text followed by the written text, and a video version with audio, images, and full text subtitling. For assessing learners' ability to interpret written texts, for example, regardless of the means of representation chosen, learners would answer questions about the text with the questions being posed in a similarly differentiated style. Depending on the time frame for the entire online project, it may only be possible to incorporate a couple of differentiated lessons with corresponding assessments at first. Creating a ready set of three ways to differentiate instructional materials allows the project team a handy means to produce differentiated lessons and modules. Over time, however, based on student reactions and performance, more can be added. Creating a design framework open enough to accept additional instructional materials facilitates such expansion and improvement.

By beginning with the final summative assessment and backward designing instructional materials and interactions all the way to the start of the course, the project team ensures that learners are primed to succeed. Their success is bolstered by integrating similar forms of assessment throughout the course. Where designers create a proficiency-based course, they should assess communicatively using performance-based assessments. Chapter 5 provides full details regarding the research on performance-based assessments with examples of how to integrate them in online language courses. Performance rating should look much like the Can-Do targets in LinguaFolio. If needed, rubrics and their ratings can be converted to percentages or scores for grading. Figure 1.11 is drawn from the CARLA site on assessment in world languages and visualizes a group activity with its Can-Do statement for interpersonal speaking and a rubric for evaluating student performance.

For the final summative assessment, there might be achievement testing or the completion of a project with stated skill targets and performance modes. In the event that a proficiency rating is also needed, the instructional team can either create their own testing or use existing ones, like the ACTFL oral proficiency interview (OPI) and the written proficiency test (WPT), the reading proficiency test (RPT), the listening proficiency test (LPT), or those from testing companies like the OWL and AVANT Stamp tests (see more in Chapter 3 on proficiency testing).

CENTER FOR ADVANCED RESEARCH ON LANGUAGE ACQUISITION

Task and multiple trait *mini-rubric*

Activity Description:

If language teachers were paid every time they had to remind students to speak the target language (TL), they could probably retire.

With this in mind, you will be a part of a group that will meet at the beginning of each class (groups will change from time to time). Your teacher will have an activity prepared for the groups to complete each day (this gives your teacher the opportunity to take attendance and finish all those other time-consuming tasks).

Each group should elect a leader to take charge and keep the group on task, making sure that everyone participates. Always speak as much TL as possible during your warm-up. Help and learn from each other. Use the TL to greet and say your farewells to your group members at the end of the activity.

Primary Activity Standard: Communication Standard 1.1 (Interpersonal Communication)

Students engage in conversations, provide and obtain information, express feelings and emotions, and exchange opinions.

	Excellent	Average	Needs Work
Time on Task	The group forms immediately to work on activity until the teacher indicates otherwise; if group finishes early, members discuss topics related to TL. 10 9	The group forms fairly soon to work mostly on activity until the teacher indicates otherwise; if group finishes early, members are either silent or discuss topics not related to TL. 8 7 6	The group takes a long time to form; they do not work on activity (unless the teacher walks by); if group finishes early, members discuss topics not related to TL. 5 4 3 2 1 0
Participation	All group members participate equally throughout the entire activity. 5	All group members but one participate equally throughout the activity. 4 3	More than one group member does not participate equally throughout the activity. 2 1 0
Group Cooperation	All members cooperate to help each other learn; if anyone has been absent, the group helps him/her; no one acts "superior." 10 9	Most members cooperate to help each other learn; if anyone has been absent, the group sometimes helps him/her; no one acts "superior." 8 7 6	Members do not cooperate to help each other learn; if anyone has been absent, the group does not help; some members act "superior." 5 4 3 2 1 0
Use of TL	Members use as much TL as possible (also to greet and say farewells). 5	Members use some TL during activity (also to greet and say farewells). 4 3	Members rarely use TL during activity (neither do they greet nor say farewells). 2 1 0

© 1999 Wade Petersen

*The source for this activity and rubric is *50 French Oral Communication Activities with Mini-Rubrics* by Wade Petersen. References to *French* in the original were changed to *target language* or *TL* above so that the activity can be adapted for any language. Petersen has also written activities and rubrics for Spanish and German.

Petersen, W. (1999). *50 French oral communication activities with mini-rubrics.* Auburn Hills, MI: Teacher's Discovery.

Petersen, W. (1999). *50 Spanish oral communication activities with mini-rubrics.* Auburn Hills, MI: Teacher's Discovery.

Petersen, W. (1999). *50 German oral communication activities with mini-rubrics.* Auburn Hills, MI: Teacher's Discovery.

Close Window

Figure 1.11 Interpersonal task with assessment rubric.

Created for CARLA, University of Minnesota (Peterson, n.d.).

Finding a balance between efficiency and effectiveness may be difficult when designing an online course. There are, however, an increasing number of automated testing programs and applications that can facilitate test taking and grading. The major publishing companies like Pearson, Cengage, and Vista Higher Learning incorporate automated grading features for many tests and some student writing. Extempore offers a robust tool for oral testing along with good feedback mechanisms for teachers. Good instructional design can improve assessment routines by affording the learners models of and resources for interpersonal and presentational writing. For example, it can demonstrate how to create and revise compositions using tools like the Wordreference.com site or *BonPatron*, a French writing assistant (O'Neill, 2019). More information on assessment tools is provided in Chapter 2.

The final design issue regarding assessment is that of assessment and exam proctoring. Where traditional forms of testing are expected, the online course may offer on-campus or distance proctoring. If students can be expected to submit to examination in a specific place, say a testing center on a campus, there are fewer difficulties. Many online campus programs set up a 50-mile radius policy for onsite testing. Yet, this may defeat the idea of a course offering distance learning. Many public community colleges across the United States have testing centers where proctored exams might be arranged even if the course is offered from another institution, even in a different state. Some public libraries and churches, too, may offer proctoring services. For military students, the authors have managed to arrange proctoring at a duty station under strict control. Off-campus sites may charge fees; thus, the testing is best worked out during the analysis and design phases. Some of the language publishers offer online testing with screen lockdown. With a locked down screen, once students start the exam, they can only work on the test, with no other tabs or browsers being open. Nonetheless, there is no way to preclude the use of a cell phone or another device. There are also online proctoring services like ProctorU, Proctorio, Examity, Pearson Vue, among others (Dimeo, 2017). Generally, the online proctoring services set up a rigorous student identification protocol, time limits for the testing, room checks to assure there are no forbidden resources or aids, and either ongoing video interfacing and/or keystroke captures to ensure that the test-taker looks primarily at the screen and stays on task. Anomalies are signaled to the instructor at the end of the session. Still any of these workarounds can be hacked; no surveillance method is foolproof. Some schools simply rely on their honor code to stop cheating.

Performance-based and portfolio-based assessments such as LinguaFolio, however, can circumvent the need for proctoring. However, LinguaFolio is designed as a learner's ePortfolio and not as an institutional assessment tool. Given the philosophy and intended use of LinguaFolio as a tool for aggregating evidence of student learning and reflective self-assessment (with subsequent teacher review of the student's self-reported success), some instructors, such as the authors, have been able to incorporate it as a part of individual student contracts and graded tasks, rather than ascribing a point system to the assigned Can-Do targets. To do so, it is necessary to align the tasks (graded) with LinguaFolio Can-Do targets, grading the evidence in a final submission, but not grading the student's self-assessment.

Anti-plagiarism program like Safe-Assign (free in Blackboard), Grammarly, or TurnItIn, among others compare a student's written work to a massive Internet archive of digitized texts to discover large scale identical or nearly identical phrasings. The system assigns a percentage of similarity and the programs cite the original text so the instructors can make their own determinations. The best defense against cheating and plagiarism is tailoring the course and its assessment to authentic, engaging communication that inspires students to express themselves in the L2.

Designing for Accessibility, Usability, and Inclusivity

This section addresses three aspects of online course design that touch on the rights, responsibilities, and perspectives that ensure that all learners are treated equitably and respectfully. Accessibility relates to persons with disabilities and it is a legal issue in instructional contexts within the United States. Usability concerns the effective, efficient, and satisfying design of a product, educational or otherwise, and may or may not address issues of disability. Finally, inclusivity is about learner diversity and often includes a discussion of UDL, known as design for all. The discussion of usability and inclusivity below will fall under UDL.

What is accessibility? According to the Civil Rights Act of 1960 and the United States Department of Education:

> "Accessible" means a person with a disability is afforded the opportunity to acquire the same information, engage in the same interactions, and enjoy the same services as a person without a disability in an equally effective and equally integrated manner, with substantially equivalent ease of use. The person with a disability must be able to obtain the information as fully, equally, and independently as a person without a disability.
>
> (Office for Civil Rights, 2013)

Regulations and resources with respect to accommodations vary across secondary, postsecondary, public, private, and commercial arenas and from country to country. In the United States, Section 508 of the Rehabilitation Act, updated in 2018, now includes the incorporation of the Web Content Accessibility Guidelines (WCAG) 2.0, with two levels, Level A and Level AA. It means that not only must there be closed captioning for online courses, but also videos must conform to the latest requirements. Language education, which necessarily includes listening, speaking, reading, and writing, must include possible and needed types of interventions. In the analysis phase, the designer or team identifies institutional policies, for example WCAG2.1 A or AA, and affordances available to their institution. They list all assistive technologies needed for learner input and output, noting any limitations for languages online. Burgstahler (2017) offers 20 tips for creating ADA-compliant online learning sites, documents, and resources. Listed below are ones not yet covered in this chapter, but that bear attention:

- Use descriptive wording for hyperlink text (e.g., "DO-IT Knowledge Base" rather than "click here").
- Avoid using PDFs, especially those presented as images (i.e., the text cannot be copied); if a PDF is used, design it to be accessible or create an accessible alternative. Consider using accessibly designed HTML or Word documents.
- Provide concise text descriptions of content presented within images.
- Make sure all content and navigation is accessible using the keyboard alone and choose IT tools that are accessible.
- Caption videos and transcribe audio content.
- Make examples and assignments relevant to learners with a wide variety of interests and backgrounds.
- Offer outlines and other scaffolding tools to help students learn.
- Provide adequate opportunities to practice.

Accessible, inclusive education involves deliberate design, instruction, and assessment to meet the needs of all learners, whatever their background, ability, orientation, marital status, health, or cognitive and learning style may be. Focusing on physical disabilities in federal legislation since 1990, Section 504 of the Rehabilitation Act of 1973 and the Americans with Disabilities Act have expanded to broader dimensions of social, cultural, and economic factors that limit educational access and success. Whether online, blended, flipped, or face-to-face, exclusionary design elements must be recognized, confronted, dismantled, or avoided whether technological, pedagogical, or socio-cultural. In the analysis phase detailed above, questions for identifying the breadth and depth of learner diversity are suggested. Others may certainly be added as society grows ever more inclusive. Given the iterative process of ADDIE design, attention to accessibility and inclusivity can and should be a focus throughout the life of every program, course or module (Glynn & Wassell, 2018).

Designing with differentiation is designing for accessibility. Online instructional design pays a great deal of attention to universal design and accessibility. The MLA, in its Guidelines for Information and Technology Access and Support for the Modern Languages (MLA, 2013), has stipulated that departments and their institutions should: "support best practices in universal design and accessibility. Technologies that permit persons with disabilities to conduct research, teach, learn, and carry out other professional and educational responsibilities effectively should be made available. Institutions must be aware of and comply with federal regulations regarding accessibility" (Guideline #4). However, accessibility is not just about defined disabilities.

UDL guidelines were first elaborated in the 1990s by Meyer and Rose at CAST to provide, "a tool that can be used to design learning experiences that meet the needs of all learners" (CAST, 2018a). Educational, cognitive, and neuroscientific research have established that learners vary significantly in their response to instruction. Thus, instruction must strive for multiple ways to engage learners, represent the information to be learned, and to allow learners to express what they have learned. The goal is to develop learners to be purposeful, motivated, resourceful, and knowledgeable in their learning (CAST, 2018b).

There are tools for designing and checking LMS sites for accessibility and usability. Blackboard has produced an online UDL tool called Ally, an add-on feature that can be purchased and integrated directly into their LMS and in Sakai, Moodle, D2L Brightspace, and Canvas, among others, to address accessibility. It can automatically check course materials for accessibility issues based on WCAG and give feedback on the accessibility of course content. It will also suggest multiple means of representation of content by alternative formats: tagged PDFs for use with assistive devices; ePubs for reading as ebooks on iPads and other e-book readers; audio versions for listening on personal devices (for example for students to listen to readings when they cannot use their eyes); HTML for viewing in browsers and on mobile devices; electronic braille (BRF) versions for e-braille displays. It can also offer students a translated version of materials, which would not be appropriate for a language class, except where instructions or prompts in the institutional L1 could be translated into an international student's home-based L1, but should not include the L2 content being taught. Ally also works on websites to offer the same suite of accessibility indicators and alternative formats for content. Ally may well improve accessibility and inclusivity for those who can afford to integrate it, although at the time of this writing it is still in its early stages. CIDI labs has created DesignPLUS to help in the design of Canvas learning sites. It integrates seamlessly into Canvas and includes an accessibility checker. D2L Brightspace offers an onboard HTML and accessibility checker in versions above 10.7.1.

The design team should take care to represent all learners, irrespective of gender, race, ethnicity, religion, sexual orientation, ability, age, family status, etc. In language learning, target cultures and ethnicities—each with its own products, practices, and perspectives, and some of which may appear contrary to those of the L1 or L2 culturality—should be introduced to the learners in sensitive, non-judgmental ways that neither ignore nor under-play L1 biases that the learners will have to navigate to increase their inter-cultural competencies.

Alpha and Beta Testing

An important part of evaluation is testing in alpha and beta modes. Alpha testing identifies issues before a course is released to real students. It simulates students engaged in the course in various functions: course navigation, instruction, following a task, or taking an assessment. As a design issue it must be programmed into the workflow at strategic times. For example, an alpha test might be an instrument that checks the course flow for ease of navigation and logical progression.

The second stage, called beta testing, should provide input on the course products as they reach their final forms. A cross-section of beta testers should resemble the students who are expected to take the course. A careful review of their performance across the instructional materials and assessments helps refine those elements. Furthermore, their reflections on navigation, their satisfaction with course structure and its elements, and the like, help the designer or project team fix major problems and issues before real students register for the course. Beta testing, like alpha testing, must be programmed into the design and development timetable.

Evaluating the Design

This chapter has covered the essentials of design for online language courses and programs using the ADDIE process. The design of an online course should be robust, coherent, accessible, learner centered, and learning focused. During the development phase, changes can be made. A sound, comprehensive analysis phase followed by healthy design protocols, like those listed above, and open, collaborative engagement and communication with all stakeholders—designers, administrators, faculty, students, and community partners—promotes success.

Questions that can bring a team back on track are: Which path will result in the learners attaining the designated goals? What will be the impact of a given choice on the learning process and the eventual success of the learners? They should be followed by: What does current research tell us about the effectiveness of the overall course design and its major components; about the efficacy of technologies and online learning modalities that the team has chosen; about proven student learning outcomes for current online language learning pedagogies and media? Using data-driven research to check assumptions and traditional ways of delivering language learning will result in healthier and more robust, and eventually successful, online language instruction, as Chapter 5 will show. Moreover, online learning in the digital environment, with its increasing access to learning analytics, is particularly primed for data collection on individual and group activity. For example, the Open University in England, known for its leadership in online learning worldwide, is heading a multi-year project that will draw upon ten years of data collection and research. It plans to explore the usefulness of learner analytics and learning design data for faculty and students, the optimal balance of learning design and analytics for retention, where student voice is located in design and analytics, and best ways to support faculty and institutions in using both (Institute of Educational Technology, n.d.). Their work will undoubtedly move the field of online education forward in significant ways.

Suvorov stated during the BOLDD workshop at the 2019 CALICO conference that evaluation determines the merit of a program and measures observed outcomes in light of program objectives. It assigns value to results. One may (and often does) gather learner assessment data as part of a program evaluation (Murphy-Judy, Hromalik, Russell, & Suvorov, 2019). Each step in the ADDIE process should include its own evaluation. If at all possible, securing outside observers to consider and challenge assumptions and practices as the project evolves will lead to improvement. Outside resources can help with quality assurance in each phase. Evaluation, however, has to be designed into each step of the ADDIE process. During and after integration, data gathered from summative assessments, learner satisfaction surveys, faculty evaluation reports, technical reports, and feedback from learner participation and formative performances and the like all funnel into a well-designed plan for evaluation.

Organizations like Quality Matters offer evaluation resources for institutions and individuals looking to create and deploy eLearning in the United States and abroad. In Europe, ERASMUS has commissioned the European Higher Education Area (ESG, 2015) to provide quality assurance guidelines. Huertas et al. (2019) describe the "constituting elements of quality" across ten areas: institutional support, course development, teaching and learning, course structure, student support, faculty support with compulsory eLearning training for new members of staff, technological infrastructures, student assessment (learner authentication, work authorship, and examination security) and certification and electronic security measures (pp. 6–7). Of note is the attention they pay to what we call te(a)chnologies: "In the eLearning context, it is well to consider innovation strategies, rapid iterative review, and connections between research and pedagogy and/or learning design (which requires knowledge of the latest innovations in order to select the most appropriate means for achieving learning objectives)" (p. 6). Still, students and student learning must always be the driving force behind any kind of educational program, whatever the mode of delivery. Student activity in eLearning and assessment, as noted in the revised European Standards and Guidelines for Quality Assurance (2015) Standard 1.3, is central to evaluation of an entire program: "Institutions should ensure that programs are delivered in a way that encourages students to take an active role in creating the learning process, and that the assessment of students reflects this approach" (p. 12).

Vlachopoulos (2016) undertook a comprehensive literature review of quality assurance and roadmaps for eLearning. His article provides a wealth of information from the four corners of the globe on what quality eLearning design looks like and includes. His graphic representation of best practices in Figure 1.12 includes five focal areas: conceptual investigation, assurance, face-to-face and eLearning, quality in distance/online education, and quality design standards in eLearning courses.

The eResources for this chapter offer several checklists for effective online design as well as for more general project evaluation. Below, however, is a short checklist based on the major points of this section on design.

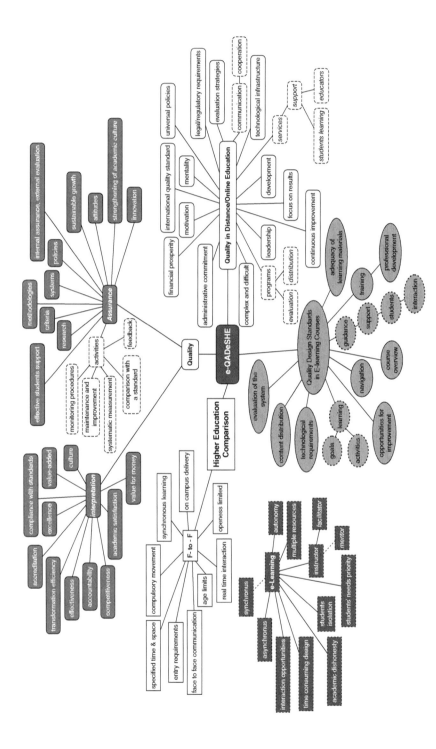

Figure 1.12 The roadmap of e-QADeSHE project.

Created by Dimitris Vlachopoulos for Athabasca University (Vlachopoulos, 2016).

Checklist

☐ The LMS is chosen and has consistent and easy-to-use navigation plus an area for course information and the Getting Started module;

☐ Clear course goal(s) and targeted learning outcomes are defined (in proficiency terms, i.e., Can-Do benchmarks);

☐ Summative assessments for the entire course and for each module are aligned with the course goals and learning objectives for each major module;

☐ The plan for integrating teaching, social, and cognitive presence throughout the course and appropriate te(a)chnologies are chosen;

☐ Types of scaffolded and differentiated instructional materials and interactions are in the planning stage;

☐ A plan to ensure accessibility, usability, and inclusivity for the course/program is set;

☐ A plan to evaluate the design of the entire program or course is under construction.

Conclusion

There are many ways to design for online, blended, and flipped language learning. The ADDIE process presented here is time tested and, if used in concert with a backward design model, offers a solid foundation for creating an eLearning program, course, or module. By beginning the whole project with the end in mind—which is to create standards-based instruction that engages learners in authentic communication within a meaningful cultural context—a virtual learning environment can be created to engage learners in a healthy, humane community of inquiry, one that includes and supports their diverse learning and social needs.

Key Takeaways

1. The design of an online language program is a serious, time-intensive endeavor best undertaken by a financially and professionally supported team. Many online language educators may not find themselves in such circumstances. Referring to the information in this chapter to analyze and design an online course or program will help ensure that a good design emerges.

2. Asking the right questions and honestly appraising the context(s) in which an online program will be delivered are fundamental to building a successful, sustainable product.

3. With a meta-perspective of the design phase, developers, faculty, and administrators can envision possible ways to adapt or improve an emerging or established online program.
4. Learning and the learners should always be at the heart of the creation of an online program, course, or module.

Discussion Questions

1. What is your role in the design, adaptation of a design, or re-design of the online program, course, or module? Which aspects of the overall course creation are in *your* hands: all of it from start to finish; a single course within an existing framework; a few lessons or modules; evaluation and suggestions; consulting? What would you like your level of input to be?
2. Which of the ADDIE steps do you find the most important given your role in the online program?
3. In your project, who will be your team members and what do they bring to the project? Who are the leaders in online education at your institution? How can you engage them to be part of your support network?
4. Which offices or individuals may not support your online language program or course? How and why are they pushing back? What can you say or do to reduce their opposition? What information could you supply them that might make them more supportive?

Suggestions for Further Reading

Bates, A. (2019). *Teaching in the digital age.* Chapter 4 and the Appendix A. Retrieved from https://opentextbc.ca/teachinginadigitalage/

Burgstahler, S. (2019). 20 Tips for teaching an accessible online course. Retrieved from https://www.washington.edu/doit/20-tips-teaching-accessible-online-course

Growth Engineering. (n.d.). Bloom's Taxonomy and online learning. Retrieved January 30, 2020, from https://www.growthengineering.co.uk/what-can-blooms-taxonomy-tell-us-about-onlineLearning/

Simon, E., & Fell, C. (2013). *Going hybrid: A how-to manual.* Boulder: Anderson Language Technology Center, University of Colorado. Retrieved from https://tinyurl.com/goinghybridatcu

Wiggins, G., McTighe, J., & Gale Group. (2005). *Understanding by design* (Expanded 2nd ed.). Alexandria, VA: Association for Supervision and Curriculum Development.

References

American Council on the Teaching of Foreign Languages (ACTFL). (2012). *Proficiency guidelines*. Retrieved from https://www.actfl.org/resources/actfl-proficiency-guidelines-2012

American Council on the Teaching of Foreign Languages (ACTFL). (2015). *Performance descriptors for language learners* (2nd ed.). Retrieved from https://cms.azed.gov/home/GetDocumentFile?id=5748a47daadebe04c0b66e64

American Council on the Teaching of Foreign Languages (ACTFL). (2017). *Use of the target language in language learning*. Retrieved from https://www.actfl.org/resources/guiding-principles-language-learning/use-target-language-language-learning

Anderson, L.W. (Ed.), Krathwohl, D.R. (Ed.), Airasian, P.W., Cruikshank, K.A., Mayer, R.E., Pintrich, P.R., Raths, J., & Wittrock, M.C. (2001). *A taxonomy for learning, teaching, and assessing: A revision of Bloom's Taxonomy of Educational Objectives* (Complete edition). New York: Longman.

Armstrong, P. (2016). *The new Bloom's taxonomy*. Website of the Vanderbilt University Center for Teaching. Retrieved from https://cft.vanderbilt.edu/guides-sub-pages/blooms-taxonomy/

Association of Departments of Foreign Languages (ADFL). (2014). *Suggested best practices and resources for the implementation of hybrid and online language courses*. Retrieved from https://www.adfl.mla.org/Resources/Policy-Statements/Suggested-Best-Practices-and-Resources-for-the-Implementation-of-Hybrid-and-Online-Language-Courses

Bates, A.W. (2019). *Teaching in a digital age* (2nd ed.). Retrieved from https://pressbooks.bccampus.ca/teachinginadigitalagev2

Blake, R. J. (2010). The use of technology for second language distance learning. *Modern Language Journal, 93*(5), 822–837.

Blake, Robert J. (2011). Current trends in online language learning. *Annual Review in Applied Linguistics, 31*, 19–35.

Boettcher, J., & Conrad, R.M. (2016). *The online teaching survival guide*. San Francisco, CA: Jossey-Bass.

Bonilla-Silva, E. (2006). *Racism without racists: Colorblind racism and the persistence of inequality in the United States*. Lanham, MD: Rowman and Littlefield.

Bowers, J., & Kumar, P. (2015). Students' perceptions of teaching and social presence: A comparative analysis of F2F and online learning environments. *International Journal of Web-Based Learning and Teaching Technologies, 10*, 27–44. doi:10.4018/ijwltt.2015010103

Burgstahler, S. (2017). *ADA compliance for online course design*. Retrieved from https://er.educause.edu/articles/2017/1/ada-compliance-for-online-course-design

Burns, M. (2019, April 14). To read or not to read: Text in an online world. *eLearning Industry* [Blog post]. Retrieved from https://elearningindustry. com/text-in-an-online-world-read

Center for Applied Second Language Studies (CASLS). (2017). *LinguaFolio online unit planner guide*. Retrieved from https://lfonetwork.uoregon.edu/wp-content/ uploads/sites/5/2016/03/Unit_Planner_Guide_Final_Updates.pdf

Center for Applied Special Technology (CAST). (2018a). *Universal design for learning guidelines version 2.2*. Retrieved from http://udlguidelines.cast.org

Center for Applied Special Technology (CAST). (2018b). *Universal design for learning guidelines version 2.2* [Graphic organizer]. Retrieved from http:// udlguidelines.cast.org/binaries/content/assets/udlguidelines/udlg-v2–2/ udlg_graphicorganizer_v2–2_numbers-yes.pdf

Chickering, A. W., & Gamson, A. F. (1987). *Seven principles for good practice in undergraduate education*. Racine, WI: Johnson Foundation.

Christensen, C. M. (2011). *The innovative university*. San Francisco, CA: Jossey-Bass.

Cisco. (2019). *The Cisco Visual Networking Index (VNI) global mobile data traffic forecast, 2017–2022 white paper*. Retrieved from https://www.cisco.com/c/ en/us/solutions/collateral/service-provider/visual-networking-index-vni/ white-paper-c11-738429.html

Clark, D. (2015). ADDIE (ISD). *The performance juxtaposition*. Retrieved from http://www.nwlink.com/~donclark/history_isd/addie.html

Clement, J. (2020, January). Share of global mobile website traffic 2015-2019. *Statistica*. Retrieved from https://www.statista.com/statistics/277125/share-of-website-traffic-coming-from-mobile-devices/

Clementi, D. (n.d.). *Flowchart for developing an IPA: Create a standards-based integrated performance assessment unit step-by-step*. Retrieved from carla.umn.edu/ assessment/vac/CreateUnit/p_1.html

Clinefelter, D. L., Aslanian, C. B., & Magda, A. J. (2019). *Online college students 2019: Comprehensive data on demands and preferences*. Louisville, KY: Wiley.

Cook, V. (2001). Using the first language in the classroom. *Canadian Modern Language Review, 57*(3), 402–423.

Council of Europe. (2011). *Common European framework of reference for languages: Learning, teaching, assessment*. Cambridge, UK: Cambridge University Press.

Council of Regional Accrediting Commissions (C-RAC). (2011). *Interregional guidelines for the evaluation of distance education*. Retrieved from https://www. nc-sara.org/files/docs/C-RAC%20Guidelines.pdf

Covey, S. R. (1989). *The 7 habits of highly effective people: Powerful lessons in personal change*. New York, NY: Free Press.

Department of French, University of Texas at Austin. (n.d.). *Français interactif.* Liberal Arts Technology Services (LAITS) and the Center for Open Educational Resources and Language Learning (COERLL). Retrieved from https://www.laits.utexas.edu/fi/.

Dick, W., & Carey, L. (2014). *The systematic design of instruction* (8th ed.). New York, NY: Pearson Education.

Dimeo, J. (2017, May 10). Online exam proctoring catches cheaters, raises concerns. *Inside Higher Ed.* Retrieved from https://www.insidehighered .com/digital-learning/article/2017/05/10/online-exam-proctoring-catches-cheaters-raises-concerns

Distance Education Accrediting Commission (DEAC). (n.d.). Retrieved from https://www.deac.org/.

Downes, S. (2005). *An introduction to connective knowledge.* Retrieved from https://www.researchgate.net/publication/248290359_An_Introduction_to_ Connective_Knowledge

Downs, L. R. (2018, May 17). Federal regulations Groundhog Day [Blog post]. Retrieved from https://wcetfrontiers.org/2018/05/17/federal-regulations-groundhog-day/

Edutechnica. (2019). *7th annual LMS data update.* Retrieved from https:// edutechnica.com/2019/10/07/7th-annual-lms-data-update

European Higher Education Area (ESG). (2015). *Standards and guidelines for quality assurance in the European higher education area.* Brussels, Belgium. Retrieved from https://enqa.eu/wp-content/uploads/2015/11/ESG_2015.pdf

Garrison, D. R. (2006a). Online collaboration principles. *Journal of Asynchronous Learning Networks, 10*(1), 25–34. doi:10.24059/olj.v10i1.1768

Garrison, D. R. (2006b). Online community of inquiry review: Social, cognitive, and teaching presence issues. *Journal of Asynchronous Learning Networks, 11*(1), 61–72. Retrieved from https://eric.ed.gov/?id=EJ842688

Garrison, D. R., & Arbaugh, J.B. (2007). Researching the community of inquiry framework: Review, issues, and future directions. *Internet and Higher Education, 10,* 157–172. doi:10.1016/j.iheduc.2007.04.001

Garrison, D. R., Anderson, T., & Archer, W. (2000). Critical inquiry in a text-based environment: Computer conferencing in higher education. *The Internet and Higher Education, 2,* 87–105.

Glisan E. W., & Donato, R. (2017). *Enacting the work of language instruction: High leverage teaching practices.* Alexandria, VA: American Council on the Teaching of Foreign Languages.

Glynn, C., & Wassell, B. (2018). Who gets to play? Issues of access and social justice in world language study in the U.S. *Dimension,* 18-32. Retrieved from https://www.scolt.org/images/pdfs/dimension/2018/2_Dimension 2018.pdf

Gustafson, K. L., & Branch, R. M. (2002). *Survey of instructional development models* (4th ed.). Washington, DC: Educational Resources Information Center.

Harel, I., & Papert, S. (1991). *Constructionism: Research reports and essays, 1985–1990.* Westport, CT: Praeger.

Hart, C. (2012). Factors associated with student persistence in an online program of study: A review of the literature. *Journal of Interactive Online Learning, 11*(1), 19–42.

Hromalik, C. (2016). BOLDD Workshop CALICO 2016 [Presentation slides]. Retrieved from https://docs.google.com/presentation/d/1QpqxKHRCgmlS 08flX1-Ms1wjlKpeAISFceOwHI8tRuk/edit#slide=id.ga0403043a_1_17

Hromalik, C. D., & Koszalka, T. A. (2018). Self-regulation of the use of digital resources in an online language learning course improves learning outcomes. *Distance Education, 39*(4), 528–547. doi:10.1080/01587919.2018.1520044

Huertas, E., Biscan, I., Ejsing, C., Kerber, L., Kozlowska, L., Ortega, S., ... Seppmann, G. (2019). *Considerations for quality assurance of eLearning provision* (Report from the ENQA Working Group VIII on quality assurance and eLearning Occasional Papers 26). Retrieved from the ENQA website: http://www.enqa.eu/index.php/publications/papers-reports/occasional-papers

Institute of Educational Technology, Open University. (n.d.). *Learning analytics and learning design.* Retrieved from https://iet.open.ac.uk/themes/learning-analytics-and-learning-design

Jabr, F. (2013, April 11). The reading brain in the digital age: The science of paper versus screens. *Scientific American.* Retrieved from https://www.scientificamerican.com/article/reading-paper-screens/

Kelly, R. (2014, February 27). Feedback strategies for online courses. *Faculty Focus.* Retrieved from https://www.facultyfocus.com/articles/online-education/feedback-strategies-online-courses/

Kenny, J., & Fluck, A. (2017, September 21). Online courses more time-consuming, to prepare for, study says. *The Times Higher Education Supplement.* Retrieved from https://www.timeshighereducation.com/news/online-courses-more-time-consuming-prepare-study-says

Kuh, G. D. (2005). *Student success in college: Creating conditions that matter.* San Francisco, CA: Jossey-Bass.

Looney, D., & Lusin, N. (2019). *Enrollments in languages other than English in United States institutions of higher education, summer 2016 and fall 2016: Final report.* Modern Language Association (MLA). Retrieved from https://www.mla.org/content/download/110154/2406932/2016-Enrollments-Final-Report.pdf.

Ma, R. (2019). *The emergence of China's nationally-recognized MOOCs.* Classcentral .com. Retrieved from https://www.classcentral.com/report/china-national-moocs/

Magliaro, S. G., & Shambaugh, N. (2006). Student models of instructional design. *Educational Technology Research and Development, 54*(1), 83–106. doi:10.1007/s11423-006-6498-y

McKenzie, L. (2018, December). EdX's struggle for sustainability. *Inside Higher Education.* Retrieved from https://www.insidehighered.com/ digital-learning/article/2018/12/18/quest-long-term-sustainability-edx-tries-monetize-moocs

Modern Language Association (MLA). (2013). *Guidelines for information and technology access and support for the modern languages, committee on information technology.* Retrieved from https://www.mla.org/About-Us/Governance/ Committees/Committee-Listings/Professional-Issues/Committee-on-Information-Technology/Guidelines-for-Information-Technology-Access-and-Support-for-the-Modern-Languages

Moore, M. (1991). Editorial: Distance education theory. *American Journal of Distance Education, 5*(3), 1–6.

Murphy-Judy, K. (2020). An ADDIE model for online world language course or program creation. (Author-created image from personal archive).

Murphy-Judy, K., & Johnshoy, M. (2017). Who's teaching which languages online? A report based on national surveys. *The IALLT Journal, 47*(1), 137–167.

Murphy-Judy, K., Hromalik, C., Russell, V., & Suvorov, R. (2019, May). *Basic online language design and delivery.* Workshop presented at the CALICO 2019 Conference, Montréal, Canada.

National Council for State Authorization Reciprocity Agreements (NC-SARA). (2019). *Standards and policies.* Retrieved from https://www .nc-sara.org/resources/sara-manual-192-effective-06012019

National Council of State Supervisors for Languages, & American Council on the Teaching of Foreign Languages (NCSSFL-ACTFL). (2017). *NCSSFL-ACTFL can-do statements.* Retrieved from https://www.actfl.org/resources/ ncssfl-actfl-can-do-statements

National Standards Collaborative Board. (2015). *World-readiness standards for learning languages* (4th ed.). Alexandria, VA: Author.

North, B. (2006, March). *The common European framework of reference: Development, theoretical and practical issues.* Paper presented at the symposium A New Direction in Foreign Language Education: The Potential of the Common European Framework of Reference for Languages, Osaka, Japan.

Office for Civil Rights. (2013). Resolution agreement: South Carolina Technical College System, OCR Compliance Review No. 11-11-6002. Retrieved from https://www2.ed.gov/about/offices/list/ocr/docs/investigations/11116002-b.pdf

Official Journal of the European Union. (2019, June). L151. "Legislation" (English ed.). *62*(7), 70–115. https://eur-lex.europa.eu/legal-content/EN/TXT/?uri=OJ:L:2019:151:TOC

Ohio Department of Education. (n.d.). *Backward design of a thematic unit.* Retrieved from http://education.ohio.gov/Topics/Learning-in-Ohio/Foreign-Language/World-Languages-Model-Curriculum/World-Languages-Model-Curriculum-Framework/Instructional-Strategies/Backward-Design

O'Neill, E. (2019). Training students to use online translators and dictionaries. *International Journal of Research Studies in Language Learning 8* (2), 47–65.

Pascarella, E. T., & Terenzini, P. T. (2005). *How college affects students* (2nd ed.). San Francisco, CA: Jossey-Bass.

Patra, S. (2019). *A complete list of SWAYAM free online courses and MOOCs.* Retrieved from https://www.classcentral.com/report/swayam-moocs-course-list/#Humanities

Peterson, W. (n.d.). *Interpersonal task assessment rubric.* CARLA website on assessment. Retrieved from https://carla.umn.edu/assessment/vac/improvement/rubrics/figure7.html

Reinders, H., & White, C. (2016). 20 years of autonomy and technology: How far have we come and where to next? *Language Learning and Technology, 20*(2), 143–154. Retrieved from http://llt.msu.edu/issues/june2016/reinderswhite.pdf

Ribbe, E., & Bezanilla, M.-J. (2013). Scaffolding learner autonomy in online university courses. *Digital Education Review, 24,* 98–113. Retrieved from http://revistes.ub.edu/index.php/der/article/view/11279

Rose, D. H., Meyer, A., Strangman, N., & Rappolt, G. (2002). *Teaching every student in the digital age: Universal design for learning.* Alexandria, VA: ASCD.

Shea, P. (2006). A study of students' sense of learning community in online environments. *Journal of Asynchronous Learning Networks, 10*(10), 35–44. doi:10.24059/olj.v10i1.1774

Shea, P., Pickett, A., & Pelz, W. (2003). A follow-up investigation of "teaching presence" in the SUNY Learning Network. *Journal of Asynchronous Learning Networks, 7*(2), 61–80. doi:10.24059/olj.v7i2.1856

Shearer, R. (2003). Instructional design in distance education: An overview. In M. G. Moore (Ed.), *Handbook of distance education.* Mahwah, NJ: Erlbaum.

Shrum, J. L., & Glisan, E. W. (2010). *Teacher's handbook: Contextualized language instruction* (4th ed.). Boston, MA: Heinle.

Siemens, G. (2005). *Connectivism: Learning as network creation* [Master's thesis]. Retrieved from http://masters.donntu.org/2010/fknt/lozovoi/library/article4.htm

Singer, L. M., & Alexander, P. A. (2016). Reading across mediums: Effects of reading digital and print texts on comprehension and calibration. *Journal of Experimental Education, 85*(1), 155–172.

Skinner, B. F. (1974/2011). *About behaviorism.* New York, NY: Vintage.

Smaldino, S. (n.d.). *ASSURE.* Retrieved from http://www.instructionaldesign.org/models/assure.html

Sneed, O. (2016, May 9). Integrating technology with Bloom's taxonomy. *TeachOnline.* Retrieved from https://teachonline.asu.edu/2016/05/integrating-technology-blooms-taxonomy/

Southern Association of Colleges and Schools (SACS), Commission on Colleges. (1997/2012). *Distance and correspondence education policy statement.* Retrieved from http://www.sacscoc.org/pdf/DistanceCorrespondenceEducation.pdf

Southern Association of Colleges and Schools (SACS), Commission on Colleges. (2016). *Principles of accreditation.* http://www.sacscoc.org/pdf/2012PrinciplesOfAcreditation.pdf

Southern Region Educational Board (SREB). (2012). *Principles of good practice: The foundation for quality of southern regional education board's electronic campus.* Retrieved from https://www.sreb.org/sites/main/files/file-attachments/principles_of_good_practice_6.22.2012_final.pdf

Stephens, N. M., Fryberg, S. A., Markus, H. R., Johnson, C. S., & Covarrubias, R. (2012). Unseen disadvantage: How American universities' focus on independence undermines the academic performance of first-generation college students. *Journal of Personality and Social Psychology, 102*(6), 1178–1197. doi:10.1037/a0027143

Stockwell, G., & Hubbard, P. (2013). *Some emerging principles for mobile-assisted language learning.* Monterey, CA: International Research Foundation for English Language Education. Retrieved from http://www.tirfonline.org/english-in-the-workforce/mobile-assisted-languageLearning

Traxler, H. (1983). *Chancengleichheit* [Cartoon]. Hans Traxler, Chancengleichheit. Schul-Spott: Karikaturen aus 2500 Jahren Pädagogik by M. Klant.

Vlachopoulos, D. (2016). Assuring quality in e-learning course design: The roadmap. *International Review of Research in Open and Distributed Learning, 17*(6), 183–205. doi:10.19173/irrodl.v17i6.2784

Vygotsky, L. S. (1980). *Mind in society: The development of higher psychological processes*. Boston, MA: Harvard University Press.

Western Interstate Commission for Higher Education (WICHE). (2018). *WICHE state authorization reciprocity agreement (W-SARA)*. Retrieved from https://www.wiche.edu/sara.

Wiggins, G., & McTighe, J. (2005). *Understanding by design* (Expanded 2nd ed., Gale virtual reference library). Alexandria, VA: Association for Supervision and Curriculum Development.

World-Class Instructional Design and Assessment (WIDA). (2012). *Amplification of the English language development standards kindergarten–grade 12*. Retrieved from https://wida.wisc.edu/sites/default/files/resource/2012-ELD-Standards .pdf

World-Class Instructional Design and Assessment (WIDA). (2016). *K-12 can do descriptors, key uses edition*. Retrieved from https://wida.wisc.edu/teach/ can-do/descriptors

World-Class Instructional Design and Assessment (WIDA). (2018a). *Performance definitions: Listening and reading grades K–12*. Retrieved from https://wida .wisc.edu/sites/default/files/resource/Performance-Definitions-Receptive-Domains.pdf

World-Class Instructional Design and Assessment (WIDA). (2018b). *Performance definitions: Speaking and writing grades K–12*. Retrieved from https:// wida.wisc.edu/sites/default/files/resource/Performance-Definitions-Expressive-Domains.pdf

Zhang, A. (2003). *Transactional distance in Web-based college learning environments: Toward measurement and theory construction* (Doctoral dissertation). Retrieved from https://www.learntechlib.org/p/117282

Zhong, Q. M. (2018). The evolution of learner autonomy in online environments: A case study in a New Zealand context. *Studies in Self-Access Learning Journal, 9*(1), 71–85.

Ziegler, N., & Moeller, A. (2012). Increasing self-regulated learning through the LinguaFolio. *Foreign Language Annals, 45*(3), 330–348. doi:10.1111/ j.1944-9720.2012.01205.x

Chapter 2

What Are the Nuts and Bolts of Online Teaching?

Introduction

Development begins once a design plan with a reasonable timeline has emerged. The development phase in the ADDIE process—which includes analysis, design, development, integration, and evaluation (see Chapter 1 for a full description of ADDIE)—populates the learning platform or learning management system (LMS) with materials and opportunities for learner engagement and reflection. The foundation of good design builds upon professional standards (both for language education and for online education) and careful attention to universal learning design (UDL) processes. Moreover, effective online language courses should incorporate core practices for language instruction (Glisan & Donato, 2017), which Chapter 3 describes, as well as best practices for online course delivery, which are presented in Chapter 5. Given the communicative learning goal and the online mode of delivery, a two-pronged question stays central throughout the development phase:"How will these materials deploy in the target language grounded in its authentic culture(s) in an online environment?"

Online language learning is a new academic landscape for many students. Although those born after 2000 may appear tech savvy, they are less so in academic and professional uses of technologies and media. Online language learners, as noted in Chapter 1, often face hurdles, which include the following: the foreignness of the language as well as its perspectives, practices, and products; deficits in how to go about learning a language; not yet adequate online learning behaviors (e.g., not staying on pace in the course); and/or the fledgling ability to take responsibility for their own learning (e.g., setting aside time each week to read materials, view lectures, and complete assignments). Conole (2013), part of the Open University (OU) Learning Analytics and Learning Design team, defines learning design as a methodology for creating pedagogically sound activities and interventions by what we are calling te(a)chnologies. With respect to online language design and development, te(a)chnologies refer to having knowledge of the current educational technologies that are available as well as the ability to select and use the ones best suited for students to master the course learning objectives. The overarching focus of online course development should be on what learners will be able to do rather than on what teachers do. In other words, the student's development both as a language learner and as an online learner should be foremost in the developer's mind. This chapter details the process of online course development with significant attention to strategies, tools, techniques, and procedures to develop a successful online language learner.

Chapter 2 covers the development of: (1) the learner, (2) the learning management system, (3) the course structure, and (4) interaction and course activities. In addition, assessment routines and appropriate tools, further resources, ancillary materials to support and expand student learning, and te(a)chnologies and tools to open readers' minds to what is possible today and tomorrow in the world of online language education are presented.

Developing the Learner

Successful online learning is a 21st century skill for lifelong learning. It goes far beyond watching videos and navigating through links. In line with the Center for Applied Special Technology (CAST, 2018) UDL Guideline #6, Executive Functioning, better learning arises from effective goal setting, planning and strategy development, managing information and resources, and self-monitoring one's progress. Whether students are learning language, acquiring skills, or building content knowledge, they draw immediate and future benefit from guidance in how to learn well online, manage their own learning, and grow in self-regulation and learning autonomy.

As set forth by Dabbagh (2007), a successful online learner displays the following characteristics:

- A strong academic self-concept
- Fluency in the use of online learning technologies
- Interpersonal and communication skills
- Understanding and valuing interaction and collaborative learning
- An internal locus of control
- Self-directed learning skills
- A need for affiliation (p. 220).

She adds skills in collaborative learning, social learning, as well as discursive/dialogical abilities and the ability to engage in self and group evaluation and reflection to the list (pp. 220–221). Of course, these attitudes and competencies do not develop on their own; they must be fostered and developed with the guidance of competent online instructors.

Developing into a competent and successful online learner entails growing in self-regulated learning (SRL), which is characterized by learning how to plan, set goals, and organize and manage one's workload. This occurs through self-monitoring and self-evaluation, whereby learners increasingly rely on themselves rather than on others. SRL develops in tandem with metacognition, motivation, and effective habits (B. J. Zimmerman, 1990, p. 11). Incorporating a learning ePortfolio with special attention to goal defining and reflection goes a long way to bolster students' academic self-concept; it also helps them recognize the value of interactions, improve their communication skills, and increase their internal control (Ziegler & Moeller, 2012). With LinguaFolio and other vetted ePortfolio systems like the European Language Portfolio (ELP) and the Language Integration Through the ePortfolio (LITE) of the Linguistic & Cultural Diversity Reinvented (LINCDIRE) group, learners are guided toward language acquisition and self-regulation. (Council of Europe, Language Policy Division, 2020; Linguistic & Cultural Diversity Reinvented, 2020).

To promote learner development, administering short surveys to students regarding their satisfaction with the interface and tools, their sense of growth, and their growing efficacy in language learning provides invaluable feedback to both students and faculty. Elsewhere, a short questionnaire or end-of-lesson classroom assessment technique (CAT), which is a simple, non-graded and anonymous in-class activity, supplies a handy snapshot of how things are going in the class (Angelo & Cross, 1993). In the online environment, these can be delivered using an LMS quiz, Google Forms, Socrative, Mentimeter, Kahoot, Quizlet, or similar apps. Surveys tell learners that the instructor cares about them and their learning, which increases learner engagement and promotes autonomy. Asking learners to think about the technologies and media in the course may prompt an awareness that, besides linguistic and cultural knowledge, they are also acquiring important digital literacies and learning skills. Such surveys, of course, also funnel into the central and ongoing evaluation process of the entire course. There are more formal tools, like the Online Self-regulated Learning Questionnaire (OSLQ), developed by Barnard, Lan, To, Paton, and Lai (2009) to measure SRL at both the start and finish of a course should such quantification be sought.

The major LMSs collect user data on student and faculty activity in the system. Student user data provides an optic on student behavior for praise or remediation. For example, a student who only logs onto the system once a week—and then only to take a test—is not showing effective learning behaviors. Language educators know steady language acquisition arises from regular exposure to and production of the language. By looking at user data and statistics in the LMS and gathering information from other integrated learning materials (publisher online materials, for example), instructors can better guide learners toward more effective strategies and behaviors. However, some learners may find activity tracking to be "creepy" or invasive (Jutting, 2016). Thus, it is a good practice to explain to them how and why their student data is captured and reviewed and how it is kept safe. Collecting, reviewing, and giving feedback based on student data is a powerful tool to improve teaching and learning online and to help learners grow in SRL and autonomy (Rientes, Lewis, Mcfarlane, Nguyen, & Toetenel, 2018).

Developing the Learning Management System (LMS) Interface

Readability and Usability

Whichever LMS or platform is used, background choices to improve readability, usability, and accessibility are part of the development phase. A student's first encounter with an online course is usually text-based. Studies by Rello and Bigham (2017) show that interfaces that are designed for people with dyslexia and/or other neurological reading issues positively impact all readers. There are a variety of ways to address dyslexia on webpages (Rello, Kanvinde, &

Baeza-Yates, 2012). Of particular interest to online language instruction are the studies regarding linguistic differences in dyslexia and written word processing across languages. English has what Rello et al. (2012) call an opaque or deep orthography where spelling and sound are anything but consistent. Languages like Spanish, Italian, and Finnish, however, have a transparent or shallow orthography that make their decoding (i.e., comprehension) process less difficult. Developers of courses in these transparent languages might consider using more of the second language (L2) throughout. For non-alphabetic languages like traditional Chinese writing, neurological reading processing takes place in a different part of the brain from that of alphabetic languages. Hence, dyslexia manifests differently and warrants adaptations that are suited to that language, language family, or writing system (alphabetic, logographic, etc.). With regard to the content, Rello et al. (2012) further note that it is not just transparency that lessens readability, but also complicated syntax and phrasing. Learner orientation materials, how-to guides, and instructions should all use clear, easy-to-digest writing, regardless of language.

Color and contrast also affect on-screen readability. Recent studies show warm backgrounds (light yellow, orange, peach, or cream) with a black or off-black font improve readability and reading speed for all online readers (Rello & Bigham, 2017). High contrast pairs (white/black or black/white) make words seem to vibrate and should be avoided (Rello et al., 2012). The British Dyslexia Association (2012) advises sans serif font, monospacing, and roman fonts with font sizes from 12–14 points for online reading. Font size 18 is deemed optimal by other experts (Rello & Baeza-Yates, 2013, 2015; Rello, Bautista, Baeza-Yates, Gervás, Hervás, & Saggion, 2013a; Rello, Pielot, Marcos, & Carlini, 2013b). Research varies on spacing within and between words. Regular (0%) spacing inside a word and greater spacing between words is preferable to condensed spacing within a word and regular spacing between words. Paragraphs should be offset by at least one empty line, even if there is only one line of text. Narrow columns are to be avoided, whereas intermediate-sized columns (+/-44 characters) are better than longer-sized ones (66 > characters) for struggling online readers (Rello et al., 2012).

When creating text-based content online, consistent formatting is optimal, which applies to the font size and type (e.g., bold, italic) as well as to the colors used for specific tasks (e.g., orange background for resources, cream background for learner-learner interactions, and light green background for assessments). Mixing more than three fonts is not recommended. Users navigate sites better, find resources more quickly, and trust their learning more deeply when typefaces and fonts are well chosen and consistent. Font sizes and the use of boldface, italics, and underlining, too, should become consistent signals for the entire site, from module to module, even from course to course in a multi-course program. Underlining, especially with blue font, indicates hyper-links. Large font sizes (over 18 points) typically indicate headings and titles. An average-sized font (usually around 12 points) is used for the main text, with smaller sizes for footnotes (under 12). Italics are hard to read on screen and in colored text, unless the text is a very dark color that contrasts with the back-ground. Using all caps should be avoided since it signals shouting in the short message service (SMS) world (i.e., texting) and mid-sentence capitalization slows down reading, as does centered text rather than right or left justified text (Pappas, 2015). Whatever formatting is chosen, links should be in a single color and style, like the underscored blue of most word-processing utilities. A bolded or all caps typeface can, however, be used to indicate due dates for assignments. All visual signals should remain as consistent as possible.

Although text may be a critical medium for delivering course content, two facts should be kept in mind:

1. Today's learners are less likely to read lengthy texts and may actually be put off by explanations, instructions, and announcements that are overly long in the text-based medium (Burns, 2019).
2. The primary instructional goal of an online language course is the language and/or content learning in the language.

Regarding the first fact, the reading load of an online course often imposes a heavy literacy burden on learners who must read for both content and everything else (e.g., instructions, course navigation directions, guides to using technologies and interfaces, task and assignment models, rubrics and their criteria, etc.). Much of what is conveyed visually in a face-to-face course can be converted into images, videos, screencasts, and various interactive modalities for online delivery. For the second item, the majority of the learning activities should be in the target language. The section below on developing interaction and course activi-ties using audiovisual and interactive means shows how developers and teachers can avoid overly long text-based instructions and move quickly and effectively to presenting content that is comprehensible for learners in the L2.

Common LMSs

In Chapter 1, common LMSs and platforms were presented in detail. Most of these are user friendly and relatively simple for faculty and students to use.

The majority of secondary and postsecondary institutions adopt a common LMS that is primarily geared for their traditional, brick-and-mortar courses. These platforms allow instructors to create an online grade book, an online assignment drop box, and online discussion boards to supplement in-class discussions, to name a few of the more common features. With traditional, brick-and-mortar classes, LMSs are sometimes used for administering tests and quizzes so as not to take up valuable class time. In order to use an LMS for effective online delivery, however, some rethinking and retooling needs to take place. For example, even though the overall look of the LMS is usually determined by the institution, most LMS interfaces allow customization of banners, layouts, and other details. It is important to choose a consistent appearance and structure that is intuitive for learners and easily adopted by other faculty who may teach the course in the future. In this chapter, the authors mainly refer to Blackboard and D2L Brightspace due to their access to and familiarity with them, and not as a recommendation of either.

Upon creating or copying a course, an LMS like Blackboard prompts the course creator or person modifying the copied course to customize it. Blackboard organizes information by buttons (or tabs) and folders as shown in Figure 2.1.

In Figure 2.1, the instructor's Control Panel on the left offers a "Customization" tab. It includes student enrollment (self or automatically through the institutional student information system), access for outside guests

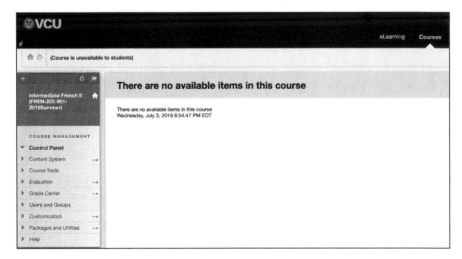

Figure 2.1 Screenshot of a standard Blackboard control panel and launch page for developing a course.

This image is the property of Blackboard. Printed with permission from Blackboard.

or observers, properties (colors, button styles, arrangements, labels), and tool availability. The tool availability sub-tab gives access to tools such as blogs, journals, discussion boards, e-mailing options, as well as institutionally available packages like VoiceThread (a text-, audio-, and video-based discussion board), Kaltura (a repository to post and share videos), Zoom (an online meeting space), and SoftChalk (a content authoring platform). The complete list of available tools is located under the "Course Tools" tab (second under the Control Panel options in Figure 2.1). Developers should be aware of their options in order to decide early in the development phase which ones to incorporate into their courses. The learning goals should always drive the choice of the tools and media, and those that are the most effective and efficient for achieving those goals should be chosen.

Still within the "Customization" tab, under the "Teaching Style" sub-directory of styles, developers can choose from among various teaching approaches such as case studies, constructivism, experiential learning, project-based learning, cooperative learning, guided discussions, etc. Choosing any one of these results in a learning interface designed for that style and its subsets. Figure 2.2 shows the communicative teaching style based on Web 2.0 (i.e., interactive web activity). It divides activities into discussion, sharing, and meeting up. It contains folders for course materials and for a wiki, which is a collaboratively created website on a particular topic. Students can easily access recent activity in the course, review earlier materials and instructions, and work with a course mentor such as a teacher, teaching assistant, or tutor. They have access to all their course tools and to a "Start Here" button that links to the all-important Getting Started documents

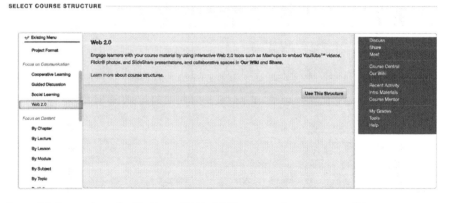

Figure 2.2 Screenshot of a Blackboard Web 2.0 "Focus on Communication" format.

This image is the property of Blackboard. Printed with permission from Blackboard.

folder. It should be clearly visible from the launch page. The "Start Here" button is described below.

The developer can use or modify any one the prepopulated styles or build a course style from the bottom up. Figure 2.3 shows a screenshot of a French course. The Blackboard interface has remained stable over many years, allowing for easy transfer from year to year, course to course, and instructor to instructor. Blackboard tends to look the same from year to year if one keeps the same theme and style.

The left side shows links/buttons for the major sections of the course. Announcements are topmost as the first line of communication with students. Announcements, reminders, events, invitations, and the like are created by the faculty. Announcements can be sent simultaneously as an e-mail through the composition window. The announcements button is followed by one of the most important elements of an online course interface, the "Start Here" button that locates all the "Getting Started" information, training, and resources a new online student needs to get off to a strong start. Figure 2.3 shows an additional "HELP!" label for students to see that this button is their "first line of defense" for the course. It replaces the immediacy of a classroom response to questions and confusion. The Getting Started module offers a clear overview of the interface and the curriculum and often includes links to the syllabus and course calendar. The syllabus and calendar may reside under the Course Documents button or under a separate button. Blackboard allows as many buttons as needed. Still, for usability, five to eight buttons with logically nested subsets is "cleaner." The Start Here button lets students quickly

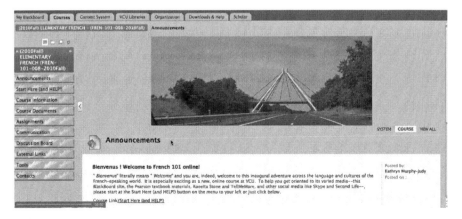

Figure 2.3 Screenshot of a Blackboard launch page for a novice-level online French course.

This image is the property of Blackboard. Printed with permission from Blackboard.

access a comprehensive course overview. The rest of the buttons should be self-evident. Most LMSs offer a similar interface. Both the D2L Brightspace and Blackboard platforms allow users to create their own names for folders that appear in the left-hand navigation bar. They both also allow nested folders, which means that there can be subfolders under main folders. However, in Canvas, an add-on like Atomic Curriculum Tools is needed display folders and modules as if they are nested. Most of the other common LMSs that are

available on the market today offer similar tools and capabilities to the ones described above.

Mobile Learning

Students today "live" on their phones. Many LMSs have a mobile option and some entirely mobile LMSs do not offer a computer-based option. In most schools, however, the computer is the base device. Since students want at least some of their learning to be mobile, developers should explore how course materials display on devices like smartphones and tablets (Masterson, 2019). Phones, more often than tablets, may not display everything properly. It is particularly important to let students know which parts of the course do not port well to mobile devices. Based on their market penetration with the targeted learner population, course delivery on various mobile operating systems should be tested by the developer. These include Google's Android, the Apple iOS, Bada by Samsung, and less so, the Blackberry and Windows Phone operating system, and for the large Chinese market, Huawei's Harmony. Providing students with a specific icon to indicate activities that are suitable (or unsuitable) for mobile learning will help guide learners to the appropriate devices for their online learning.

Developing the Course Structure

Choosing the curriculum and developing the overall course structure generally occur during the design phase. Secondary and postsecondary schools often depend on departmental or divisional curriculum, policies, and procedures for determining the direction of their course structure. The State University of New York (SUNY) provides its SUNY Learning Network (SLN) as a framework for course development in their course management system. The SLN includes advice and strategies for faculty to promote student success. It specifies that the sequence, quantity, and pacing of learning activities can be problematic in online courses (Shea, Pickett, & Pelz, 2003). Still, much of the information is similar to what is normally found in a face-to-face course syllabus and calendar. Where an online course is expected to stay on pace with an on-campus course or program, the number of units, materials, and other learning resources usually stay the same and they should coincide to ensure program coherence. Nevertheless, online course developers need to review the existing sequencing, quantity, and pacing of course materials to adapt and scaffold them for the specificity of online delivery.

What follows describes setting up basic course information and orientation material including: (1) choosing the number of units and their pacing within time parameters; (2) selecting or creating instructional materials and appropriate technologies, with a special focus on video and interactive media; (3) developing interactions, course activities, and assessments; and (4) finding or creating resources and ancillaries for student success.

Basic Course Information

Presenting a course overview and student orientation occurs in brick-and-mortar courses the first week of instruction. With online courses that are synchronous (i.e., those with pre-set, real-time class meetings or interactions), instructors can conduct the orientation session during the first class meeting. However, for courses that are delivered asynchronously (i.e., anytime/anyplace instruction without any required real-time class meetings or interactions), there is no predetermined, first-day class meeting for this to take place. In its absence, developers must carefully craft the introductory and basic course information folders or modules.

A strategy supported in Quality Matters training is the Getting Started module with its "Start Here" tab or button mentioned above. It links to an overview of the entire course. Its landing page should clearly show where and how to start the course. It should also offer access to information on the course structure and content, including the course overview, course goals, expected learning outcomes, the types and timing of assessments with the criteria for grading, the location of the learning units or modules, and the training materials (or links to them) for all of the technologies and media that are used in the course, as recommended by Quality Matters in their standards. A video tour of the course works well to show the whole structure and layout of the course and to help students locate all of the course resources and ancillaries. Another video can be designed to showcase effective online learning skills and SRL strategies. Moreover, "breadcrumbs"—the secondary navigation system that is displayed at the top of the webpage and that shows a user's location on the website—should be available for learners to retrace their clicks and thus avoid getting lost in cyberspace. Shea et al. (2003) noted, "faculty … create course-level and section-level overviews of documents with the goal of reminding students where they are and what they will be working on throughout each section of the course" (p. 9). Redundancy of information allows learners more than one avenue to pursue their learning. Learners should be able to locate information in more than one place, without getting confused or sidetracked. For example, information on course grading may be found in the "Getting Started" module, on the syllabus, and in a video orientation for the course.

Online learners need ready access to the instructor's contact information, office hours, and response time expectations. These topics are addressed more fully below. Online students also need information and access to support services, such as technical help, which are best delivered in their own folder or module. These resources can be located under the "Start Here" button, reside in a course resources folder or module, or be in their own folder or module. There should be a list of support services for the LMS, publisher materials, software, and applications, with links to their website support pages (e.g., technical help, live help, etc.), including their contact e-mail addresses, social media connections, and phone numbers wherever possible. Frequently asked questions (FAQs) and flowcharts for potential problems and their resolution are also recommended. Delays due to technical issues negatively impact a learner's progress and engagement in the course. While the instructor's primary role is to address instructional issues, not technical ones, students should be instructed to copy the instructor on requests for technical support should a major problem arise. Developers and faculty are advised to keep such inquiries in a special folder for the end-of-course evaluation in light of revising the support guides, FAQs, and troubleshooting pages.

In courses with learners in the Novice to Intermediate Low, or the A1–A2 range, posting orientation materials, welcome messages, and course information documents, as well as general policies and procedures in the first language (L1) is generally appropriate. Moreover, using the L1 for materials shared across multiple courses and languages may be the most effective approach. Still, developers might consider providing the instructions for course routines and standard operating procedures in the target language with supportive visuals. Their introduction and consistent use throughout a course reduces the cognitive load that arises when shifting between the L1 and the L2. For learners with special needs, it is "very cognitively inefficient for them to move back and forth between languages" and "too much of the students' first language will demotivate their second language learning" (Virginia Department of Education, 2017, p. 27). The same document suggests an important strategy for accommodating language learners with special needs, which also is valid for online learners:

> [S]etting up routines and procedures in the beginning of the year before transitioning to target language, will help with the process of moving from English to target language instruction. As you transition into the target language, students may feel less anxious about what is expected of them if care is given to scaffold the process... Just assuming that the students can figure out the management without explicit support—or thinking that you cannot do classroom management in the target language—are not reasons to avoid doing it.
>
> (p. 27)

Upper-level courses designed for Intermediate Mid, or B2, learners and above should consider providing introductory information in the L2. Other options and opinions are discussed below and in Chapter 3, but where it concerns content learning activities, according to the American Council on the Teaching of Foreign Languages (ACTFL), they should be delivered in the L2 at least 90% of the time, regardless of learner proficiency level (ACTFL, 2017). It is up to instructors to make the L2 comprehensible for learners at each level of proficiency (see Chapter 3 for more information on teaching online communicatively).

Learner Orientation

Depending on the design plan and location of the student body, learner orientation may take place on campus or online. If it is delivered online, it can be in a synchronous, asynchronous, or mixed mode. For flipped and blended learning, orientation is less of an issue than in entirely online environments because students spend at least some time having face-to-face interactions with their instructors on campus, where learner orientation to the course will normally take place. Some institutions offer an orientation module for all online learners, regardless of discipline, others are created by specific academic units or by individual course developers. These are often institutional decisions that are determined in the analysis and design phases. Once the type of orientation is decided or created, student access to its materials can be available within a welcome message, course announcement, or in its own "orientation" folder or module; however, it is preferable to locate this important information across all three of these areas. Student access to the entire course is advised at least two to three weeks before the start date, if possible. At some institutions, however, student access is not available until the first day of classes. In these instances, a welcome e-mail prior to the start date that presents the course structure and expectations to learners is even more important.

Ideally, the welcome e-mail should be delivered seven to ten days before the official course start date. A short instructor introduction, some of the getting started and basic course information, and/or links to them are standard. Links have an added benefit of prompting learners to visit the actual course to discover its structure and the location of important information before the official start date, if allowed. This welcome message or e-mail sets the tone for the course. Addressing each student by name and asking them for their preferred names and pronouns fosters inclusivity and acceptance from the beginning. It also models inclusive netiquette, that is, the protocols for civil communication online (e.g., not using all caps, which is considered shouting online). Since enrollments tend to stay open for the week preceding and often at least a week after the official start date, instructors should consult their roster daily to identify newly enrolled students. Developing an e-mail message or announcement for late enrollees can relieve the stress on faculty during those first hectic few weeks of a course.

Location of the folder or tab for student orientation materials should be immediately visible and readily accessible to the learners as soon as they enter the online course. If an orientation module is required, a graded assignment emphasizes that learners are responsible for its content. An interactive video (using H5P, Camtasia, Snagit, or the like) can provide the orientation information with integrated pop-up quizzes. Orientation minimally includes:

- A welcoming and personal introductory video or text biography on behalf of the primary instructor;
- A description of the online/blended/flipped learning environment for the present language course;
- A list of the technical skills the students need for the course and where to get training or support if needed;
- Advice on the study skills that the course requires and how to improve such skills;
- Advice on workload management and indicating when to contact the instructor, a tutor, or a help center for timely support;

- An explanation of how best to communicate for course purposes, including netiquette and timeliness in group work;
- Location of resources and support, including technical help and other campus resources;
- A library of resources on issues affecting online learning, such as time management, computer accessibility, and willingness to reach out with questions, etc.

Several LMSs, like Blackboard, D2L Brightspace, and Canvas offer course announcements as a landing page, tab, and window. With Blackboard, there is a selection option in its announcement creation window to send the announcement out as an e-mail to all registered students. Selecting this option would kill two birds with one stone by providing a landing page announcement and sending out the welcome letter at the same time. For instructors with large or multiple class sections, such an option offers a significant time savings.

Modules and Pacing

Chapter 1 noted a warning by Bates (2019) that experts in a field may underestimate the amount of time online students need to process instruction and transfer learning experiences from short- to long-term memory. For online language learning, this caveat is all the more important. Chapter 3 will delve more deeply into this area.

Shea et al. (2003) urge developers and faculty to recognize the importance of establishing time parameters. The SLN course management system provides standard documents to help set such parameters. It provides preformatted course schedules for learning activities, topics, assignments, and due dates that are recorded. Within units or modules, a "What's Due?" document is set up and brought to learners' attention. Moreover, clear start and end dates, with reminders, help keep students on track and all assignment documents should offer clearly visible due dates and reminders. Many LMSs offer a feature for faculty to activate and deactivate learning modules to manage the pace of a course or to ensure mastery learning through the adaptive release of lessons or modules. SoftChalk and similar lesson/module builders allow developers to "drip" lessons based on built-in assessments. Similarly, the D2L Brightspace platform allows instructors to hide lessons or modules until learners are ready for them.

The backward design phase of development generally directs how to divide up the online course, the number of modules, and the number and extent of lessons within modules. Much depends on whether there will be a tight or loose structure to the course. Bates (2019) uses the term, "tight," to indicate "a very strong structure, with specific topics assigned for study at particular points in the course, with student work or activities tightly linked" (p. 0, section 11.9.1). Basic language courses often need this kind of structuring. Upper-level courses, however, may benefit from a loose structure where it is "part of the student's responsibility to manage and organize their study, or [where they have] some choice about what they study and the order in which they do it, so long as they meet the learning goals for the course" (p. 0, section 11.9.1). He concludes that the decision between tight or loose structuring also depends on the level of student self-regulation and the faculty/student ratios. The more students there are, the less time there will be to provide the individualized support and feedback needed in a loose structure. The more students need help developing SRL, the more time will be needed to dedicate to that aspect of their learning.

Online learners, in general, thrive where there is consistency. Whatever number of units or modules chosen for a given course, keeping each one more or less the same duration with a similar flow of activities develops a rhythm for student workflow and therefore lets them manage their learning more effectively. Where a module demands more time or a different workflow, its change of pacing and scheduling should be highlighted. For each module, an advance organizer, which is a visual representation of the content that will be covered, helps learners to see the big picture. This practice is especially helpful for holistic learners, but also allows all learners to grasp the logical flow of the online lesson or module. A checklist of the learning objectives that correspond to specific tasks and assessments motivates learners to achieve the targeted outcomes. Additionally, by providing guidelines, performance expectations, and rubrics for each activity, learners are primed to reflect on their learning in a timely fashion. Using LinguaFolio, or another ePortfolio, structures the sequencing of learning objectives and encourages reflection. See Chapter 1 for more details on how to use LinguaFolio in an online language class.

In a brick-and-mortar classroom, the class meeting schedule is predetermined. This rarely happens in online courses where learners interface with learning opportunities more individually. Still, set time frames and clearly defined deadlines are essential for students to engage in good online time management. Indicating what is due, when, as well as how to break down tasks into smaller chunks helps online learners begin to take responsibility for their own learning.

Some online language courses are set up for anytime/anyplace instruction. This allows advanced learners to work ahead, which could free up their time to work on other classes. While online instructors may allow students to work ahead, they are strongly advised not to allow students to fall behind. Once learners disengage from the online course, it becomes very difficult for them to catch up. The workload may seem to build up more quickly in an online course than in traditional, brick-and-mortar classes because online learners receive their instruction online (via instructional videos, podcasts, readings, etc.) in addition to figuring out and completing all of their assignments, assessments, and interactions online. The practice of not allowing students to submit work late—except for documented emergencies—may help keep students on pace and minimize online course attrition rates.

Where traditional students often meet up or communicate with each other outside of the classroom, an online course can offer weekly socialization for students and an outlet for addressing issues and problems. A course developed with compensatory strategies (e.g., weekly cafés, jam sessions, Twitter feeds, class Facebook chats, synchronous session group notes, etc.) provides powerful alternatives to the conversations that occur both within and outside of the brick-and-mortar classroom. If such opportunities are created for an online class, reminders and links announcing their availability should also be included on calendars and checklists, in module and assignment instructions, and in weekly announcements. It is vitally important to address academic and social issues that are raised in a timely fashion. The authors note that the current generation of students tend to use their social media to arrange study groups and to use back channels for information exchange. They should be encouraged to do so because these practices foster social presence in the course and validate students' need for connectedness to one another. Moreover, they should be urged to invite classmates to join, especially if there are older generation students who are less accustomed to such digital sociability.

The Course Calendar

The online course calendar is an important visual tool that serves as a reminder of key course assignments, assessments, and interactions. Where multiple links to the calendar information are accessible, care needs to be taken to ensure that identical dates, deadlines, and the like are maintained. Except in extraordinary circumstances, calendars should remain stable throughout the course. Consistency and predictability are absolutely essential to learner success in the online learning environment. A checklist of what is due also has great value for online students. Some LMSs offer checklist functions for tasks and deadlines. Canvas, among others, allows the developer to indicate if an assignment is required. The DesignPLUS product from CIDI Labs provides "progress bars" that display the percentage of completed assignments in a module for some LMSs. Publisher sites also typically furnish a running list of all work to be done as well as the upcoming due dates. Many publisher sites even allow instructors to add calendar items and due dates for work outside the textbook and workbook materials. As such, it could be used as the single calendar for the entire course. If the main calendar is kept on the LMS, it should link out to or embed any other calendars not integrated into its interface. Whatever other materials and sites are chosen (e.g., TalkAbroad, FlipGrid, VoiceThread, Padlet, Edmodo, NearPod, etc.), a checklist that includes their tasks, steps, due dates, and the like should be integrated with all other assignments and be clearly marked and readily accessible in the LMS. It is easy for students to get "lost" when there are too many moving parts to a course. Moreover, they should not waste time searching for where to locate course content and interactions.

Online learners are often frontloaded with a heavier learning load than their on-campus peers. They have to learn how to navigate the course and the course technologies, all the while learning new content in the L2. In the first few weeks, they face a significant cognitive load and instructors should provide them with sufficient processing time to figure out the technical details (e.g., the LMS, online resources and applications, etc.), learn the logic behind the LMS interface, understand the course layout, as well as to learn the new content in the L2. By the third unit or module, the average learner will have settled into the groove and should be able to handle more content exposure, new skill acquisition, even the introduction of new resources. Still, the time to engage in new skills and technologies must be factored in at all times with that of content instruction so as not to be detrimental to the prioritized learning targets.

The Center for Advanced Second Language Studies (CASLS) offers a planning document along with its calendar and pacing guide in the LinguaFolio Blended Unit Planner that accompanies the LinguaFolio Online (LFO) site and materials (Figure 2.4). It can be used to organize an entire course and then be reused for each unit or module under development.

Step 1 gathers the basic unit information such as the title of the activity, its duration, and the student proficiency level. Step 2 clearly follows a backward design process (see Chapter 1 for information on backward design). Targeted learning goals derive from a broad concept that frames the entire lesson or

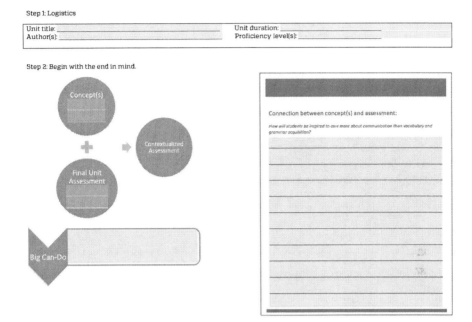

Figure 2.4 CASLS LinguaFolio planning guide template (Center for Applied Second Lange Studies [CASLS], 2015).

Reprinted with permission.

module and toward which the learners are being guided throughout. The contextualized assessments elicit evidence of learner performances across a variety of integrated learning activities and practice that, all together, sufficiently scaffold student learning so that they can confidently and successfully execute the final assessment. The full LinguaFolio Blended Unit Planner explains how to integrate the ACTFL World-Readiness Standards (National Standards Collaborative Board, 2015), choose and use appropriate Can-Do Statements (NCSSFL-ACTFL, 2017), create integrated performance assessments (IPAs)—which are assessments that connect to classroom instruction across three modes of communication (they are detailed in Chapter 5)—and provide the types of interactions needed for students to demonstrate their learning outcomes via the LinguaFolio Online platform. Step 3 (not included in Figure 2.4) involves various levels of questioning and thinking, similar to the PACE model that is discussed in Chapter 3. For Step 4, the day-to-day template, the authors have provided Table 2.1, adapting the CASLS Unit Planner to specify assistive technologies used for online delivery.

Table 2.1 Day by day module planning

Big Can-Do:					
Content:					
			Activities & Assessments		
Day/ Date	Can-Do Statement(s)	Student task(s)	Connection to final assessment (rubric criterion, appropriate descriptor)	Feedback tool(s)	Technologies or apps needed

*Note. Adapted from the CASLS Unit Planner (CASLS, 2015).
Permission granted.

The CASLS Blended Unit Planner includes a model lesson and descriptions of best practices for unit creation and delivery. The authors will return to this model in the section below on learner-content interaction.

Developing Interaction and Course Activities

The literature on online language education cites three types of interactions arising from the Community of Inquiry (COI) theory (Garrison, 2006a, 2006b; Saadatmand, Uhlin, Hedberg, Åbjörnsson, & Kvarnström, 2017). According to Anderson (2016), carefully chosen interactions lead to "presence" in the COI Model. Its three main actors are the learner, the instructor, and the content. Thus, the interactions are: learner-instructor, learner-learner, and learner-content. As discussed in Chapter 1, good design attends to the three presences—teaching, cognitive, and social—to create a community of inquiry. Interactions can be mapped onto presences to visualize how they all work together, as shown in Figure 2.5.

In the diagram below, Figure 2.5 is a visual shorthand for thinking about the three presences, the three sets of interactions, and their intersections while developing modules, activities, and assignments for an online course or module. Anderson (2016) notes what he calls "the enigma of interaction"

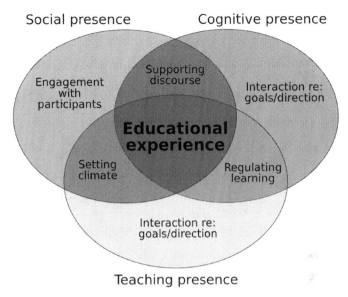

Social presence   Cognitive presence

Engagement with participants

Supporting discourse

Interaction re: goals/direction

Educational experience

Setting climate

Regulating learning

Interaction re: goals/direction

Teaching presence

Figure 2.5 Bury's (2014) community of inquiry model.
CC BY SA 3.0.

based on research that indicates that online learners really do not need more than one well-designed interaction for learning to take place (p. 1). Yet, for a language course where language is both content and medium, research shows that all three are needed: learner-teacher interactions for modeling interpersonal communication, practice, and feedback; learner-learner interactions for negotiation of meaning and interpersonal practice and performance; and learner-content interactions for direct instruction and interpretive mode work.

The Three Types of Interaction

There are three types of interaction: learner-instructor, learner-learner, and learner-content. Sometimes interactions may include more than one pair of actors. Online materials—such as course readings, audio clips, or videos—may well include built-in interactivity. Including a mix of interaction types is the best way to optimize online language learning and to build presence in the online course.

Learner-Instructor Interaction

Learner-instructor interactions take place primarily in the space called teaching presence, which is the learner's perceptions of feeling connected to the

Figure 2.6 A humanizing avatar (Lachmann-Anke & Lachmann-Anke, n.d.).
Reprinted from Pixabay with permission.

instructor in an online course. Fostering teaching presence is a powerful way to promote learning. The developer looks for ways to insert teaching presence into the materials to give a human "feel" to the information being presented. An instructor avatar (i.e., an iconic image or photo of a real person) could be included with a tagline to pay attention to the "talking teacher head" whenever it shows up in lesson materials, as in Figure 2.6.

Then, each time student attention is called for, a comic book style speech bubble or a link with written, audio, or video instructions connects the important information to the avatar. It is a simple graphic device, but it humanizes otherwise dry instructions and descriptions. Additionally, it visually captures the learner's attention. It is worthwhile to ask other online course developers about their ways to humanize screen-mediated materials, as Jones (2019) recommends in her article on emojis in the foreign language classroom.

The following infographic by Pacansky-Brock (Figure 2.7) visualizes many of the ways discussed in this chapter to humanize an online course and acknowledges the all-important elements of teaching presence, empathy, and awareness.

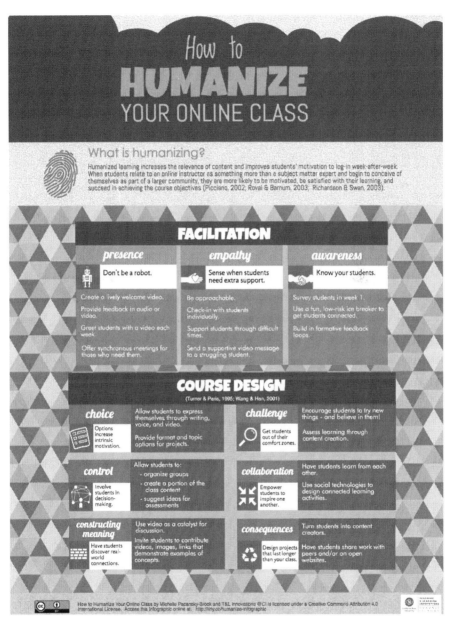

Figure 2.7 "How to humanize your online class," (Pacansky-Brock, 2015).

CC BY 4.0 International License.

Kumar and Skyrocki (2016) list eight ways to humanize an online course and develop teaching and social presence through learner-instructor interactions:

- Set a warm, welcoming tone right in the beginning of the course to connect with students.
- Do ice-breaking activities to create a community of learners; ask students to share personal profiles, bios, stories, and other examples of personal information.
- Offer a "live" orientation session through Skype or any other web conferencing tool so students have the opportunity to interact with the instructor in real time.
- Provide a discussion forum for non-course-related social interactions.
- Encourage peer-to-peer support.
- Incorporate group work.
- Provide a personal response to students on their personal profile.
- Encourage students to contact the instructor after digesting feedback on their assignments or discussion postings; a short note to contact the instructor with any questions leads students to feel comfortable seeking additional help.

The authors have used Learner Support Agreements (LSA) and learning contracts with students in online, blended, and flipped classrooms. The essential elements in an LSA, or contract, line up with the grading scale. After having determined their current proficiency level, the students are asked to set realistic end-of-course targets. At the end of the semester, the authors use the contracts with their embedded grading scale to compute the final grade, which students have indicated that they appreciate. As part of the bidirectional contract, learners are also asked to write up targets for the instructor to work toward throughout the course. This practice promotes their buy-in into the process. By using LFO, learners actively see their progress on the proficiency wheel. Figure 2.8 shows an imaginary student's proficiency wheel from the LFO platform. Learners can see their growth over the duration of the course as the color of their level fills in.

If the course contains synchronous interactions, there will be occasions for learner-instructor, real-time interactivity, especially when virtual classroom sessions are scheduled into the curriculum via Blackboard Collaborate, Adobe Connect, or some other virtual meeting room/webinar tool like Zoom or Google Meet. The use of synchronous sessions is determined in the design phase, but the timing, frequency, placement, and content are set during the

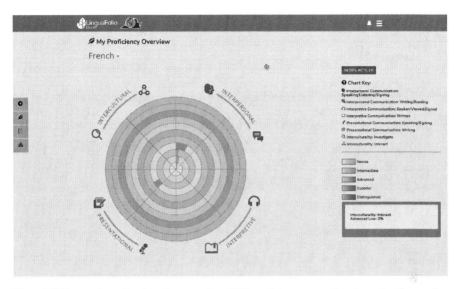

Figure 2.8 Screenshot of an imaginary student LFO proficiency overview from the Center for Applied Second Language Studies (n.d.). My Proficiency Overview.

Permission granted.

development phase. For synchronous sessions, consistency in scheduling lets students plan ahead for the days and times that they need to be present online. In the communicative classroom, teacher-led explanations of grammar would be rare, except when the class collaborates to co-construct a rule or when a difficult concept warrants additional scaffolding. Synchronous class meetings in an online class are similar to the flipped classroom, where learners discover forms, structures, and vocabulary prior to the synchronous class session; during the class meeting, these items are used to engage learners in target language communication. Through pre-session comprehension and readiness checks, the instructor can target misconceptions and common mistakes after the icebreaker, or even as the icebreaker or warm-up activity. With misunderstandings cleared up, students then engage together in real-time communicative activities in pairs, small groups, and/or as a whole class. Authentic activities that extend the topic could also be completed during synchronous sessions; and most importantly, these sessions provide opportunities for immediate teacher feedback, an important feature of learner-instructor interaction. Overall, synchronous sessions are well suited to fostering interaction in an online language course; however, synchronous sessions should rarely be instructor-dominated lectures.

In asynchronous courses, learner-instructor interactions are mediated through the LMS or through other media and apps like Google Docs,

VoiceThread, FlipGrid, Padlet, and GoReact, among others. Despite the screen mediation of such interactions, instructors are still able to communicate regularly and personally with learners to provide feedback and encouragement. In addition to e-mails and text messages, regular communications may take the form of whole-class announcements, Twitter tweets, or other social media options that are current. Great care, however, must be exercised not to expose personal student information in such messages. Online instructors need to provide virtual office hours, which, depending on the type of course and the location of the student body, may include synchronous virtual office hours in the LMS or via virtual conferencing. Entirely asynchronous discussion boards, chat rooms, or VoiceThreads can also serve as points of contact for students to ask for and receive help from their instructors. For students who reside on or near campus, a physical time and place at the instructor's office or at an agreed upon location (e.g., the campus cafeteria)—where such physical interaction is permitted and feasible—is also a good way to provide instructor support for online leaners. However delivered, office hours should be regular so that the learners know when the instructor is available, as online learners are reassured by that knowledge and access. There should also be a way for learners to connect outside the prescribed hours, with a defined protocol and response time set forth in orientation and course information documents.

Shea et al. (2003) underscore the importance of facilitating discourse as a part of teaching presence. They suggest facilitating online discourse by:

1. identifying areas of agreement and disagreement;
2. seeking to reach consensus and understanding;
3. encouraging, acknowledging, or reinforcing student contributions;
4. setting the climate for learning;
5. drawing in participants and prompting discussion; and
6. assessing the efficacy of the process (pp. 11–12).

Item 4 is especially important (setting the climate for learning); and in order to do so, Shea et al. (2003) advise stress-free, ungraded activities that enable learners to practice the skills needed for the course. Repeated practice and rehearsal of learned material and skills consolidate them in long-term memory. Practice in retrieving or rehearsing information across multiple episodes promotes consolidation and reconsolidation in long-term memory (McGaugh, 2000; Parle, Singh, & Vasudevan, 2006; Racsmány, Conway, & Demeter, 2010; Roediger & Butler, 2011).

Shea et al. (2003) suggest the following six strategies for eliciting student success from whole-class discussions online.

1. Provide an overview of what is due each week to keep students working in their cohort and staying interested in the topic.
2. Keep the topics provocative and relevant to students' lives and studies.
3. Try to reach consensus and understanding; yet, before consensus can arise, ideas have to be fleshed out and interrogated.
4. Include a grade for participation with clear guidelines for quantity, quality, and timeliness. Students need to engage early and often (a minimum amount stipulated). Late students might be asked to summarize the entire discussion, giving students impetus to participate early!
5. The instructor keeps the discussion on track by guiding without "pontificating" because that stymies discussions.
6. Assign a product based on the discussion that leads them to synthesize, integrate, and apply what has been discussed (pp. 70-71).

For the language classroom, one might add links to resources for lexical and grammatical scaffolding. Moreover, the instructor will need to be particularly attentive to noting cultural differences and nuances to advance the learners' intercultural competencies while not dominating the conversation.

Besides setting up good discussion routines, the Right Question Institute offers a compelling technique to get learners, whether face-to-face or online, to find meaning and relevance in what they are studying. It is called the question formulation technique (QFT) (Rothstein & Santana, 2011). It begins with a prompt asking learners to pose questions, individually, in groups, or as an entire class on a given topic. The next steps in the QFT build on the learners' questions, focusing their attention on how questions and language work in general. After prioritizing their questions, learners then move from inquiry into action. Their prioritized questions can serve as the basis for research, a presentational task, setting up a community project, etc. The technique builds engagement and trust between learners and instructors. It promotes learner-learner interaction (see below), bolsters student-teacher rapport, and builds a strong online community of inquiry. The QFT also humanizes learning and promotes learner autonomy. These, and the other strategies suggested for learner-instructor interaction, make online learning dynamic, engaging, and humane.

Learner-Learner Interaction

Learners should be afforded plenty of opportunities to practice what they learn with one another through both written and oral interactions. Discussion boards and chat features provide spaces for collaborative reading and writing activities. Social media, like class Twitter feeds or Facebook pages, can also be used to promote interpersonal writing (Lord & Lomicka, 2009; Miller, Morgan, & Koronkiewicz, 2018). Yet, attention also needs to be paid in the online environment to stimulate oral interactivity. As already noted, some online language learners harbor the misconception that they will encounter few listening or speaking activities in the course. It should be made clear from the outset that online language learning covers all four skills (listening, speaking, reading, and writing) across all three modes of communication (interpretive, interpersonal, and presentational). See Chapter 3 for an explanation of the modes of communication. Chat rooms and virtual cafés offer students the opportunity to engage in spontaneous language use outside the formal instructional setting, much like face-to-face class study group meetings outside of class.

Some publisher materials offer student-student activities on their websites. Vista Higher Learning, Pearson, and Cengage, for example, all provide written and oral student-student communicative exercises. They also allow instructors to create and insert their own student-student oral interactions. Note, however, that orientation materials must stipulate the hardware and software configurations that will be needed for such interactions.

Where the instructor develops student-student interactions, considerations of ease of use, Internet safety, time zones, anonymity, and privacy issues all arise. Many of these may have already been tackled during the analysis and design phases. For interactions taking place behind the LMS or institutional firewall, there tend to be fewer problems. However, with third-party apps and social networks such as FlipGrid, Padlet, NearPod, GoReact, Twitter, and Facebook, privacy and other issues must be faced well ahead of their being deployed. VoiceThread, if integrated into the LMS, ensures privacy and reliability for asynchronous oral, written, and video interactions. Yet the problem with it and apps like FlipGrid are that they lack the true negotiation of meaning that takes place in synchronous interpersonal communications. Perhaps the only way online to ensure truly interpersonal spoken communication is through a synchronous class setting or using an interface that offers real-time speaking between students, for example, GoReact. In virtual classrooms or meeting spaces, like Blackboard Collaborate or Zoom, there are breakout rooms where students can work together in real time. The instructor decides on the number of learners per room, placing students in specific rooms or assigning them randomly. As the students work together in the breakout rooms, the instructor is able to visit each room to observe and intervene as needed. The authors use synchronous virtual classroom sessions in their respective LMSs to set up communicative tasks and activities, and then they send groups of students into breakout rooms. They observe and scaffold each group as needed, and finally reconvene the whole class to share their findings and to provide feedback and further instruction to the whole class. Individual feedback can be given in real time through the virtual classroom chat function from the instructor to a single student, to selected groups of students, or to the whole class. The role of developers is to lay out which media and interfaces to use, how often, and how they should be orchestrated to achieve the learning objectives in each module.

Another way to provide learner-learner interaction is through virtual exchanges, also known as Collaborative Online International Learning (COIL), teletandem exchanges, or telecollaboration (O'Dowd, 2007). A course or module can be designed to offer intra- and inter-class exchanges between students at the same level, or between more advanced students and those at the lower levels of proficiency. The LMS can be used as well as various apps, sites, and media, like HelloTalk, the Mixxer, and FlipGrid. Otherwise, texting and/or calling can be set up once a partner has been identified (via Skype, WeChat, Viber, Google Meet, etc.). Research shows that virtual exchanges between learners of two languages benefit both partners (O'Dowd, 2007, 2011; O'Dowd & Klippel, 2006; Telles, 2015). Such exchanges connect L2 learners with L1 native speakers in sessions during which they converse in both languages. Discussion topics or learning tasks are predetermined by participating faculty and are prepared by both sets of learners. Sometimes, there can be two distinct conversation topics; nevertheless, both sets of partners engage in interpersonal communication with a native speaker. By listening and speaking in the L1 with an L2 speaker, the L1 student sees and hears first-hand how the L2 functions when used by native speakers of the language. Authentic, relevant language tasks promote linguistic and cultural exchange at a deep level. Moreover, in a tandem exchange, when a student asks her partner about her family, the response involves real families in real cultural contexts. In subsequent conversations, discussions of families and health arise from authentic concern, not just a practice exercise for specific vocabulary and phrases. Therefore, the communication that takes place is authentic, more engaging, and memorable.

Yet live language exchange is fraught with potential problems, ranging from time zone differences and Internet connectivity issues to incompatible academic and holiday schedules. There are other ways to include authentic L1-L2 dialogue, such as orchestrating conversations with native speaker informants, graduate students from a target language country, and/or upper-level undergraduate students of the language. There are also paid services that match L2 students up with well-trained L1 informants for language tutorials. They are detailed in Chapter 3.

Virtual exchanges can also be used for interpretive work. Before there was widespread literacy in the modern world, reading was a social activity. It entailed recitation, gesturing, and dramatic flourishes, as well as asides for clarification, comment, comparison, and further exploration. The notion of silent, individual reading is a recent invention. The onset of our interconnected, virtual world allows us once again to enjoy the benefits of reading socially. Using a mutually available text as their base and their phones, a Zoom session or some form of Voice over Internet Protocol (VoIP), students can be tasked with reading aloud, asking questions, and co-constructing the meaning of the text. Such interaction builds collaborative skills and a feeling of social connectedness online. The L2 learner also benefits from the scaffolding that the written (or other mediated) text affords. In virtual exchanges between L1 and L2 partners, the sharing of a common text in the target language hones interpretive and intercultural skills with a native speaker.

Learner-learner interactions require appropriate behavior online, also known as netiquette. As an icebreaker or as part of orientation, students can be asked to co-create their own netiquette, using a shared writing space or a virtual whiteboard. Such an activity promotes ownership and accountability for their interactions. Often, this strategy also improves learner engagement and attitudes toward the class as a community. The developer should make sure that derogatory or inappropriate emojis or comments, dominating conversations in the form of excessively long posts in chats and discussion boards, overt bullying, and microaggressions find their way onto the list. For collaborative and group work, attention should be paid early on to netiquette, inclusivity, collaborative dynamics, and the timely sharing of group work. During synchronous sessions and within asynchronous exchanges, faculty should circulate virtually among groups to nip potentially offensive behaviors in the bud. Most LMSs archive all written student work, thus leaving proof of transgressions should it, unfortunately, come to that. Note, however, that breakout rooms in synchronous live classrooms generally are not recorded.

Learner-Content Interaction

Learner-content interaction refers to the course materials and resources that the learner engages with to realize the course learning goals. T. D. Zimmerman (2012) notes that students who "interact with the content more frequently achieve higher success in online courses" (p. 162). In learner-content inter-action, the UDL notion of multiple means of representation and expression comes into play. What is essential in the online learning environment is the availability of multimodal and differentiated instructional materials, in other words, multiple means of representation of the course content. Equally impor-tant is that learners are able to respond and interact in ways suited to their learning and circumstances such as through multiple means of expression (CAST, 2018). Furthermore, the Virginia Department of Education (2017) document on support for students with disabilities notes that students are best supported by multimodal instruction with research confirming that all language learners "benefit from instruction that joins listening, speaking, see-ing/reading, and writing the language as quickly as possible in the classroom" (p. 32). What facilitates learning for students with disabilities often promotes better learning for everyone. In the broadest sense, the entire online course or module involves learner-content interaction.

Online lessons or modules arising from the QFT and/or project-based learning (PBL) offer multiple ways for learners to access and express their learning. The National Foreign Language Resource Center (NFLRC) offers stellar materials, webinars, and courses on PBL (see Chapter 4). Multimodal technologies and applications—such as interactive video, FlipGrid, Padlet, Kahoot, VoiceThread, SoftChalk, and Twine—encourage learner interactions as suggested in the UDL guidelines. Multiple means of writing and reflec-tion, including blogs, reflective journals, online discussions, self-reporting sur-veys, and digital storytelling are effective for interpersonal and presentational writing. The Virginia Department of Education (2017) report mentions the use of tactile approaches to language learning (pp. 28, 32). How might an instructor insert tactile elements into a virtual classroom? Two thoughts come to mind: (1) ask the learner to assemble common household or classroom objects (pencils, Legos, paper, post-its) for activities built around their manip-ulation (drawing, labeling, etc.) and (2) use a virtual whiteboard, a shared Google Drawings document, or any number of iPad/tablet apps for simulating tactile activities online.

Interpretive modes of communication lend themselves readily to multiple means of representation and learner-content interaction. The text should be presented for optimal visual access and offer multiple representations (font sizes, annotations, highlighting, cartoon versions, etc.). Although an inter-pretive mode task may target the written word, for students with dyslexia, vision problems, or who are auditory learners, they need options for working through the text whatever their limitations or challenges. A written text can easily be accompanied by an audio clip or a braille rendition (e.g., using a braille accessory). Otherwise, software packages like SoftChalk and Twine can break the text up, annotating it visually and/or aurally. Google Docs, Microsoft Word, and other text processing packages can also insert comments, images, links, and sidebars. Moreover, the eComma reading package from the Center for Open Educational Resources and Language Learning (COERLL), MIT's Annotation Studio, or the Hypothesis overlay for social media reading also provide options for sharing and scaffolding readings for students. For an authentic reading passage, there should one or more pre-reading activities, such as a group chat on the topic, vocabulary brainstorming, a discussion of the text's illustrations to predict their relationship to the text, and/or outlining the major topic and subheadings to preview the textual organization and flow. Any new cultural information that the students will encounter in the text should also be pointed out at the pre-reading phase. Post-reading exercises and tasks check for comprehension at the appropriate proficiency level. Thereafter, students can be brought to interact with the text in engaging ways at their current proficiency level or at the next higher one. One or more activities should engage the learners in communicative activities related specifically to the text. Relating text to the unit concept encourages learners to transfer their learning, thus engaging higher order thinking skills and literacies, as the LinguaFolio Lesson Planner has suggested.

Listening is a major component in second language acquisition, often treated as the lesser of the four skills. Conti and Smith (2019) note that listening is the skill that teachers understand the least, usually have fewer resources for, feel the least confident teaching, and neglect the most often (p. 4). Further, they contend that listening is, "important for the development of second language proficiency. Our brains are wired to pick up language through listening" (p. 1). Their listening as modeling (LAM) approach reduces the stress of listening by helping learners focus their listening and hone it as a skill. By offering multiple listening representations through sound and/or video clips, an online course directs learners to intentional listening foci. SoundCloud and similar recording apps allow the instructor to annotate audio clips to focus on specific aspects of an oral text or they can let the students collectively interrogate and annotate the samples in a socially mediated way. The Google Add-on Kaizena allows the same kind of interactivity. Thanks also to screencasting and H5P, sound clips can be annotated so visual aids like phonetic transcriptions and subtitling, in either the L1 or the L2, can be added. Numerous academic and commercial sites offer a wide range of listening clips, often in video format and sometimes with transcripts. The enormous quantity and quality of podcasts, with a wealth of topics and accents, is an incredible resource for online educators to work with online learners on their listening skills.

In summary, when creating various kinds of interactions, the developer can use the content in Table 2.2 to figure out what kinds of interactions, activity types, and tools best suit the instructional objectives for a given lesson.

Table 2.2 Interaction types and modes with examples.

Interaction Type	Synchronous	Asynchronous
Learner - Content	**Example:** Explain proofreading of a sentence by annotating and correcting the error. Can be done with one student, a team, or the whole class. Group reading of a text. **Technology:** Writing and drawing tools in Blackboard Collaborate, Zoom, Adobe Connect; simultaneous use of Google Docs.	**Example:** Synthesize module and reading as a written reflection Shared reading of a common text. **Technology:** Wiki, blog, or forum to post the reflection Google Doc for the text w/ comment feature; Hypothesis; other social reading app like eComma.
Learner - Instructor	**Example:** Schedule a meeting during the instructor office hours. **Technology:** Online Calendar/Sign Up or Doodle poll; Google Meet, Blackboard Collaborate, or Zoom to connect and talk in real time.	**Example:** Receive feedback on an assignment from the instructor. **Technology:** Google Docs with comment feature or chat; Google Docs with chat; Laulima (Sakai=LMS Grading with feedback provided); Hypothesis for written commentary on any web page. SoundCloud to annotate audio clips; GoReact or VoiceThread to annotate student oral performance or practice.
Learner - Learner	**Example:** A meeting to work collaboratively project. **Technology:** Blackboard Collaborate + Google Docs, Google Meet, Zoom, phones.	**Example:** Peer review of assignment. **Technology:** VoiceThread, Laulima (Sakai=LMS) Forum, Google Doc with comment/chat.

(Continued)

Table 2.2 Interaction types and modes with examples. (*Continued*)

Interaction Type	Synchronous	Asynchronous
Community of Practice	**Example:** Bring in invited speakers to the class Tutor or teletandem exchanges. **Technology:** Adobe Connect, Google Meet, Zoom TalkAbroad, Boomalang; UNICollaboration.	**Example:** Join and participate in a forum or social network in the field. **Technology:** Edmodo, Facebook Group, Twitter feed.
Learner - self	Learning contract Mid-course conference summary and response Review of LinguaFolio reflections and teacher responses Course end summary of meeting personal learning goals and objectives with future plans to continue improving and growing.	

Note. Center for Language & Technology at the University of Hawai'i at Mānoa (n.d.) Permission granted.

The table includes the three main interactions as well as two more: learners interacting with a community of practice and learners interacting with themselves (self-reflection).

Visualizing Bloom's digital taxonomy is another way to think about and choose learning interactions with appropriate te(a)chnologies as Figure 2.9 below demonstrates. Many of these apps or sites involve social media and can be used both synchronously and asynchronously. It is up to the lesson developers to create the task prompts so that the learners may use them in one or the other mode, per the activity instructions. Apps that at first blush appear to be only asynchronous can be turned into synchronous tools by sharing them over Zoom or connecting simultaneously with the group via phone or any instant messaging/speaking application.

There are, obviously, myriad ways to create interactions in the online language learning environment. The developer's task is to select the type of interaction, its mode, and the best media and tools to deploy them. The section that follows takes a deeper look at online tools, applications, and resources that are appropriate for online language courses and programs.

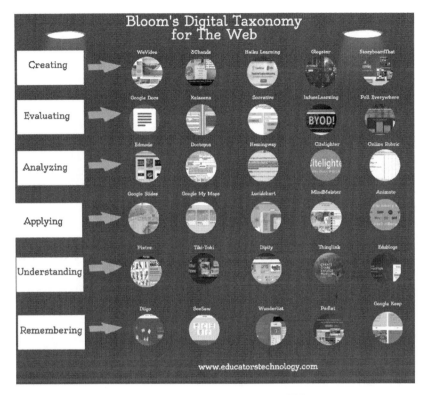

Figure 2.9 Bloom's digital taxonomy for the web (Kharbach, 2020).
CC BY SA 4.0.

Online Course Development Tools and Resources

It is important for developers to consider the various synchronous and asynchronous activities that will stimulate interaction in the course, as noted above. However, the tools that are used should depend upon the instructional goal of the activity. Table 2.3 prompts developers to ask the right questions about who, what, when, and why in the various interactional modes.

Table 2.3 Interaction modes.

Interaction Mode	What is the instructional goal?	Use/not use?	When is it appropriate?	Who is involved in the activity?
Synchronous oral				
Synchronous written				
Asynchronous oral				
Asynchronous written				
Combinations				

*Note. Adapted from Quinlan (2017)
Permission granted.

Interaction Tools

Some possible tools to stimulate interaction in an online language class include:

- Synchronous oral tools: Skype, virtual classrooms, GoReact, virtual tutoring, teletandem sessions
- Synchronous written tools: "Chats" within Google Docs, Facebook, "texting" etc.
- Asynchronous oral tools: VoiceThread, Voki, Lingt, SpeakEverywhere, LMS Voiceboards, GoReact
- Asynchronous written tools: Blogs, discussion boards, wikis, social media (Facebook, Twitter), journaling

In addition to the tools mentioned above, the NFLRC has created a handy online tool for language educators to select the type of interaction, activity, or assessment they wish to integrate and the various online tools and resources that will enable its delivery: the Personal Learning Network Tool (PLN). It can also be extremely useful in creating and deploying assessments. Another useful resource is Jane Hart's comprehensive site with over 2000 online teaching and learning tools.

The various activities, tools, and their uses and configurations should be considered as developers create opportunities for learner–instructor, learner–learner, and learner–content interaction. An in-depth look at the various tools and resources that may help instructors create online activities that stimulate interaction are described below.

Video, Multimedia, and Interactive Media Tools

In order to address the three types of interaction, it is helpful to examine the te(a)chnologies that may serve as a foundation. This section probes the use of audiovisual and interactive media for instruction, activities, and interactions because of their enormous potential and usability in online language teaching and learning.

Today's students are visual learners. It is estimated that around 65% of the population favors visual learning input. Short-term, or working memory, processes words and bits of information and stores them temporarily until new information replaces them. On average, working memory actively retains around seven to nine bits of information at a time. More can be held in the prefrontal cortex by means of chunking and using mnemonic devices before it moves through the hippocampus and integrates into the long-term memory network of the cerebral cortex. Images, however, are processed directly and retained in long-term memory, thus allowing much more information to come in and stay put. This makes sense since the human brain is wired for visual information, with 40% of our nerve fibers linked to the retina, which can register 36,000 visual messages per hour (Jensen, 2008). Researchers in neuroscience have stated that the processing speed of visuals is 60,000 times faster than text-based processing, as fast as 13 milliseconds (Potter, Wyble, Hagmann, & McCourt, 2014; Wilmes, Harrington, Kohler-Evans, & Sumpter, 2008). Visual information positively impacts student learning regardless of the delivery method. Although the literature notes a general preference for visual learning among learners of all ages and that the brain processes visual information rapidly into long-term memory, teaching to a predominant style (visual, aural, read/write, or kinesthetic), called "meshing," does not improve performance or retention as was previously believed (Newtown & Miah, 2017; Pashler, McDaniel, Rohrer, & Bjork, 2008; Rogowsky, Calhoun, & Tallal, 2015). Nevertheless, differentiating instruction through multimodal lessons, practice, interactions, and assessments maximizes human brain power, but visual information is simply processed faster and more deeply. This section focuses mainly on video and interactive video, although illustrations, infographics, cartoons, gaming, and virtual reality experiences are also effective visual tools in online education.

The simplest and most widely used video creation tool in online education is the recorded slideshow presentation that uses embedded tools to record audio narration and annotations to the slides in PowerPoint and Keynote, the two main slide presentation programs. The capturing feature records the slide presentation as a video. It can be saved as a video file or as an audio PDF. Both can be added to the LMS or linked from another service like YouTube or SlideShare. Google Slides recently added ways to provide voice narration (Curts, 2019); however, the process of recording audio onto Google Slides at the time of this writing is still laborious.

Another common video source is YouTube. There are other video servers like TeacherTube, Daily Motion, Vimeo, and the nearly defunct MySpace. Other languages and countries have tried to rival YouTube: Vkontacte and Rutube (Russia), Globo (Brazil), Iqiyi and Bilibili (China), among many others. YouTube, however, is the most ubiquitous and it overflows with how-to videos, documentaries, and more in many languages. Developers can look there for instructional videos for both content and training purposes. For educators, however, sustainability and copyright issues should be investigated before relying on any of its videos for a course.

Sometimes a suitable video in the target language cannot be located or may need to be adapted for a specific course or module. In this instance, a screen capture with or without audio can be made. Several screen capturing applications offer additional tools to create callouts, lines, arrows, active highlighting, annotation, captioning, and/or labeling. They can add layers of information strategically to focus student attention on pertinent information. For video or scrolling captures, options exist like Screencast-O-Matic, with both free and paid versions (see more in Chapter 3); the TechSmith™ gamut of screen and lecture capturing tools (e.g., Jing, a free tool with limited support); Snagit, an upgraded, wallet-friendly tool with a toolbar app; Relay for lecture captures; and Camtasia with its full blown, expensive, but highly performative suite of tools. Kaltura is another video capture and annotation software that some institutions offer to their faculty. Camtasia can even insert gradable quizzes into a video that interactively link learners to remediation based on their quiz results. In the Apple world, there is QuickTime (free), iMovie (free with Mac OS), Final Cut Pro, Captur, and Skitch (free and paid versions) to name but a few. On PCs, one can use the Windows snipping tool (from the Vista operating system and above), as well as free and paid software like FastStone Capture, Greenshot, and LightShot among others. Video and lecture capture systems that produce MP4s and other standard video formats produce clips that play across devices and are not LMS- or software-dependent. Some current capture systems limit interoperability and transferability, but a new standard called Open Video Capture Standard will make videos, hardware, and software independent according to the IMS Global Learning Consortium (n.d.).

Course developers may create original videos for their online courses, but video production takes substantial time and effort to plan, schedule, storyboard (i.e., a sequence of images that depict the flow of the video), write and practice scripts, film, and edit. They entail significant forethought about language, language pedagogy, and film production. Often, however, online courses simply need quick, easy, self-made videos to address learners' immediate needs and to scaffold their learning as questions arise during the course. Such videos offer an added benefit of feeling personalized and engaging for learners.

Using tools like Camtasia, SoftChalk, or H5P, a regular video becomes interactive by interspersing it with annotations, callouts, pop-up interactive quizzes, and surveys. Such interactivity ratchets up learners' attention and thus improves learning and retention. Besides the time spent crafting how-to and content videos, developers need to keep in mind how much time the learners need to process the information. Instructors must be careful not to overload the students. A more technical issue is that of copyright. Knowing fair use laws for the United States and any other country from which videos originate is essential. The Berkeley Language Center Library of Foreign Language Film Clips, now called Lumière, is an online library of 20,390 clips drawn from 5,615 films in 62 languages. Its contents may only be used as part of a course at a not-for-profit educational institution by students registered for credit at that institution. Educators applying for an account on Lumière should check to see if their institution is on the list of participating institutions. If not listed, an educator/institution may apply. The Lumière platform allows registered educators to create clips and add scaffolding to them as well. Despite its technical difficulties, interactive video is an extremely powerful tool in the online developer's toolkit. Chapter 3 provides additional examples of how video applications can be used to teach language communicatively online.

Another use of video as a learning medium in the online environment is the virtual meeting. Some LMSs, like Blackboard, have virtual classrooms (Blackboard Collaborate). Adobe offers Adobe Connect®. Other services like Go-to-Meeting, Google Meet, and Zoom offer whole-class connections for webinar-like, synchronous interactions. A powerful benefit to virtual encounters is the recording function, which allows the instructor to capture live class interactions for those who are absent, for review and repetition, or for insertion into other courses. Inserting a recorded virtual class session allows learners to stop and rewind the instructor and their classmates as often as needed.

Another pedagogically and communicatively effective use of video is to capture student participation and performance, for example asking the learner to create a recording on a smartphone. Some examples of learner videos include:

- an interpretation of a listening or reading activity like acting out a story (interpretive),
- a conversation with a peer or native speaker partner (interpersonal), or
- an oral presentation with or without slides or other visuals (presentational).

That recording is then uploaded to the LMS or ePortfolio as performance evidence. Social and collaborative platforms and applications like VoiceThread, Padlet, and FlipGrid also capture and share video performances and they provide easy ways for students to comment and interact with each other's work. VoiceThread has a limited free version as well as institutional integrations for LMSs like Blackboard, Moodle, or Canvas. Padlet has a powerful paid version, but the free version will suffice for students to share their work. FlipGrid is free to educators. All three apps have user community groups for sharing ideas, lessons, tasks, tips, and tricks. It is important to remember that online students can get sidetracked if they have to navigate to several different websites. For instructors, too, finding students' work, providing feedback, and grading work that is dispersed over many sites and applications can unnecessarily complicate their instructional mission and overburden their workload.

Textbook Platforms

Many world language publishers have designed their textbook platforms for online, hybrid, and flipped delivery with calendars, robust workbooks, interactive activities, synchronous and asynchronous oral work, and secure testing features. The major North American publishers that produce language learning content are Cengage, Pearson-Prentice Hall, McGraw Hill, Wiley, and Vista Higher Learning. They offer products with interactive e-textbooks and workbooks. Several integrate smoothly with LMSs like Blackboard Learn, Moodle, D2L Brightspace, and Canvas. Moreover, major publishers have excellent resources for student orientation, offer 24/7 online technical support, and ensure student privacy.

Smaller publishing houses such as Georgetown University Press, Breaking the Barrier, and Wayfair Books also offer online versions of textbooks. In Europe and Asia, there are Cambridge, Hachette, Santillana (recently acquired by Vista Higher Learning), and Cheng and Tsui, among others. Other language courseware distributors provide multimedia materials that are well-suited—if not specifically designed for—online learning. These include This is Language, FluentU, and Discovery. This is Language, for example, offers over 5,000 authentic, unscripted, nicely scaffolded videos in five languages (English, French, Spanish, German, and Italian) of interactions with young adults who mirror in age and interests with our diverse language learners. Prompt Cards are designed for younger students (PK-8). Videos are tagged for proficiency level and include pre-viewing, viewing, and post-viewing activities. Numerous formative and summative assessments are offered along with jigsaw, gap-fill, comprehension, grammar, and vocabulary exercises. Games can also stimulate student interactions with the materials and with one another. Various media companies like Rosetta Stone and Mango Languages, too, offer online resources for languages. Ready-made materials and activities, like those offered by publishers, reduce the time and effort of content development.

Media Companies, National Governments, Libraries, and Museums

Communications companies or organizations like the BBC, TV5Monde, Radio France Internationale, Deutsche-Welle, the Asia Society, and the Canadian Government, among others, also offer exciting, up-to-date teaching resources with easy online access. Such government and telecommunication giants provide state of the art te(a)chnologies. Several, like TV5Monde, even have the materials categorized by learner level (according to CEFR scales). Many offer free language level or proficiency assessment tools. The Virginia Museum of Fine Arts, the J. Paul Getty Museum, and other national, state, and local museums and libraries offer free, online educational materials based on their holdings that may be readily adapted for language learning.

In-House Content Creation

Some online course designers and developers create their own materials inside the LMS or on another platform like WordPress; however, this approach may lengthen and complicate development time and effort. The recent upsurge in open educational resources (OER) means online educators can pick from reliable, vetted resource pools, such as those listed with Multimedia Educational Resource for Learning and Online Teaching (MERLOT) and COERLL. EDUCAUSE in its library links to at least nine OER sites. In addition, sites like the OER Commons not only provide access to a host of language learning resources, but also include module builders to splice resources together into coherent suites of lessons or to offer them as ancillaries. Another distributor of open resources of potential interest to the world language community is the World Digital Library, hosted by the United States Library of Congress with support from the United Nations Educational, Scientific and Cultural Organization (UNESCO). Several national educational and library systems like the *Bibliothèque Nationale* in France also host high-quality, open teaching and learning resources. However, authentic resources that are intended for native or near-native users often demand scaffolding for L2 lessons or modules. Nonetheless, some are developed for immigrants and thus integrate nicely into language classrooms.

Assessment and Assessment Tools

Assessment is a critical element in online course development. In backward design, it is where the development of a module or lesson begins once the learning goals have been determined. Assessment of student learning begins and ends with what students can do with the language. In ePortfolios like LinguaFolio, student evidence of achieving Can-Do targets is student-driven, as they select, upload, and self-assess their performance to the LFO site. The instructor then reviews student input and responds to students' self-evaluation with their expertise in second language acquisition and proficiency-based teaching. Setting up performance-based assessments takes considerable time and effort in the design and development phases, more so during integration, when the instructional staff evaluates ePortfolios and task-based learning assignments and submissions. The extent to which an online language program will adhere to best practices in proficiency-based course construction and evaluation is normally worked out during the analysis, design, and development phases. Chapter 5 thoroughly describes them and reviews the best practices for online course delivery. A clear recognition of the time needed for assessment creation, correction, and feedback for the teaching staff, as well as attention to security and verifiability of student work, are essential. Performance-based assessments, like Integrated Performance Assessments (IPAs), as opposed to traditional achievement testing, is often more time intensive, but it supports the goals of communicative language teaching far better and results in better student learning outcomes. See Chapter 5 for a detailed description of IPAs.

Once a learning target has been identified, developers choose acceptable forms of evidence of student learning and the criteria for evaluating the performance. Next, they create the assessment tools and tasks to elicit student performance. Assessment can be formative, as part of the learning process, or summative, to determine the extent of learning at the end of a module or course. Formative assessment includes all types of quizzes, games, and even session icebreakers that allow for quick comprehension and skill-growth checks to determine if the learners are ready to move forward in their learning process. For an entirely asynchronous course, as mentioned above, a video can be interspersed with quizlets using H5P, Camtasia, Snagit, or other video enhancing tools. These allow the learner to work through an authentic text or a lecture-like lesson, checking for comprehension at important moments, as in Figure 2.10 below.

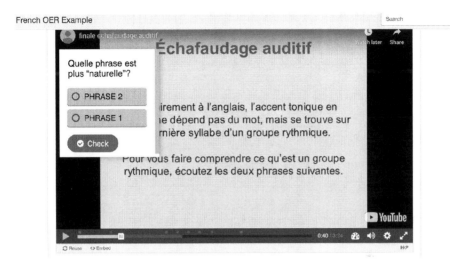

Figure 2.10 Screenshot of an H5P embedded comprehension check.
CC BY.

For comprehension checks of readings, interactive quizlets can be embedded into the text itself. Hot Potatoes, a free application, allows developers to create six different types of interactive quizlets: multiple-choice, short-answer, jumbled-sentence, crossword, matching/ordering, and gap-fill exercises. Learners also benefit from feedback for correct and incorrect answers. Google Forms can be coupled with Flubaroo to do much the same thing, with the added value of gathering the points for grading into a spreadsheet. The spreadsheet data can then be imported into an LMS gradebook. Standard LMSs offer quizzing features that insert into lessons and modules. Socrative, Mentimeter, and other online quizzing and polling apps also create embedded quizzes for readings and PowerPoints. Many institutions have a Respondus account, which also allows quizzes to be inserted into lesson materials and gathers response data for the instructor. Go Conqr, Riddle, Edmodo, and Revision Quiz Maker are other online quizzing and polling apps whose links can be embedded into calendars, lesson plans, and module instructions. For interpersonal and presentational speaking, listening, and/or writing assessments, some online language programs opt for synchronous, one-on-one, or group video/microphone sessions. Extempore and GoReact offer oral activity and testing environments for a minimal per-student fee. They also facilitate the grading process and thus ease the instructor's workload. By providing feedback to learners throughout modules, instructors scaffold student learning more effectively. Larger assignments, tasks, and projects should all include smaller milestones to help students manage their workload better. Early feedback keeps students on track and reinforces the criteria for success. Also, through smaller, ongoing assessments, the instructor can nip common errors in the bud using class announcements, weekly chats, quick video lessons, links to websites and/or pages, or videos that offer alternate explanations.

Summative assessment comes at the end of a lesson, unit, or course. It is meant to determine the extent and quality of learning. Of special note for online language learning, almost all major publishers offer language workbooks and testing online that coordinate with their materials. This will be explored more in Chapter 5, which covers the research on effective assessment practices. Summative assessment should offer a variety of means of expression for students to display their learning, such as a final project, a class presentation, an internship report from both the learner and the supervisor, a publishable article submission, and the like. Assessment, however, should not be confused with course evaluation, which is part of the ADDIE model and is addressed in Chapter 1; nevertheless, data drawn from assessments of student learning do play an important role in overall program evaluation.

While considering assessment and its place in developing self-regulated learners, the question of the use of online dictionaries, online translators (OT), and grammar/spelling checkers arises, especially for interpretive and presentational tasks. All three tools are exactly that: tools. They are part of the 21st century professional toolkit. Moreover, they are free and ubiquitous, and, frankly, widely used by students and teachers alike! In his research, O'Neil (2019) confronts the question of how best to deal with them in the language classroom, including their use for graded activities and tasks. From his research, he concludes that training in OT raises performance levels on writing tasks and that banning OT is simply ineffective as a learning tactic (O'Neil, 2019). He provides web-based learner training tools adaptable to the online learning venue. Working through such training materials—and then engaging in the task or activity—takes learners more time and must be factored into their workload. Then again, competent use of online dictionaries, spelling and grammar checkers, and translators, in the long run, improves overall student performance and will eventually ease student workload and reduce time on task.

Good feedback on assessments is critical for online language learners. Several factors, some depending on the type of assessment, make the feedback "good." The first is providing quick, meaningful feedback on student work. If the assessment or practice routine is formative, then rapid, correct/incorrect responses that are easily programmed into online exercises or quizzes are effective. Most online workbooks offer machine-graded practice and quizzes. Quizzing features in the

LMS or module creator like SoftChalk, H5P, or web-based forms (e.g., Google Forms) on a website, embedded quizzes on PowerPoints (Mentimeter, Poll Everywhere), and stand-alone gaming quizzes (Kahoot, This is Language's Nutty Tilez, etc.) also offer programmed correction. Giving individual feedback on the initial processes of interpretive, interpersonal, and especially, presentational activities, is good for learning. Such feedback, however, is time intensive for the instructor. Certain apps, software, and websites can simultaneously support learning and reduce faculty labor. For example, the VoiceThread interface allows faculty to observe and comment on students' pronunciation, grammatical and syntactical errors, and word choice before they submit their final version of a presentational assignment or engage in a graded tandem exchange. Go React, too, allows students to video record their preparatory work and receive comments before submitting a final product. Google Docs has an add-on tool called Kaizena that allows voice commentary on documents. Given the interactivity inherent in Google documents, students and instructors can exchange questions and comments on both written content and oral recordings. The instructor side of Kaizena and GoReact have the added feature of pre-recorded or instructor-created responses to common student errors. The learning task, too, can be scaffolded by preparational steps that guide learners toward better performance. For example, in a writing task, students can be taught to effectively use L2 grammar and spelling correctors that are available in most word-processing programs (Google Docs, MS-Word, Keynote, etc.). In French and Spanish, there are wonderful websites for error detection. The French one is called Bon Patron and the Spanish one is called Spanish Checker. Based on a large corpus of student composition errors in French and now in Spanish, the site analyzes student work for common errors, but does not correct them. Rather, it annotates the error so that the student can learn to self-correct. Below is a screenshot of the French page where students submit their text (Figure 2.11). The paid version allows for longer texts and greater depth of scaffolding and error correction.

Apps, sites, and software like BonPatron, LinguaFolio, GoReact, and Extempore are ideal for capturing student performances. Furthermore, quiz creators like Quizlet, H5P, SoftChalk, LMS test makers, as well as those in publisher materials, can contribute to online assessment.

Resources and Ancillaries

In the online world, the issue of resources has more than one meaning. Sometimes it refers to all the technologies, media, institutional support, support units, and the like that are at the disposition of designers and developers

Figure 2.11 Screenshot of the BonPatron site by Nadaclair Language Technologies (n.d.).
Reprinted with permission.

(Bates, 2019). Here, however, it refers to additional learning materials and instructional support, beyond those assigned as part of a course curriculum. Often these lend to differentiated learning and open up even greater means of representation of course content. However, a compendium of such resources and ancillaries takes time to accumulate and vet. Some may eventually come from being retired from a previous version of a course or module, maintaining value as a resource, but no longer as primary material. Extra resources and ancillaries might also include archived synchronous session recordings, links to or embedded publisher-produced PowerPoints, models of successful past student performance, and synchronous session class notes to name a few. The number and types of additional resources should be organized so learners can access what they need when they need it and not be confused by what is assigned and what is ancillary (or extra).

The authors have found that student-curated ancillaries work well as resource materials in intermediate to advanced online, blended, and flipped language courses (Mathieu, Murphy-Judy, Middlebrooks, Boykova, & Godwin-Jones, 2019). With student-curated ancillaries, learners share discovered sources with classmates, usually on a social media site that can aggregate all of their input and/or through an oral presentation. Social bookmarking sites like Diigo, Digg,

Pinterest, or StumbleUpon, as well as a class Google Doc or an LMS wiki, are great places to aggregate, display, archive, and share the class "finds" (Godwin-Jones, 2015).The task leads to developing autonomy in language learning while creating a set of very useful course ancillaries. It also provides another means of engagement, as recommended in the CAST (2018) UDL Guidelines. Many students, upon discovering such sites from classmates, start to access them on their own to further their learning. Important sites for supporting student work like Bon Patron and Spanish Checker, if not already part of the course materials and resources, may emerge from curation. Finally, through the many eyes and searching techniques of the whole class, the instructor, too, benefits from the students' discoveries.

Other Tools

New tools and apps appear on the educational technology scene constantly. It is important to stay abreast of emerging technologies and media. Although the news of Google's quantum supremacy for computers was announced in October 2019, its impact on human lives and communication has yet to be felt (Arute, Arya, & Babbush, 2019). Still, the fact that it performed mathematical calculations in three minutes twenty seconds that would take supercomputers over 10,000 years promises new heights in artificial intelligence, analytics, holography, corpus linguistics, and the like. As new quantum computers come online and processing accelerates, there may be no limit to development possibilities that combine the neuroscience of learning with second language acquisition research and learner analytics, thus providing new applications, connectivity, and heretofore unimaginable affordances.

In the current moment, online educators can browse the following sources: Godwin-Jones' regular column on emerging technologies in the online journal, *Language Learning & Technology (LLTI)*; the Tech Watch column in ACTFL's *The Language Educator, Edutopia; FLTMAG*, as well as other techie magazines. Educational technology blogs are another good resource; or better yet, one can set up an aggregator program for online publications using keywords like "educational technology," "world languages," "second language acquisition," "teaching languages online," etc. Once feeds are collected daily, weekly, or monthly, educators can skim through the newest and latest in the field at their leisure. As Chapter 4 details, national language resource centers (LRCs) that focus on new technologies and media for language instruction also offer newsletters about emerging te(a)chnologies. Reading about new products is a great way to think about and develop new online language teaching and learning approaches and tools.

Gaming and augmented reality (AR) attract many learners. An online course can actually be designed as a game with each module moving learners-as-gamers toward communicative goals while being immersed in a safe learning environment. One AR course in French called *Paris occupé* takes place in a recreated Paris under Nazi occupation during World War II. It covers all three modes of communication and integrates neatly into an online French course at the Intermediate or Advanced Low levels. In his LLTI column on AR where he presents *Paris occupé*, Godwin-Jones (2016) also explains how commercial games like Pokémon Go can be turned into powerful learning tools, in part because learners get to play the games they already know and enjoy. Simulations and 3D gaming worlds, like Second Life, Minecraft, and Day-Z are all filled with the potential for language learning. Godwin-Jones (2016) addresses other marker-based and place-based language games and game creation apps in his column. If online developers want to include gaming in a program, course, or module, they can seek existing ones or create their own. Sites like Augmented Reality and Interactive Storytelling (ARIS) offer free, open-source game editors that reduce the time and costs of developing or modifying gaming programs. Note, however, that building an engaging, effective online language learning game from scratch is extremely time intensive and usually requires a very large project team and deep funding resources. Finally, most digital creation tools are audiovisual. The upsurge in maker-spaces, where learners create physical objects though digital media, means that tactile—and perhaps eventually olfactory and even gustatory—learning opportunities and adventures may one day populate the educational arena.

Since this section on tools is gazing toward a wide-open horizon of teaching and learning opportunities, it should include robots and holograms. Actually, robots are already being used in distance learning for mobility impaired learners or for telecommuting into learning spaces to work in teams. An iPad or other tablet mounted onto a robot can be controlled by a student off-site such that she can interact with fellow learners in real time and shared space, with both audiovisual presence and movement. Holograms, on the other hand, although part of cinematic, futuristic landscapes, are still a few years off for widespread classroom or online integrations. Yet, having access to 3D real-time and archived images can bring a whole world of cultural practices, products, and perspectives into a student's learning space, whenever and wherever it may occur. In the meantime, 3D tools, like Google Glass, and 3D spaces, like Second Life and virtual worlds, allow for exciting immersive experiences (Godwin-Jones, 2014; Reinhardt & Sykes, 2012).

Given the focus in this chapter on developing not just robust online language learning environments but also autonomous, self-directed learners, a review of tools should include not only what they push out toward the learners but also, and perhaps more importantly, how they engage learners through te(a)chnologies.

Conclusion

The concluding activity for development is evaluation. Still, as frequently noted, ADDIE is an iterative process in which evaluation is a key element each step of the way. Once a course has been developed, it is ready to be beta tested and, barring major revisions, deployed. Chapter 3 fleshes out that fourth ADDIE step of implementation. To evaluate a program, course, or module that has been fully developed, it is best to start with reviewing the goals because as each section or module is considered, the overarching question is, "Does it work to reach the stated goals?" Questions of usability, accessibility, and inclusion remain at the forefront of the evaluation of the project developed. Development in this guide includes developing the overall structure, layout, and interface, as well as content development of modules and lessons within modules. Most importantly, in the development phase, instructional designers always pay careful attention to developing the learner toward self-regulation and autonomy. Several institutions offer checklists for online course development that can be found in the eResources for this chapter.

Key Takeaways

1. A good online language course develops a broad array of materials, learning opportunities, and interactions within a clear, consistent, learner- and learning-friendly interface.

2. While an online language course develops learners' linguistic and cultural capacities, it should also be developing learners' self-regulation and sense of autonomy. Online students need to regulate their own learning.

3. With the centrality of evaluation in the ADDIE model, a good online course undergoes frequent revision based on data collection and critical reflection throughout its design, development and deployment.

4. Good language teaching is good language teaching and transfers regardless of the mode of delivery. Many online instructors note that their face-to-face classrooms improve significantly from their work on online language courses, especially now, as digital content and online resources and applications are used for all modes of course delivery, whether traditional, online, hybrid, or flipped.

Checklist

☐ The overall structure is coherent, accessible, usable, and inclusive.

☐ Course timeframes are realistic for the average learner.

☐ Developed materials will meet or exceed accessibility standards (WCAG 2.0, A, or AA), quality online learning standards (QM, in-house, or other), world language education standards (ACTFL, CEFR, WIDA, other), and any other standards and criteria required (e.g., professional certification).

☐ There is a defined protocol and calendar for the following: welcoming students, orientation, the course of study, assessments, and course evaluation(s).

☐ Modules, interactions, tasks and assignments, and assessments adhere to the UDL standard of multiple means of engagement, representation, and expression.

☐ Modules, interactions, tasks, and assignments also target the development of learner self-regulation and increasing autonomy as an online learner.

☐ Assessment of student learning derives directly from the stated learning goals and objectives that have been sufficiently presented and scaffolded through lessons and other learning opportunities.

☐ Technologies and media suit the learning objectives and processes, that is, they are effective te(a)chnologies for the course.

Discussion Questions

1. Which facets of learner development are the most important in your circumstances? How do you plan to address them in course information documents and in the individual modules?

2. What is more appropriate for your course, strong or tight structuring of the course or module? Where might tasks and interactions be more loosely defined, allowing for more learner autonomy and choice?

3. What kind of tasks and assessments might encourage learners to go beyond the requirements toward self-directed learning?

4. Which te(a)chnologies are the most mind-opening for you as you begin the development process?

5. Choose and review a list of standards or a checklist from the eResources site that applies well to your situation. Then, consider the following questions:

   a. Which of the listed items have you already considered? Which are most important for your context?

   b. What will you need to add for the specificity of your online language course or module?

Suggestions for Further Reading

Bates, A. W. (2019). *Teaching in a digital age* (Chaps. 4, 7, 9, 11). Vancouver, CA: Bates. Retrieved from https://opentextbc.ca/teachinginadigitalage/

Center for Applied Special Technology (CAST). (2018). *Universal design for learning guidelines* (Version 2.2). Retrieved from http://udlguidelines.cast.org

Wandler, J. B., & Imbriale, W. (2017). *Promoting undergraduate student self-regulation in online learning environments.* doi:10.24059/olj.v21i2.881

References

American Council on the Teaching of Foreign Languages (ACTFL). (2017). *Use of the target language in language learning.* Retrieved from https://www.actfl.org/resources/guiding-principles-language-learning/use-target-language-language-learning

Anderson, T. (2016, March 3). The enigma of interaction [Blog post]. Retrieved from https://virtualcanuck.ca/2016/03/03/the-enigma-of-interaction/

Angelo, T. A., & Cross, K. P. (1993). *Classroom assessment techniques: A handbook for college teachers.* San Francisco, CA: Jossey-Bass Publishers.

Arute, F., Arya, K., Babbush, R., Bacon, D., Bardin, J. C., Barends, R., ... Martinis, J. M. (2019). Quantum supremacy using a programmable superconducting processor. *Nature, 574,* 505–510. doi:10.1038/s41586-019-1666-5

Barnard, L., Lan, W., To, Y., Paton, V., & Lai, S. (2009). Measuring self-regulation in online and blended learning environments. *The Internet and Higher Education, 12*(1), 1–6. doi:10.1016/j.iheduc.2008.10.005

Bates, A. W. (2019). *Teaching in a digital age.* Vancouver, CA: Bates. Retrieved from https://opentextbc.ca/teachinginadigitalage/

British Dyslexia Association. (2012). *Dyslexia style guide.* Retrieved from https://www.bdadyslexia.org.uk/advice/employers/creating-a-dyslexia-friendly-workplace/dyslexia-friendly-style-guide

Burns, M. (2019, April 14). To read or not to read: Text in an online world. *eLearning Industry* [Blog post]. Retrieved from https://elearningindustry.com/text-in-an-online-world-read

Bury, M. (2014). *Community of inquiry model.* Retrieved from http://https://en.m.wikipedia.org/wiki/Community_of_inquiry

Center for Applied Second Language Studies (CASLS). (2015). *LinguaFolio online: Unit planner guide.* Retrieved from https://lfonetwork.uoregon.edu/wp-content/uploads/sites/5/2016/03/Unit_Planner_Guide_Final_Updates.pdf

Center for Applied Special Technology (CAST). (2018). *Universal design for learning guidelines* (Version 2.2). Retrieved from http://udlguidelines.cast.org

Center for Language & Technology at the University of Hawai`i at Mānoa (n.d.). *BOLDD Workshop.* CALICO Conference 2017. Flagstaff, Arizona.

Center for Language & Technology at the University of Hawai`i at Mānoa. (n.d.). *Interaction blueprint.* Retrieved from https://clt.manoa.hawaii.edu/projects/online-learning-design-studio/interaction/

Conole, G. (2013). *Designing for learning in an open world.* New York, NY: Springer

Conti, G., & Smith, S. (2019). *Breaking the sound barrier: Teaching language learners how to listen.* Independently published.

Council of Europe, Language Policy Division. (2020). *European language portfolio.* Retrieved from http://languageportfolio.weebly.com/european-language-portfolioelp.html

Curts, E. (2019, May 29). *4 free and easy audio recording tools for Google Slides in tech and learning* [Blog post]. Retrieved from https://www.techlearning.com/news/4-free-and-easy-audio-recording-tools-for-google-slides

Dabbagh, N. (2007). The online learner: Characteristics and pedagogical implications. *Contemporary Issues in Technology and Teacher Education, 7*(3). Retrieved from https://citejournal.s3.amazonaws.com/wp-content/uploads/2014/05/v7i3general1.pdf

Garrison, D. R. (2006a). Online collaboration principles. *Journal of Asynchronous Learning Networks, 10*(1), 25–34. doi:10.24059/olj.v10i1.1768

Garrison, D. R. (2006b). Online community of inquiry review: Social, cognitive, and teaching presence issues. *Journal of Asynchronous Learning Networks, 11*(1), 61–72. Retrieved from https://eric.ed.gov/?id=EJ842688

Glisan, E. W., & Donato, R. (2017). *Enacting the work of language instruction: High leverage teaching practices.* Alexandria, VA: American Council on the Teaching of Foreign Languages.

Godwin-Jones, R. (2014). Games in language learning: Opportunities and challenges. *Language Learning and Technology, 18*(2), 9–19. Retrieved from http://llt.msu.edu/issues/june2014/emerging.pdf

Godwin-Jones, R. (2015). Contributing, creating, curating: Digital literacies for language learners. *Language Learning and Technology, 19*(3), 8–20. Retrieved from http://llt.msu.edu/issues/october2015/emerging.pdf

Godwin-Jones, R. (2016). Augmented reality and language learning: From annotated vocabulary to place-based mobile games. *Language Learning and Technology, 20*(3), 9–19. Retrieved from http://llt.msu.edu/issues/october2016/emerging.pdf

IMS Global Learning Consortium. (n.d.). *The open video capture standard.* Retrieved from https://www.imsglobal.org/OpenVideoCallforParticipation .html

Jensen, E. (2008). *Brain-based learning: The new paradigm of teaching* (2nd ed.). Thousand Oaks, CA: Corwin Press.

Jones, L. (2019, November 1). Three innovative approaches to integrating emoji into your language lessons. *FLTMAG.* Retrieved from https:// fltmag.com/integrating-emoji-into-your-language-lessons/

Jutting, C. (2016, August 3). Universities are tracking their students. Is it clever or creepy? *The Guardian.* Retrieved from https://www.theguar dian.com/higher-education-network/2016/aug/03/learning-analytics-universities-data-track-students

Kharback, M. (2020). *Bloom's digital taxonomy for the web.* Retrieved from https://www.educatorstechnology.com/2016/12/blooms-digital-taxonomy-for-web.html

Kumar, P., & Skyrocki, M. (2016, May 6). Ensuring student success in online courses. *Faculty Focus.* Retrieved from https://www.facultyfocus.com/ articles/online-education/ensuring-student-success-online-courses/

Lachmann-Anke, P., & Lachmann-Anke, M. (n.d.). *Teacher schools university* [Cartoon]. Retrieved from https://pixabay.com/illustrations/teacher-school-university-board-1015630/

Linguistic & Cultural Diversity Reinvented Group. (2020). *Language integration through e-portfolio (LITE).* Retrieved from https://lite.lincdireproject .org/

Lord, G., & Lomicka, L. (Eds.). (2009). *The next generation: Social media networking and online collaboration in foreign language learning.* San Marcos, TX: CALICO.

Masterson, K. (2019). 5 Trends in mobile technology. *Chronicle of Higher Education.* Retrieved from https://connect.chronicle.com/rs/931-EKA-218/images/ MobileTrends_Snapshot_mkto.pdf

Mathieu, L., Murphy-Judy, K., Godwin-Jones, R., Middlebrooks, L., & Boykava, N. (2019). Learning in the open: Integrating language and culture through student curation, virtual, exchange, and OER. In A. Beaven, A. Comas-Quinn, & B. Sawhill (Eds.), *New case studies of openness in and beyond the language classroom* (pp. 1–18). Research-publishing.net. doi: 10.14705/ rpnet.2019.37.967

McGaugh, J. L. (2000). Memory: A century of consolidation. *Science, 287*(5451), 248–251. doi.org/10.1126/science.287.5451.248

Miller, A. M., Morgan, W. J., & Koronkiewicz, B. (2018). Like or tweet: Analysis of the use of Facebook and Twitter in the language classroom. *Tech Trends, 63,* 550–558. doi:10.1007/s11528-018-0341-2

Nadaclair Language Technologies. (n.d.). *Bon patron.* Retrieved from https://bonpatron.com

National Council of State Supervisors for Languages, & American Council on the Teaching of Foreign Languages (NCSSFL-ACTFL). (2017). *NCSSFL-ACTFL can-do statements.* Retrieved from https://www.actfl.org/resources/ncssfl-actfl-can-do-statements

National Standards Collaborative Board. (2015). *World-readiness standards for learning languages* (4th ed.). Alexandria, VA: Author.

Newtown, P., & Miah, M. (2017). Evidence-based higher education: Is the learning styles "myth" important? *Frontiers in Psychology, 8,* 444. doi:10.3389/fpsyg.2017.00444

O'Dowd, R. (Ed.). (2007). *Online intercultural exchange: An introduction for foreign language teachers.* Bristol, England: Multilingual Matters. Retrieved from https://www.degruyter.com/view/product/523863

O'Dowd, R. (2011). Intercultural communication competence through tele-collaboration. In J. Jackson (Ed.), *The handbook of language and intercultural communication* (pp. 340–356) Abingdon, England: Routledge.

O'Dowd, R., & Klippel, F. (2006). *Telecollaboration and the development of intercultural communicative competence.* Berlin, Germany: Langenscheidt.

O'Neill, E. (2019). Training students to use online translators and dictionaries: The impact on second language writing scores. *International Journal of Research Studies in Language Learning, 8*(2), 47–65. doi:10.5861/ijrsll.2019.4002

Pacansky-Brock, M. (2015). *How to humanize your online class.* T&L Innovations. Retrieved from https://brocansky.com/humanizing-infographic

Pappas, C. (2015, July 21). Typography in eLearning: 5 key tips for eLearning professionals. *eLearning Industry* [Blog post]. Retrieved from https://elearningindustry.com/typography-in-elearning-5-key-tips-for-elearning-professionals

Parle, M., Singh, N., & Vasudevan, M. (2006). Regular rehearsal helps in consolidation of long-term memory. *Journal of Sports Science & Medicine, 5*(1), 80.

Pashler, H., McDaniel, M., Rohrer, D., & Bjork, R. (2008). Learning styles: Concepts and evidence. *Psychological Science in the Public Interest, 9*(3), 105–119. doi:10.1111/j.1539-6053.2009.01038.x

Potter, M. C., Wyble, B., Hagmann, C. E., & McCourt, E. S. (2014). Detecting meaning in RSVP at 13 ms per picture. *Attention, Perception, and Psychophysics, 76*(2), 270–279. doi:10.3758/s13414-013-0605-z

Racsmány, M., Conway, M.A., & Demeter, G. (2010). Consolidation of episodic memories during sleep: Long-term effects of retrieval practice. *Psychological Science, 21*(1), 80–85. https://doi.org/10.1177/0956797609354074

Reinhardt, J., & Sykes, J. M. (2012). Conceptualizing digital game-mediated L2 learning and pedagogy: Game-enhanced and game-based research and practice. In H. Reinders (Ed.), *Digital games in language learning and teaching* (pp. 32–49). Basingstoke, UK: Palgrave Macmillan.

Rello, L., & Baeza-Yates, R. (2013). Good fonts for dyslexia. In *Proceedings of the 15th ACM SIGACCESS international conference on computers and accessibility* (pp. 1–8). Bellevue, Washington: ACM Press. doi:10.1145/2513383.2513447

Rello, L., & Baeza-Yates, R. (2015). How to present more readable text for people with dyslexia. *Universal Access in the Information Society, 16*, 29–49. doi:10.1007/s10209-015-0438-8

Rello, L., Bautista, S., Baeza-Yates, R., Gervás, P., Hervás, R., & Saggion, H. (2013a). One half or 50%? An eye-tracking study of number representation readability. In P. Kotzé, G. Marsden, G. Lindgaard, J. Wesson, & M. Winckler (Eds.), *Proceedings of the 2013 IFIP conference on human–computer interaction (Lecture notes in computer science, vol. 8120)*. Berlin, Germany: Springer. doi:10.1007/978-3-642-40498-6_17

Rello, L., & Bigham, J. P. (2017). Good background colors for readers: A study of people with and without dyslexia. In *Proceedings of the 19th international ACM SIGACCESS conference on computers and accessibility* (pp. 72–80). New York, NY: Association for Computing Machinery. doi:10.1145/3132525.3132546

Rello, L., Kanvinde, G., & Baeza-Yates, R. (2012). Layout guidelines for web text and a web service to improve accessibility for dyslexics. In *Proceedings of the international cross-disciplinary conference on web accessibility* (pp. 1–9). Lyon, France: ACM Press. doi:10.1145/2207016.2207048

Rello, L., Pielot, M., Marcos, M. C., & Carlini, R. (2013b). Size matters (spacing not): 18 points for a dyslexic-friendly Wikipedia. In *Proceedings of the 10th international cross-disciplinary conference on web accessibility* (pp. 1–4). New York, NY: Association for Computing Machinery. doi:10.1145/2461121.2461125

Rientes, B., Lewis, T., Mcfarlane, R., Nguyen, Q., & Toetenel, L. (2018). Analytics in online and offline language learning environments: The role of learning design to understand student online engagement. *Journal of Computer Assisted Learning, 31*(3), 273–293.

Roediger, H. L., & Butler, A. C. (2011). The critical role of retrieval practice in long-term retention. *Trends in Cognitive Sciences, 15*, 20–27. doi.org/10.1016/j.tics.2010.09.003

Rogowsky, B., Calhoun, B., & Tallal, P. (2015). Matching learning style to instructional method: Effects on comprehension. *Journal of Educational Psychology, 107*(1), 64–78. doi:10.1037/a0037478

Rothstein, D., & Santana, L. (2011). *Make just one change: Teach students to ask their own questions.* Cambridge, MA: Harvard Education Group.

Saadatmand, M., Uhlin, L., Hedberg, M., Åbjörnsson, L., & Kvarnström, M. (2017). Examining learners' interaction in an open online course through the community of inquiry framework. *European Journal of Open, Distance and e-Learning, 20*(1), 61–79. doi:10.1515/eurodl-2017-0004

Shea, P., Pickett, A., & Pelz, W. (2019). A follow-up investigation of "teaching presence" in the SUNY learning network. *Online Learning, 7*(2). doi:10.24059/olj.v7i2.1856

Statistica Research Department. (2019, July 23). *Mobile phone internet user penetration worldwide.* Retrieved from https://www.statista.com/statistics/284202/mobile-phone-internet-user-penetration-worldwide/

Telles, J. A. (2015). Learning foreign languages in teletandem: Resources and strategies. *DELTA: Documentação de Estudos em Lingüística Teórica e Aplicada, 31*(3), 603–632. doi:10.1590/0102-4450226475643730772

Virginia Department of Education, Office of Special Education Instructional Service and the Office of Humanities and Early Childhood Education. (2017). *Supporting world language learning for students with disabilities.* Retrieved from http://www.doe.virginia.gov/instruction/foreign_language/resources/world-language-swd.pdf

Wilmes, B., Harrington, L., Kohler-Evans, P., & Sumpter, D. (2008). Coming to our senses: Incorporating brain research findings into classroom instruction. *Education, 128*(4), 659–667.

Ziegler, N., & Moeller, A. (2012). Increasing self-regulated learning through the LinguaFolio. *Foreign Language Annals, 45*(3), 330–348. doi:10.1111/j.1944-9720.2012.01205.x

Zimmerman, B. J. (1990). Self-regulated learning and academic achievement: An overview. *Educational Psychologist, 25*(1), 3-17. doi:10.1207/s15326985ep2501_2

Zimmerman, T. D. (2012). Exploring learner to content interaction as a success factor in online courses. *International Review of Research in Open and Distributed Learning, 13*(4), 152–165. doi:10.19173/irrodl.v13i4.1302

Chapter 3

What Is Special about Teaching Language Online?

Introduction

Chapters 1 and 2 covered the basics of designing and developing online or blended language courses. This chapter explains how to deliver instruction by applying sound pedagogical practices to the online teaching and learning environment. The practices described in this chapter may be applied equally to the delivery of online, blended, and/or flipped language courses. Teaching language is different than teaching other disciplines online because students must engage in speaking, reading, writing, and listening practice while learning rich cultural content that enables them to develop intercultural communicative competence (ICC). ICC refers to the ability to understand cultures, including one's own culture, and to be able to use this understanding to communicate appropriately with people from other cultural backgrounds; speakers who possess ICC not only attempt to gain an inside view of another's culture, they also attempt to understand their own culture from an alternate cultural perspective (Byram, 1997). This may be achieved by investigating the world beyond the learners' immediate environment, identifying and evaluating perspectives, obtaining and applying both disciplinary and interdisciplinary knowledge, expressing ideas, and taking action (ACTFL, 2014).

With many other disciplines, only reading and writing are necessary to learn the course content online. However, with language learning, listening and speaking are also critical components of the course that are necessary for students to build their proficiency in the target language; moreover, all four skills are also needed for students to develop their knowledge and understandings of cultural practices and products and the perspectives that underpin them. Therefore, special consideration must be given to the technology tools and applications that are used to facilitate the acquisition of language and culture online. Many effective tools and resources were presented in Chapter 2 and several others are highlighted in this chapter. However, language educators must keep in mind that technology tools and applications will change over time; therefore, online pedagogy is not tied to a particular piece of technology. It is more important to develop an understanding of the teaching practices that facilitate students' language acquisition as well as how to enact them in the online environment. In addition, language courses also require instructors to deliver instruction on culture through literary, historical, and geographical content while simultaneously teaching language within a meaningful or real-world context. Online language instructors must perform all of these functions in the online environment; therefore, highly specialized knowledge, skills, and expertise are required to deliver quality online language courses that are effective, efficient, and engaging for both students and instructors alike. The authors aim to help language educators develop the key knowledge and understandings that underpin successful online language instruction in this chapter.

Teaching in Online and Blended Environments

This chapter focuses on online language pedagogy, or how to teach language in the online or blended environment. In order to be proficient at online language teaching, instructors must acquire a broad base of knowledge across three domains: knowing how to teach language (language pedagogy), knowing how to teach online (online pedagogy), and knowing how to use educational technologies to deliver online teaching (pedagogy for educational technology). The intersection of these three domains are the competencies that are required of online language teachers; namely, knowledge of the pedagogy and technology for teaching language online or online language pedagogy. Figure 3.1 provides a visual representation of the competencies that are needed for effective online language instruction.

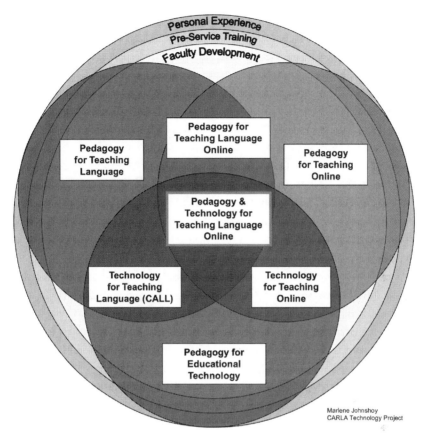

Figure 3.1 Competencies for effective online language teaching, graphic created by Marlene Johnshoy, Online Education Program Director, Center for Advanced Research on Language Acquisition (CARLA), University of Minnesota.

Used with permission.

All language educators take coursework to become experts in their discipline. In addition to their content knowledge, they also receive training on language pedagogy—or how to teach content in traditional, brick-and-mortar classrooms—in their teacher preparation programs. However, very few teacher education programs address the specific skills that are needed to teach language in online or blended learning environments. With the proliferation of virtual K-12 schools as well as the tremendous growth of online course delivery at the community college and university levels in recent years, online and hybrid courses are in great demand (Allen, J. Seaman, Poulin, & Straut, 2016). Moreover, enrollment rates for online courses continue to outpace enrollments in traditional, brick-and-mortar classes; since 2012, online enrollments have increased steadily, while enrollments in traditional courses have declined (J. E. Seaman, Allen, & J. Seaman, 2018).

As the demand for online courses grows, the need for qualified online language educators will also continue to expand. Often, instructors with no knowledge of online pedagogies are asked to teach online to fill the high demand for online courses. The authors do not recommend teaching in the online environment without sufficient support and training, as it will lead to much frustration for the instructor and for the students. Language educators who are called upon to enter into the online language teaching environment are in need of significant professional development on pedagogy and technology for teaching language online. Similarly, those who are already experienced online language instructors need to keep up with the latest technologies and pedagogies for online language teaching. Chapter 4 provides a wealth of resources for obtaining professional development in online language pedagogy. Those with little or no experience teaching online are strongly encouraged to utilize the resources that are available in Chapter 4.

This chapter provides the foundation for teaching language communicatively in online, blended, or flipped learning environments. It covers communicative competence (Canale, 1983; Canale & Swain, 1980; Hymes, 1972), pragmatics-focused instruction, the notional/functional syllabus, lesson design, professional standards and proficiency guidelines, and Glisan and Donato's (2017) core practices, with specific strategies for implementing them in the online environment. All of the key components of effective language teaching must be enacted in the online environment and this chapter will help instructors to do so.

Teaching Language in Flipped Learning Environments

In addition to those who teach in online and blended environments, language teachers who incorporate the flipped learning approach also need to develop competencies for designing, developing, and delivering language instruction outside of class time. In a traditional brick-and-mortar classroom, the teacher presents new material in a lecture format and students engage in practice activities outside of class. However, in a flipped classroom, students are introduced to the new material prior to class meetings using online delivery methods and class time is used to deepen students' understanding through group or pair work, discussion, and/or oral or written practice activities (Higher Education Academy, 2015). Therefore, the flipped learning approach reverses the traditional classroom because students learn the new material prior to class and class time is used for activities that would have been assigned for homework in a traditional classroom. However, with the flipped model, the practice activities are typically more communicative and interactive than traditional homework activities because learners can easily interact with their peers to complete assignments during class time. With traditional homework, students generally work alone in the written modality. Therefore, the flipped model has the potential to provide students with more speaking and listening practice compared to the traditional delivery model.

According to King (1993), the teacher becomes the guide on the side, rather than the sage on the stage, with the flipped learning approach. The flipped classroom is possible due to the use of learning management platforms, video-based lectures, and other online tools that allow students to approach new content on their own outside of class and at their own pace. With respect to second language (L2) classrooms, flipped learning allows for more interactive, engaging, and meaningful instruction because classroom time is used to develop communicative goals while learners focus on grammar, vocabulary, syntax, and other linguistic features outside of class on their own (Cowie & Sakui, 2015; Egbert, Herman, & Chang, 2014). The main purpose of adopting the flipped learning approach is to enable class time to be used for the development of learners' communicative competence; therefore, flipped language instructors need a deep understanding of this concept. They also need to acquire knowledge of online methods, tools, and resources to provide language instruction for students outside of class time and to differentiate their instruction to meet their students' diverse learning needs.

The Components of Communicative Competence

The main goal of online language teaching should be for students to acquire communicative competence in the target language. Hymes (1972) defined communicative competence as learners' grammatical knowledge as well as their knowledge of the social context in which language is used, which includes knowing how to use language appropriately in social situations. Canale and Swain (1980) expanded upon Hymes' definition to include three components of communicative competence: grammatical competence, sociolinguistic competence, and strategic competence. Canale (1983) later added an additional component: discourse competence. Grammatical competence involves knowledge of grammatical forms (such as verb tenses and moods), sentence structure, vocabulary items, and pronunciation among other linguistic features. Given that the treatment of grammar is so thorough in many secondary and postsecondary language textbooks, language educators may be tempted to focus heavily on the instruction of grammatical forms and structures. Many language textbooks devote a large portion of their content to presenting grammar rules and exceptions to grammar rules. However, an emphasis on the technical aspects of language does not lead to learners' development of communicative competence. Language courses, textbooks, and curricula are in need of content and activities that promote sociolinguistic and strategic competence.

Even if students could learn L2 grammar perfectly, this knowledge would be insufficient to develop communicative competence. Without knowledge of the social aspects of language, an individual's speech will always seem foreign to native speakers. Sociolinguistic competence refers to knowledge of pragmatics, or how to use the language in ways that are socially and culturally appropriate, and knowledge of the discourse structures of language, such as knowing how to form cohesive and coherent sentences or utterances in the target language. The majority of second and foreign language textbooks that are available today either do not teach pragmatics or their treatment of pragmatics is inadequate (Ishihara, 2010; Pinto, 2002). Therefore, it is up to language instructors to infuse their courses with instruction on the social aspects of language. While most textbooks do not include pragmatics-focused activities, there are a number of online resources available for teaching L2 pragmatics. Several links on how to teach L2 pragmatics as well as some web-based resources for teaching Japanese and Spanish pragmatics are available in the eResources for this book.

One way to teach pragmatics is to provide instruction on speech acts, which are specific language functions that are generally universal across languages, such as complimenting, complaining, greeting, inviting, refusing, requesting, and thanking to name a few. However, the way that speech acts are realized will vary greatly by language and culture. For example, requests in English typically are comprised of an ability statement such as *can I* or *could I* followed by the politeness marker *please*. Conversely, most requests in Spanish (between interlocutors who know each other) are comprised of a direct command such as *dame* [give me] or *ponme* [get me] without any politeness marker. Therefore, the Spanish language is more direct than English with respect to requests. Unless they are instructed otherwise, language students will transfer the pragmatic strategies from their first language (L1) to the L2. For example, Spanish language learners whose L1 is English tend to transfer English request strategies (inappropriately) into Spanish. Therefore, when making requests, they often say *puedo tener* [literally: can I have], which is both incorrect and inappropriate in Spanish. This English request strategy seems very strange to native Spanish speakers and it is a good example of the importance of how sociolinguistic competence contributes to learners' development of communicative competence.

The third component of communicative competence, according to Canale and Swain (1980), is strategic competence. This includes skills such as circumlocution, back-channeling cues, and word coinage. It is important for students to learn these skills so that they can maintain conversations with native speakers. Circumlocution is the ability to use other words to talk around or describe the word that is missing from the student's vocabulary knowledge. When students are learning a new language, it is very common for them to have large holes or gaps in their vocabulary knowledge. By using circumlocution, language learners are able to get their point across using the words and phrases that they do know. Online language teachers can help foster this skill by posting pictures of unfamiliar objects in discussion boards and asking students to describe them. This may be done using either written discussion boards or voice boards.

Back-channeling cues can also be taught to language learners and they refer to communication that serves a purely social function and that keeps the conversation going between the speakers. This can include small talk, social pleasantries, and nonverbal communication such as facial expressions and gestures (e.g., head nodding). Back-channeling cues also include vocal sounds such as "hmm" and "uh-huh," which vary by language. These types of vocalized sounds indicate that one interlocutor is actively listening to the other.

Word coinage is another feature of strategic competence; it is the ability to invent words when specific vocabulary items that learners need to communicate their message are unknown. For example, a language learner may say "air ball" instead of balloon. It is important for online language instructors to let their students know that they are free to use whatever words are necessary to get their point across. Students must feel comfortable making mistakes, coining words, and talking around words when they have gaps in their vocabulary knowledge. When the online course has a focus on communication rather than on grammatical accuracy, students can begin to relax and enjoy using the target language to communicate their messages.

Pragmatics-Focused Instruction

One way to teach pragmatics to online students is to have them view authentic videos of native speakers engaging in conversations on everyday topics such as shopping for food, using public transportation, and eating out. LangMedia is a repository of numerous authentic videos that show aspects of everyday life in over 25 different countries in both commonly and less commonly taught languages. Videos are organized by country and region, and transcripts for the videos are available in both the target language and in English.

To use LangMedia videos for promoting the development of strategic competence, students can listen for and list all of the back-channeling cues that they hear and/or see in the video. After listening for and recognizing back-channeling cues, students may then be asked to incorporate some of them into their own dialogue and/or role-play activities. Figure 3.2 presents a screenshot from LangMedia. In this figure, four authentic videos are available that show native speakers purchasing food items from open air markets as well as from supermarkets. Cultural information is provided about the shopping habits of native speakers who live in Mexico and examples are given for how people shop in the country and in larger cities.

An excerpt of a transcript from the video "Buying food at a small supermarket" is presented in Figure 3.3. There is one back-channeling cue, *Hmm*, as well as colloquial language, such as *'Ta bien* [It's OK], rather than the grammatically correct *Está bien* [It's OK]. Moreover, the term *bolillo* [bread roll] is used by one of the speakers. This term is frequently used in Mexico, but it is less common in other countries where Spanish is spoken. The more common term is *panecillo*

Figure 3.2 LangMedia, food shopping in Mexico.
Used with permission.

"Buying Food at a Small Supermarket"

Spanish transcript:

Jimena: ¡Flore! Hola. Me das un litro de leche y un kilo de huevo blanco. ¿Cuánto cuesta el kilo?

Flore: Doce.

Jimena: 'Tá bien.

Jimena: Hmm, pan...¿A cómo está el bolillo?

Flore: A ochenta.

Jimena: ¿Es de hoy?

Flore: Sí.

English translation:

Jimena: Flore! Hi. Can you give me a liter of milk and one kilo of white eggs? How much is a kilo?

Flore: Twelve.

Jimena: O.K.

Jimena: Hmm, bread...How much are the rolls?

Flore: Eighty.

Jimena: Is it fresh?

Flore: Yes.

Figure 3.3 Excerpt from transcript of "Buying food at a small supermarket" from LangMedia (shopping for food in Mexico) with the English translation.

Used with permission.

[bread roll]. Colloquial forms, back-channeling cues, and dialectical differences such as these do not typically make their way into language textbooks. However, in order to become proficient in the target language, it is important for students to be able to understand the language as it is spoken in its natural social and cultural context. Therefore, Internet-based resources such as LangMedia may be superior to language textbooks for fostering learners' sociolinguistic and strategic competence in the L2. Moreover, language educators—if they are not native speakers of the language(s) that they teach—are advanced language learners themselves. Therefore, English translations of the video transcripts may help them feel more comfortable using this resource with their students, especially if they are unaware of the colloquial expressions and dialectical differences that the speakers use in the videos.

If the main goal of an online language course is to help students develop communicative competence in the target language, then the main focus of instruction should not be on teaching grammar. Rather, learners should be engaged in the communicative and social aspects of language, with an emphasis on how the language is spoken in its natural sociocultural context. It is also important to include instruction on how to maintain conversations with native speakers through the use of circumlocution, word coinage, and back-channeling cues. This focus will bring the language to life for online learners and it should motivate them to learn the target language and its cultures.

The Communicative Language Teaching Approach (CLT)

Many language teacher education programs promote the communicative language teaching (CLT) approach. This is a flexible approach to teaching that prioritizes instruction on the notions and functions of language over target language forms and structures. While linguistic forms and structures are taught within the CLT paradigm, their purpose is to support meaningful communication in the L2 for the development of learners' communicative competence. The American Council on the Teaching of Foreign Languages (ACTFL), the Council of Europe, and other professional language teaching organizations advocate the use of CLT.

The CLT approach emphasizes notions, which are real-world situations in which people communicate (e.g., shopping, eating out, going to the doctor), and functions, which refer to the language that is needed to communicate in a given real-world situation. For example, if the notion is shopping, then some possible functions are asking how much something costs, asking for another size, and negotiating a price. In other words, functions are the specific aims of communication, while notions are the situations or settings in which the communication takes place.

According to Richards (2006), CLT has the following guiding principles:

- Make real communication the focus of language learning.
- Provide opportunities for learners to experiment and try out what they know.
- Be tolerant of learners' errors as they indicate that the learner is building up his or her communicative competence.
- Provide opportunities for learners to develop both accuracy and fluency.
- Link the different skills such as speaking, reading, and listening together, since they usually occur so in the real world.
- Let students induce or discover grammar rules (p. 13).

It is important to keep in mind that CLT is a flexible teaching approach and not a prescriptive teaching method because there are no clear methodological procedures. In fact, many different methods and techniques, such as task-based teaching and content-based teaching, fit well under the CLT paradigm.

Core Practices for Language Instruction

Core practices may be defined as the essential knowledge, skills, and understandings that teachers must have to carry out their core instructional responsibilities in their specific disciplines (Ball & Forzani, 2009). Therefore, core practices are discipline specific. In other words, what works for teaching one subject will not necessarily carry over into another subject. According to Glisan and Donato (2017), core practices are complex instructional actions, behaviors, and techniques that are powerful in advancing student learning; these practices are not readily transparent and they are not learnable through observations alone. Glisan and Donato (2017) asserted that core practices must be deconstructed and taught explicitly in teacher education programs and they must be rehearsed and coached within specific contexts. Finally, teacher educators must be able to justify the instruction of these practices for the development of professional expertise (Glisan & Donato, 2017).

Six core practices for language instruction were identified by Glisan and Donato (2017) as follows: "(1) facilitating target language comprehensibility, (2) building a classroom discourse community, (3) guiding learners to interpret and discuss authentic texts, (4) focusing on form in a dialogic context through PACE [grammar is taught as a concept], (5) focusing on cultural products, practices, and perspectives in a dialogic context, and (6) providing oral corrective feedback to improve learner performance" (p. 11). These core practices are advocated by ACTFL.

Glisan and Donato (2017) asserted that the aforementioned practices are not an exhaustive list, as there are likely other core practices that could be identified and explicitly taught in teacher education programs. However, they suggested that these are the minimum that are necessary to begin instructing language effectively (Glisan & Donato, 2017). Furthermore, the core practices listed above would be considered large-grain core practices. In order to enact them, language teachers would need to engage in many other small-grain core practices. For example, under the Core Practice *facilitating target language comprehensibility*, some small-grain practices would include speaking slowly and clearly in the target language, using input that is just beyond the learners' current level, and using gestures, facial expression, and other visual cues to facilitate students' comprehension to name a few. Consequently, there are numerous small-grain core practices that could be identified, deconstructed, and explicitly taught to L2 teacher candidates under each of the six large-grain core practices listed above.

Regarding Glisan and Donato's recommendation to use the PACE model to teach grammar, this is a novel technique that was proposed by Donato and Adair-Hauck (Adair-Hauck, 1993; Donato & Adair-Hauck, 1992, 1994, 2016), where grammar is taught dialogically. This means that teachers and students co-construct grammar rules. With traditional teacher-fronted instruction, grammar is taught deductively with the teacher explaining the grammar rules followed by the presentation of target language examples. With the inductive approach to grammar instruction, the teacher shows the students target language examples, and then the students try to figure out the rules by themselves. With the dialogic approach, scaffolding is provided by the language instructor in the form of guiding questions that prompt students to reflect upon, predict, and make generalizations about how the language works. In other words, students write grammar rules using their own words with the guidance of the teacher, who ensures that the students' explanations are appropriate.

PACE stands for Presentation, Attention, Co-Construction, and Extension. For the presentation aspect of this model, teachers do not present grammatical rules and structures. Rather, they focus on an authentic piece of text or on an oral dialogue that contains the targeted grammatical form or structure. The focus remains on meaning, but the text or dialogue is flooded with the targeted grammatical form. Students' attention is then drawn to the targeted forms or structures through input enhancement (highlighting, bolding, etc.) or through the use of visual cues. This is the attention piece of the model. The co-construction phase is when the teacher scaffolds the students in the development of their own grammar rules. Richards (2006) asserted that having students "discover" grammar rules is a guiding principle for the CLT approach. Finally, in the extension phase, the students complete a task that is related to the theme of the lesson. The task requires them to use the targeted form or structure, but the focus remains on meaning rather than on form. The PACE model allows grammar to be taught as a concept rather than as discrete points of knowledge. This technique is also known as story-based language teaching (Donato & Adair-Hauck, 2016) and it is a good fit for teaching and learning environments that adhere to the CLT approach.

While teacher candidates and novice teachers may struggle to effectively enact the core practices listed above, most experienced and effective language teachers use them daily. However, additional knowledge, skills, and expertise are necessary to enact them effectively in online, blended, and/or flipped learning environments. Therefore, language educators who wish to teach in these environments may need additional professional development opportunities, training materials, and resources.

CLT in Online, Blended, and Flipped Learning Environments

Creating online, blended, or flipped courses that follow the principles of CLT (Richards, 2006) as well as the core practices for world language instruction (Glisan & Donato, 2017) is a complex task that requires a myriad of knowledge, skills, and competencies. While it may seem overwhelming to transition initially from traditional to online, blended, or flipped learning environments, following the ten guidelines listed in Table 3.1 will help language educators teach communicatively online. In this chapter, the authors provide guidance and examples regarding how to implement these guidelines online. This list is not meant to be exhaustive, but incorporating them will help language educators design, develop, and deliver online courses that facilitate the language acquisition process. Of note, the concept of backward design is instrumental to the online language course design process; this topic is covered extensively in Chapter 1 and readers are encouraged to review this concept as they consider the guidelines below.

Table 3.1 Ten guidelines for teaching communicatively in online, blended, and flipped language learning environments

1. Emphasize the notions and functions of language.
2. Focus on meaning over form.
3. Deliver 90% or more of the instruction in the target language.
4. Base lessons on professional standards and what students can actually do at the targeted proficiency level.
5. Avoid mechanical and pattern drill activities.
6. Facilitate student-teacher and student-student interaction to foster the negotiation of meaning.
7. Incorporate open-ended activities, such as role-plays and information gap tasks, where students engage in creative language use.
8. Integrate authentic materials, which are materials and resources that were created by and/or for native speakers of the target language.
9. Create a meaningful cultural context for language instruction.
10. Grade students holistically and provide appropriate corrective feedback.

While backward design is of paramount importance in the instructional design process for online courses across every discipline, the guidelines listed on the previous page are specific for instructing language courses in online, blended, and flipped learning environments.

The Notional/Functional Syllabus

Creating and following a notional/function syllabus rather than a structural syllabus (i.e., one that focuses on the instruction of grammatical forms, structures, and lexical items) will enable online language educators to incorporate Guidelines 1 and 2 from Table 3.1. When planning the course syllabus, Guideline 1 (emphasize the notions and functions of language) and Guideline 2 (focus on meaning over form) need to be taken into account. The course syllabus should revolve around language notions and functions and not around disconnected grammatical forms, structures, and vocabulary. With the CLT approach, language educators build course syllabi around various real-world situations, and then they teach the necessary language functions that are needed to communicate in those specific situations. Consequently, when teaching communicatively, language educators should be careful not to rely too heavily on course textbooks that take a structural approach. Most secondary and postsecondary textbooks that are available in the United States and elsewhere include both notions/functions and the structures of language. Therefore, language educators may opt to place greater emphasis on language notions and functions rather than on grammatical forms and structures in their courses. Even when instructors are required to use textbooks that focus heavily on grammar, it is still possible to teach communicatively because there are a wide range of materials and resources available online that could be used to build a notional/functional syllabus. For example, the Multimedia Educational Resource for Learning and Online Teaching (MERLOT) website contains a repository of online materials and resources, many of which are completely open access, which means that they are free of charge for instructors to download, copy, and use, but some copyright and licensing restrictions may still apply. MERLOT offers a world languages collection with over 3,000 online materials available in many commonly and less commonly taught languages. Figure 3.4 presents an example of an online material for instructing French civilization from the MERLOT website.

This particular resource includes audio, video, digital images, dialogues, and online exercises. While this online resource provides rich cultural information and artifacts, instructors may need to modify the content for learners with varying levels of proficiency. This particular resource includes information on

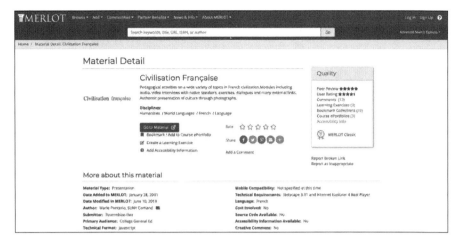

Figure 3.4 MERLOT resource for teaching French civilization.

© *Marie Ponterio, State University of New York at Cortland. Used with permission.*

several topics. Therefore, specific notions that could be taught include the following: education, family life, government, national holidays, the environment, vacations, health care, and transportation. A variety of language functions could be taught within the real-world contexts listed above, but the grammatical forms and vocabulary items that are covered would depend on the learner's proficiency level in the target language. For example, specific language functions for the notion of schooling/education could be the following: talking about current class schedules (Novice), talking about prior class schedules and comparing them to current class schedules (Intermediate), or talking about ideal class schedules and what could be improved upon in their current class schedules (Advanced). In addition to the MERLOT website, several other websites such as the Center for Advanced Research on Language Acquisition (CARLA) and the Center for Open Educational Resources and Language Learning (COERLL) offer open-access online resources for language learning and teaching. These types of resources could be employed when designing a notional/functional syllabus.

Rich Comprehensible Online Input

To integrate Guideline 3 from Table 3.1 (deliver 90% or more of the instruction in the target language), it is necessary to provide ample amounts of rich, comprehensible online input for learners. According to Krashen's input hypothesis (1980, 1985), languages are acquired subconsciously by exposure to comprehensible input and input is the only necessary factor for language acquisition to take place; therefore, students should be exposed to large amounts of target language input that is just beyond their current level of understanding ($i + 1$). Krashen (1980, 1985) asserted that there is no distinction between child L1 acquisition and adult L2 acquisition and that innate mechanisms within the human brain build an implicit linguistic system (also known as an internal grammar) when learners are exposed to sufficient amounts of comprehensible input. While some scholars may disagree with Krashen's hypotheses (Long, 1981, 1983a, 1983b; Swain, 1983, 1985, 1995, 1998), it is generally accepted that comprehensible input is a key component of the language acquisition process.

Language instructors have the responsibility of making the target language input comprehensible for learners. If exposure to the target language alone were sufficient, everyone could learn an L2 simply by watching television or listening to the radio; however, beginning-level students cannot learn an L2 this way because that would be $i + 1000$, or input that is far beyond their current level of understanding. ACTFL recommends that 90% or more of instructional time should take place in the target language (ACTFL, 2017). This does not mean that delivering instruction in the target language is sufficient for language acquisition to take place; rather, language educators must engage in strategy use to make the target language input comprehensible for learners. Some of these strategies are similar to how caretakers talk to babies and young children in their L1. Johnson (2018) reviewed the research on caretaker talk and found that caretakers do the following: (1) slow down their rate of speech, (2) repeat themselves, (3) simplify their speech, (4) use context (here and now) to support meaning, (5) use speech that is well-formed and grammatical, and (6) rough tune their speech. Rough tuning refers to using language that is approximately at learners' proficiency level, but that also includes forms, structures, and lexical items that are beyond learners' current level of proficiency. Caretakers do this naturally; however, language teachers usually fine tune their speech, which means that they tend to use only the forms, structures, and vocabulary that their students already know. Language teachers should try to avoid this pitfall so that they can optimize, rather than hinder, the language acquisition process. To make sure that their input is comprehensible to learners, language educators should incorporate the same techniques that caretakers do when speaking to babies and young children in their L1; this is especially important for beginning-level learners.

While the role of input is a major factor for language acquisition, instructors should keep in mind that producing output and interacting with others are also necessary ingredients for language learning. Several prominent scholars disagree with Krashen regarding his claim that input is the only necessary condition for language acquisition to take place. Swain (1985, 1993, 1995, 1998) proposed the output hypothesis, which asserts that L2 students must be pushed to produce output in the target language in order to process language more deeply, attending to both meaning and linguistic form simultaneously. According to Swain, learners must produce output to develop fluency and accuracy in the target language. Furthermore, she claimed that output, in addition to input, is a key factor in the acquisition process.

Similarly, Long (1981, 1983a, 1983b) set forth the interaction hypothesis, which claims that learners acquire language by talking with others. In other words, during conversations between native and nonnative speakers, the interlocutors work together to achieve mutual understanding. When misunderstandings occur, the conversation must be repaired through the negotiation of meaning (Long, 1981, 1983a, 1983b). Long (1996) revised and updated the interaction hypothesis to include cognitive factors and he stated that selective attention and processing capacity are what mediate the input that learners receive during conversational interactions. In other words, learners must pay attention to their input and as human beings, they are limited capacity processors who can only take in, attend to, and process so much new information at one time.

ACTFL (2017) provides a number of recommendations for using the target language in the classroom, which include providing large amounts of comprehensible input, ample opportunities for learners to produce output, and opportunities for learners to negotiate meaning with their instructor and their peers. ACTFL (2017) also recommends that language instructors conduct frequent comprehension checks, use contextual cues to support comprehension, and elicit students' production that increases in complexity, accuracy, and fluency over time. It is noteworthy that ACTFL does not recommend prohibiting the use of students' native language in the L2 classroom; rather, if the L1 is used, it should be in a limited way. For example, defining a vocabulary word in the L1 when all other attempts at facilitating students' understanding of the meaning of the word have failed. However, ACTFL does not recommend using the native language as the default for checking students' comprehension (ACTFL, 2017).

Online instructors should strive to adhere to ACTFL's recommendations with respect to the delivery of instructional content in the target language. However, online instructors will often need to explain the course layout, requirements, and expectations in the students' native language to ensure that they comprehend them. For example, course orientations, course policies, course grading, information on exam dates and times, project instructions, and homework deadlines may need to be delivered in L1, especially for beginning-level language students, so that they understand the course design and expectations. In other words, information on the structure and delivery of the course will be clearer for students if it is delivered in their L1. The instructional content, however, should always be delivered in the L2 in online learning environments, whether the students are Novice, Intermediate, or Advanced language learners.

There are a number of ways to provide rich comprehensible input for online and blended learners; for example, teachers can make instructional videos that tell a story using the targeted grammatical forms and structures. With video input, visual cues facilitate students' comprehension of target language meaning. It is also possible to caption videos so that students can read along in the target language while they simultaneously listen to the target language input. Of course, teachers must speak slowly and clearly when recording audio and video in the target language. Instructional videos that contain digital images are also a great way to teach new vocabulary items. According to Egbert et al. (2014), instructional videos are the central component of the pre-class materials in the L2 flipped learning approach. Similarly, instructional videos are instrumental in teaching in online and blended environments too. Figure 3.5 displays a screenshot of an instructional video that was created to teach airport vocabulary. It uses simplified language that is more comprehensible for

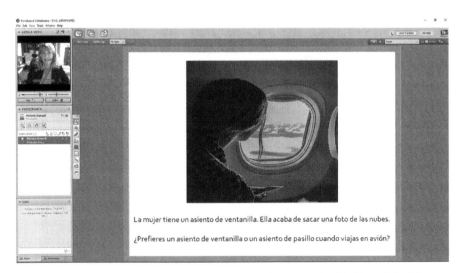

Figure 3.5 Screenshot of a captioned instructional video using the Blackboard Collaborate tool on D2L's Brightspace platform.

D2L product screenshot reprinted with permission from D2L Corporation.

language learners. The target language input, in this case Spanish, was captioned and it appears at the bottom of the screen. This not only makes the instructional video accessible for students who are deaf or hard of hearing, but it also facilitates all students' comprehension of the target language because they are able to listen to and read the input at the same time.

There are numerous online tools and applications for creating and editing videos, but many of them are proprietary and have costs associated with them. For instructors who teach at an institution with a learning management system (LMS) in place, many of those—but not all—have screen recording capabilities. In other words, instructors may create a PowerPoint presentation, caption it, record a narration, and save it for playback as an MP4 (video) file using features of the LMS. Other software applications can also be used to create a slide presentation, including Keynote and Google slides (see Chapter 2 for information on how to do so); however, not all slide presentation software is compatible with every LMS. With Blackboard Collaborate, for example, only PowerPoint files can be uploaded into the virtual classroom space where video recordings can be made.

For those who do not have an LMS in place or if their LMS does not have the recording feature, there are several free online tools that are useful for creating instructional videos, such as Screencast-O-Matic, which has both a free and a paid version. While Screencast-O-Matic is described in this chapter, other screen capturing tools such as Camtasia, Jing, Filmora, Snagit, and Zoom are also available for making instructional videos through screen casting. Screencast-O-Matic is described here to provide an example of how online tools may be used to create instructional videos that contain rich, comprehensible input. The eResources contain links for all of the tools mentioned above.

Screencast-O-Matic is a computer-based application that allows users to capture and record their screens, edit their recordings, and share them with others. It is an ideal tool for educators who wish to create tutorials, lectures, and/or demonstration videos. The free features allow users to record up to 15 minutes from either their computer screen or web cam. The recordings may be saved as either YouTube videos or as MP4 video files, which can be stored on the user's computer or LMS.

Institutions or individuals may purchase licenses, which provide users with extended features such as unlimited recording length, captioning capabilities, and additional editing and web publishing tools. With the paid version, the length of the video recordings is only limited by the user's available hard disk space. Screencast-O-Matic is a good fit for online, blended, and flipped

Figure 3.6 Recording features of Screencast-O-Matic.

Used with permission.

learning environments because it provides captioning tools to ensure that the instructional videos are accessible for students who are deaf or hard of hearing. Moreover, the web publishing tools that are built into the application are relatively easy to use. Figure 3.6 shows the recording features of Screencast-O-Matic.

Videos may be published either on the Screencast-O-Matic website or on users' own cloud services. In addition, the Screencast-O-Matic application may be integrated into several LMS platforms and screen recorders may be launched from within the LMS for ease of delivery. Figure 3.7 displays Screencast-O-Matic's video editing features.

Given that Screencast-O-Matic has a free version and that it is able to be integrated into some LMS platforms, it is a good option for creating instructional videos that provide rich comprehensible input for online language learners. Furthermore, the video captioning capabilities enable educators to create instructional materials that are fully accessible to students with diverse learning needs.

Lesson Design and Learner Proficiency Level

According to Guideline 4 from Table 3.1, online language instructors should base all online lessons on professional standards and what students can actually do at the targeted proficiency level. As was discussed

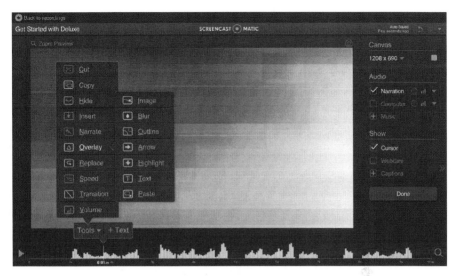

Figure 3.7 Video editing features of Screencast-O-Matic.
Used with permission.

in Chapter 1, online courses can be delivered asynchronously (anytime/anyplace learning) or synchronously (set online class meeting times). With asynchronous delivery models, lessons are typically broken down into weekly or bi-weekly modules (see Chapter 2 for a review of modules and pacing). With synchronous models, online lessons are delivered in real time during virtual class meetings.

Professional Standards

Irrespective of delivery mode, all online lessons or modules should be based on professional standards because they provide a guiding framework for the content that is covered and the skills that are developed; they also describe what learners should know and be able to do at specific levels of proficiency. Professional language learning standards create a roadmap that guides learners in their development of communicative and intercultural competence. Therefore, building lessons based on professional standards helps ensure that instruction is relevant, meaningful, and in keeping with what scholars and practitioners know about how languages are learned in instructional settings. Professional standards could also be used to create a measurable quality management system for language courses and programs, which is essential to advance foreign language teaching and learning (Bärenfänger & Tschirner, 2008). Language educators should think of professional standards as the bedrock of their instruction; a useful analogy is that teaching without the use of professional standards would be like taking a cross-country road trip without using a map. Professional standards provide the foundation for each lesson or module in quality online, blended, or flipped language courses.

In the United States, the ACTFL World-Readiness Standards for Learning Languages (National Standards Collaborative Board, 2015) are available for world language teachers and the national World-Class Instructional Design and Assessment (WIDA) Amplification of the English Language Development (ELD) Standards Kindergarten–Grade 12 (WIDA, 2012) are available for teachers of English as a second language (ESL). Many states have versions of their own standards for foreign and second language learning; however, these are typically based on national standards from ACTFL or WIDA. Europe and other parts of the world use the Common European Framework of Reference (CEFR) Standards for Languages: Learning, Teaching, and Assessment (Council of Europe, 2011), which are published in 39 languages.

Proficiency Guidelines and Testing

Both ACTFL and CEFR also provide proficiency guidelines that are used to determine students' level based on the specific tasks that they are able to perform in the target language. Similarly, the WIDA (2012) ELD standards describe six levels of proficiency for English language learners as well as what students should know and be expected to do with the language at each stage of development by grade level.

ACTFL (2015) defines proficiency as "the ability to use language in real-world situations in a spontaneous interaction and non-rehearsed context in a manner acceptable and appropriate to native speakers of the language. Proficiency demonstrates what a language user is able to do regardless of where, when or how the language was acquired" (p. 4). Given this definition, proficiency is assessed irrespective of any course, program, or curriculum, and learners must be able to use the language in both familiar and unfamiliar contexts. ACTFL breaks proficiency into five levels (Novice, Intermediate, Advanced, Superior, and Distinguished); with the Novice through Advanced levels, there are three subcategories (Low, Mid, and High). Therefore, proficiency can range from Novice Low through Advanced High prior to reaching the Superior and Distinguished levels. The ACTFL Proficiency Guidelines (ACTFL, 2012) provide detailed descriptions regarding what learners can and cannot do with language at any of the given levels. Language Testing International (LTI) is a licensee of ACTFL and they provide proficiency testing based on the ACTFL, CEFR, and the Interagency Language Roundtable (ILR) scale. The ILR is the rating scale for the State Department's Foreign Service Institute. LTI offers testing in over 100 languages and their tests include the Oral Proficiency Interview (OPI) and the computer-based Oral Proficiency Interview (OPIc) to assess speaking proficiency. The OPI is a phone interview with a certified tester, while the OPIc is a computer-based test that simulates a conversation using an avatar. OPIc tests are recorded and certified raters review the recordings to determine a proficiency rating. LTI also offers a Writing Proficiency Test (WPT), a Reading Proficiency Test (RPT), a Listening Proficiency Test (LPT), and a Listening and Reading Computer Adaptive Test (L&Rcat). All of LTIs proficiency tests use ACTFL certified raters who are subjected to rigorous training. In addition, LTI reports high levels of validity and reliability for all of the proficiency tests listed above and each test yields an official proficiency score from ACTFL.

At the K-12 level in the United States, each school district will set proficiency targets for their world language courses. Instructors can make use of the ACTFL Proficiency Guidelines (2012) to develop an understanding of where their students are currently and what they should be able to do with the language by the end of the course. They can also use these guidelines to create formative and summative assessments to measure students' progress toward meeting proficiency benchmarks. Setting common proficiency targets is also beneficial for standardizing language learning goals within departments and across institutions within a district.

Similarly, standards-based language programs at the university level set proficiency targets for all of the courses in their program, and courses are typically articulated and sequenced so that students can begin at the Novice Low level and move through the program until they reach the Intermediate High or Advanced Low level of proficiency by the end of the program, depending upon the target language studied. Proficiency benchmarks should take into account the fact that most language learners can listen and read on a higher level than they can speak and write. Proficiency targets are especially important for teacher candidates, or those who are training to become world language teachers. In order to teach a commonly taught language such as Spanish, French, or German, ACTFL recommends that instructors reach Advanced Low, which is the minimum proficiency needed to provide sufficient comprehensible input for learners, regardless of the level of language that is taught (ACTFL & Council for the Accreditation of Educator Preparation [CAEP], 2013). In other words, even if instructors are only teaching Novice students, they still need Advanced Low proficiency to teach the language well. With some of the less commonly taught languages— such as Arabic, Chinese, Japanese, and Korean—the minimum recommended proficiency level is Intermediate High (ACTFL & CAEP, 2013). This is a key factor to take into consideration when designing online language programs because fewer than half of all undergraduate teacher candidates reach ACTFL's recommended minimum level of proficiency by graduation (Glisan, Swender, & Surface, 2013). Therefore, the creation of well-articulated, proficiency-based online language programs are of paramount importance for the future of world language education.

Similar scales are available for those who teach language in settings outside of the United States and for those who teach ESL within it. World language educators in Europe and elsewhere use the CEFR scale, which is broken down into three main levels (A or basic, B or independent, and C or proficient). These levels are further broken down into subcategories that are marked with either a 1 or a 2 (e.g., A1, A2, B1, B2, C1, and C2). Similar to the ACTFL Proficiency Guidelines, the CEFR scale is used to describe proficiency at each of these levels. The CEFR proficiency scale informs planning, instruction, and assessment in Europe and beyond. Of note, research by Mosher, Slagter, and Surface (2010) found no difference in raters' ability to classify proficiency accurately between the ACTFL and CEFR scales.

For those who teach ESL in the United States, English language learner (ELL) proficiency is divided into six levels (Entering, Emerging, Developing, Expanding, Bridging, and Reaching). Similar to the ACTFL and CEFR guidelines, the WIDA (2012) amplified ELD standards document provides a detailed description of what students can and cannot do at each level of proficiency. Furthermore, the WIDA Assessing Comprehension and Communication in English State-to-State (ACCESS) test is administered yearly to ELLs in public schools. WIDA ACCESS scores are used for a variety of purposes, including placement of ELLs, establishing program entry and exit requirements, monitoring student progress, and informing instruction and assessment. A key difference between LTI and ACCESS testing in the United States relates to cost. For world languages, state and federal funding is not provided for proficiency testing and learners must cover the costs of their own testing if they wish to obtain an official proficiency rating. For example, world language teacher candidates must pay for their own OPI in states or programs that require it for certification. Conversely, Title VI of the Civil Rights Act of 1964 and the Equal Educational Opportunities Act of 1974 require public schools to ensure that ELLs can participate equally and meaningfully in educational programs. Therefore, each ELL must be assessed when entering the K-12 school system and proficiency assessment continues yearly until it is determined that the student has reached a sufficient level of proficiency to participate in mainstream classes without additional modifications or supports.

ESL instructors are provided with clear and detailed information regarding their students' proficiency levels, as the WIDA ACCESS test yields scores for listening, speaking, reading, writing, oral language (listening and speaking), literacy (reading and writing), and comprehension (reading and listening), as well as an overall score (reading, writing, listening, and speaking). This type of fine-grained analysis of student proficiency can help ESL teachers design individualized instruction to meet students' specific language learning needs. Moreover, WIDA ACCESS scores can be used to create purposeful groupings and/or pairings during lesson activities.

With respect to assessing world language students' proficiency, several open-access resources are highlighted in Chapter 4 for examining and assessing learner language. These resources can help world language educators pinpoint their students' proficiency levels with some degree of accuracy (see Chapter 4 for further details). If world language educators have a good understanding of their students' proficiency levels, then they can better meet their students' needs by differentiating their instruction (i.e., providing additional supports and/or additional challenge as needed).

Language Learning Goals

Goal setting is an important part of language learning in all instructional settings. Language educators use goals to inform their learning objectives, lesson plans, and assessments, while language students use them to identify their own learning goals and to chart their own progress. To help world language instructors and students with the goal-setting process, the National Council of State Supervisors for Languages (NCSSFL) and ACTFL created Can-Do Statements (NCSSFL-ACTFL, 2017a). The Can-Do Statements are aligned with the ACTFL Proficiency Guidelines (2012) and the ACTFL Performance Descriptors (2015) and they are broken down into proficiency benchmarks (overarching language learning goals), performance indicators (steps needed to reach goals), and examples (students' language performance for a given benchmark and indicator). These statements are not meant to be used as a checklist; rather, they are intended to describe what learners at each proficiency level are able to do over time in a wide variety of settings. They are a powerful tool to help language educators understand what proficiency really looks like in practice. The Can-Do Statements are highly specific; for example, a Can–Do performance indicator for presentational communication at the

Novice Low level is, "I can introduce myself using practiced or memorized words and phrases, with the help of gestures or visuals" (NCSSFL-ACTFL, 2017a, p. 12). A number of examples are provided under this proficiency indicator including, "I can write my name, age, and where I live on a simple form" (NCSSFL-ACTFL, 2017a, p. 12). While the benchmarks and performance indicators use some professional jargon, the examples use colloquial language that is easily understood by students and instructors alike. The authors of this book have trained and supervised numerous world language teacher candidates and it is very easy for novice teachers and teacher candidates to overestimate what students can actually do with the language, especially at the Novice through Intermediate levels. The Can-Do Statements are a highly valuable resource for ensuring that language educators assign appropriate tasks, activities, and assessments that are aligned with each level of proficiency as set forth by the ACTFL Proficiency Guidelines (2012). Students also find it meaningful when they are able to create their own learning goals and measure their own progress toward meeting them. Given that it takes many years to attain a high level of proficiency in instructional contexts, setting their own goals—and eventually meeting them—should help maintain students' focus and motivation for language learning.

In addition to language learning goals, the NCSSFL-ACTFL (2017b) Can-Do Statements also include goals for the development of intercultural communicative competence (ICC). ICC refers to students' ability to understand their own and other cultures and to use this understanding to engage in appropriate communication with those from diverse cultural backgrounds (Byram, 1997). Global competence and ICC are closely related constructs and the learning environments that foster global competence may provide the optimal conditions for students' development of ICC. According to ACTFL (2014), global competence includes the ability to speak two or more languages with cultural understanding and respect, and it is "developed and demonstrated by investigating the world, recognizing and weighing perspectives, acquiring and applying disciplinary and interdisciplinary knowledge, communicating ideas, and taking action" (p. 1). Moreover, global competence is essential for successful interactions between diverse groups of people in international, national, and local settings.

The ICC Can-Do Statements include benchmarks (overarching goals) and performance indicators (small steps needed to reach goals) that describe how well students are able to investigate cultural practices and products to gain an understanding of cultural perspectives. They also include benchmarks and performance indicators related to how well students interact with others in and/or from other cultures in terms of students' language and behavior. An example of an ICC performance indicator at the Novice level is the following: "In my own and other cultures I can identify some typical products related to familiar everyday life" (NCSSFL-ACTFL, 2017b, p. 5). There is also an Intercultural Reflection Tool that was created by NCSSFL-ACTFL (2017c) that students can use to reflect on their own development of ICC over time. The ICC Can-Do Statements and Intercultural Reflection Tool are powerful resources that enable language educators and students to set and measure goals for the development of ICC. Given that students live in an increasingly glob- alized and interconnected world, the development of ICC should be a key component of any language course or program.

Similarly, the WIDA (2016) K-12 Can Do Descriptors, Key Uses Edition, describe what ELLs can do at each level of proficiency by grade level. These statements revolve around four key language uses, as follows, with respect to the development of academic language: (1) recount, (2) explain, (3) argue, and (4) discuss. After a careful review of the literature and a linguistic analysis of the language needed for college and career readiness, WIDA selected the four aforementioned key language uses, which are also academic language functions, to be the focus of their Can Do Descriptors. One major difference between teaching ESL and teaching a world language in the United States is the focus of instruction. While world language classrooms (at the Novice Low through Intermediate Mid levels) focus on the development of basic interpersonal communicative skills (BICS), ESL instruction emphasizes the development of cognitive academic language proficiency (CALP). While both BICS and CALP are necessary to master a second language, ELLs tend to learn BICS within two years during their everyday interactions while being immersed in an English speaking context; however, it takes five to seven years for them to acquire grade-level academic language (Cummins, 1984, 1991). Given this long lag time between the development of BICS and CALP, a major goal of ESL instruction is to teach academic language so that ELLs can perform at grade level in this area. Conversely, most world language students are already operating with CALP on their grade level in their L1, and they typically do not have access to immersion in the target language environment. Therefore, they are in greater need of BICS at the Novice through Intermediate levels of instruction. The WIDA (2016) Can Do Descriptors also provide examples of tasks and activities that foster each of the key language uses.

In summary, both the NCSSFL-ACTFL (2017a, 2017b) Can-Do Statements and the WIDA (2016) Can Do Descriptors are valuable resources to assist with goal setting and to inform planning, instruction, and assessment of student learning. Moreover, both of these resources are perfectly aligned with their respective professional standards and proficiency guidelines and they both provide clear language regarding what students can actually do at their given level of proficiency. The NCSSFL-ACTFL (2017b, 2017c) Can-Do Statements also include resources for the development of ICC and global competence.

Lesson Design and the Three Modes of Communication

When designing lesson activities, Guideline 5 from Table 3.1 states that instructors should avoid mechanical and pattern drill activities. These types of activities are throwbacks from the audio-lingual method (ALM) of instruction, which is founded on the principles of behaviorism. In other words, this outdated teaching method is based on the belief that languages are learned through repetition, with learning taking place via conditioning and habit formation. Furthermore, according to behaviorism, errors should be avoided at all costs for fear that they may become ingrained. This often leads to overcorrection of students' errors. Today, it is widely understood by practitioners and scholars that ALM is not an effective instructional method. Languages cannot be learned by rote memorization and grammar drills, and it is impossible to learn a language without making mistakes. Moreover, the language acquisition process is a complex phenomenon that cannot be explained fully by the tenets of behaviorism. Unfortunately, ALM still exerts its influence today in terms of the types of activities that can be found in foreign language textbooks and resources, including those that are available online.

Pitfalls of Mechanical Drills

With ALM, lesson activities consist of mechanical or pattern drills—these are activities where students fill in a blank with a specific target language form or structure and the sentences in these activities are typically unrelated to each other. Therefore, the learner quickly understands that the purpose of the activity is simply to supply the correct grammatical form, not to make or understand meaning in the target language. With mechanical drills, the instructor has complete control over the response and there is only one possible correct answer. According to Paulston (1972), the goal of the mechanical drill is to provide practice on target language structures in order for students to move from repetition to self-expression without making grammatical errors. Paulston (1972) created a taxonomy of practice types for foreign language classrooms that includes three types of activities: mechanical, meaningful, and communicative. While learners do not need to attach meaning to the input sentences to complete mechanical activities, with meaningful activities, the learner must attach meaning to the input sentence and to the response; however, there is only one correct answer that is already known by the teacher or classmate (e.g., What color is my shirt?) Communicative activities are similar to meaningful activities, but they include open-ended items with more than one possible correct response (e.g., What are you doing this weekend?). While Paulston created his taxonomy of practice types in 1972, many foreign language textbooks that are currently available on the market in the United States and elsewhere still place a heavy emphasis on mechanical drill activities, while providing fewer meaningful and communicative activities.

A major drawback of mechanical drills is that students do not have to understand the stimulus to produce a correct answer. For example, students may conjugate the verbs correctly in mechanical drill activities by identifying the subject pronoun of each sentence and supplying the correct verb forms; however, while students' answers may be correct, it is unclear whether they understand the meaning of their responses in the target language. Research by Wong and VanPatten (2003) indicates that mechanical and pattern drills are a waste of instructional time because they do not promote L2 acquisition; therefore, they recommend that language educators bypass drills altogether in favor of more communicative lesson activities.

The authors of this book estimate that up to 80% of the activities in publisher-created materials in print and online fall into the category of mechanical or pattern drills. Therefore, extreme care must be taken when creating and/ or assigning lesson activities to ensure that students are not wasting their time engaging in ineffective grammar drills. While students may learn the targeted forms and structures in the short-term for course assessments, they will be quickly forgotten unless they have the opportunity to use them in a more meaningful way. Therefore, instructors should strive to incorporate meaningful and communicative activities into their lessons rather than relying on ineffectual and outdated mechanical drills. Language learning is promoted when students engage in open-ended communicative activities; these are activities where the teacher/peer does not know or cannot predict how the student will respond in the target language.

Moreover, language educators should keep in mind that grammar should not be the focus of instruction. Rather, grammar should be taught only to support communication, with the focus on meaning rather than on form. One way to do so is to teach grammar as a concept through story-based language learning, as was described in the section on Glisan and Donato's core practices above. Richards (2006) recommends teaching grammar inductively, which can be achieved by providing students with target language examples (aurally and in writing) and asking the students to figure out the grammar rules from the examples. Yet another inductive technique is to flood the input with the targeted forms and structures while using input enhancement techniques to draw students' attention to the targeted forms in their written input materials. According to Sharwood Smith (1991), input enhancement is any technique that highlights specific features of the written input, which can be achieved through changes in font style/size, underlining, bolding, or through the use of color. Russell (2014) found that beginning-level Spanish language learners were able to acquire the future tense with this approach. Even though the students in her study did not have any formal instruction on the Spanish future tense, they were able to use it correctly after reading several passages that were flooded with textually enhanced future tense forms.

Another way to teach grammar communicatively is to use processing instruction (PI), which is a research-based technique that requires learners to process target language forms correctly in order to extract meaning. This technique is based on VanPatten's model of input processing (1993, 1996, 2002, 2004), which is a set of principles that describe how L2 learners initially process or parse their L2 input. However, this pedagogical intervention is only effective for grammatical forms that carry semantic meaning (e.g., -ed = past tense in English) and it is not effective for targeted forms that only carry grammatical information such as definite articles. Lee and VanPatten (2003) suggested that PI should be used whenever instructors anticipate that their learners will experience a processing problem. For example, Spanish language learners who are native English speakers typically have difficulty processing object pronouns in Spanish; they often confuse subject and object pronouns in the target language input that they read or hear because the subject pronoun is frequently dropped in Spanish. While PI is a highly effective, meaning-focused technique for teaching grammar, it is somewhat challenging to design and implement. Lee and VanPatten's 2003 book is recommended reading for those who are interested in this research-based instructional technique that enables students to make form-meaning connections when learning L2 grammar (see suggestions for further reading at the end of this chapter).

A number of effective techniques for teaching grammar—such as story-based language learning, input flooding, textual input enhancement, and PI—were described above. These pedagogical interventions keep the focus on target language meaning rather than focusing on form. They should be implemented in flipped, blended, and online language learning environments as good alternatives to the mechanical drill activities that are prevalent in many of the publisher-created materials that are currently widely available in print and online.

Communicative Online Activities

Creating and delivering communicative online activities enables language educators to incorporate Guidelines 6 and 7 from Table 3.1. Guideline 6 (facilitate student-student and student-teacher interaction in the target language to promote the negotiation of meaning) and Guideline 7 (engage students in open-ended communication where they can create with language) can be promoted with meaningful and open-ended activities in which learners are engaged in three modes of communication: interpretive, interpersonal, and presentational. The interpretive mode refers to students' comprehension of written, visual, or aural target language input, the interpersonal mode encompasses all person-to-person synchronous communication in the L2, and the presentational mode denotes all spoken and written target language output that students have had time to prepare, practice, and/or rehearse in advance. Students may engage in interpretive reading, viewing, or listening and presentational speaking or writing. The interpersonal mode typically occurs in the spoken modality, but in online environments, it could also occur through texting or chatting. The interpersonal mode of communication must occur synchronously (at the same time), while the presentational mode may occur either synchronously or asynchronously (at different times). An example of synchronous communication would be two people talking on the telephone or via Skype. Conversely, an example of asynchronous communication would be one person posting a message on a discussion board and another person answering it a few hours, or a few days, later.

Some online tools for engaging students in all three modes of communication are outlined below. Please note that these tools are not meant to be prescriptive. They are included only to show examples of how to use online tools to teach communicatively. Language educators are encouraged to explore new tools and to use applications that they know or have access to in order to promote open-ended communication, the negotiation of meaning, and creative language use among students.

To facilitate practice in the interpretive mode, instructors may provide online reading and listening passages for their students, but it is important to keep a few things in mind when facilitating students' reading and listening comprehension skills in the target language. For example, comprehension skills precede production skills. This means that students will be able to listen and read at a higher level than they can speak and write in the target language. Therefore, it is OK to challenge students with written and aural target language input that is beyond their current level. L2 learners often struggle with comprehension skills because they typically engage in bottom-up processing. This means that they decode messages by paying attention to the details. In other words, L2 learners try to understand sentences and utterances by attempting to comprehend one word at a time. Conversely, native speakers usually engage in top-down processing first, which means that they decode messages by using their background knowledge to make predictions. After using top-down processing, native speakers engage in bottom-up processing to check the details of the passage against their predictions. Therefore, language teachers can promote top-down processing by helping students tap into their background knowledge in their L1. Background knowledge in the L1 can transfer over and help students comprehend input in the L2. It will be helpful to remind students to examine the type of text that they are reading in the target language (e.g., a poem, an advertisement, a diary entry, etc.) and then ask them to think about the kind of language that is used in that specific text type in their L1. There are likely to be similarities that will help facilitate their comprehension in the L2. Similarly, students' knowledge of the world can also be tapped to help them engage in top-down processing. If they are reading a passage about a young person who lives in a city in a target language country, the teacher could prompt them to think about what they know about city living (e.g., apartment buildings, public transportation, crowds, etc.). Asking students to make predictions about what they will read or hear and providing an advanced organizer (an oral, written, or visual outline of the new information that they are about to hear or read) also facilitates top-down processing. Providing visual images that coincide with reading and/or listening passages fosters students' comprehension of target language as well. It is also possible to caption videos in the target language and some video platforms such as Yabla and This Is Language (TIL), which are discussed below, even allow users to slow down the rate of speech in video input.

There are numerous online tools available that can be used to provide practice for students in the three modes of communication. For example, to stimulate the interpretive listening mode, Yabla is an application that makes authentic movies and television shows comprehensible for learners. It does this in three ways, (1) teachers may allow videos to show captions in the target language or in English, (2) students are able to slow down the videos and to rewind and replay segments of videos with Yabla's video player, and (3) written transcripts of videos are also available for students to assist their comprehension. The video content that is available on Yabla includes music videos, documentaries, interviews, travel and cooking shows, soap operas, and more.

Figure 3.8 presents a screenshot of Yabla's home page, which displays the various languages that are available on the Yabla platform.

Figure 3.8 Screenshot of Yabla's home page.
Used with permission.

All of the video content is authentic, meaning that is was made by and/ or for native speakers. This exposes students to the target language culture(s), to authentic target language accents, and to other sociolinguistic information that is socially and culturally appropriate. At this time, Yabla videos are available in Chinese, Italian, Spanish, French, German, and English. Yabla also provides a free 90-day trial for language educators. Similarly, TIL provides over 5,000 videos on common topics that are covered in the secondary and postsecondary curricula, such as friends and family, free time and leisure, education and work, home and health, and holidays and travel. TIL offers videos in ESL, French, German, Italian, and Spanish; moreover, TIL creates their own authentic videos with native speakers who are young people (not actors) talking about their daily lives. Videos are never shot twice, which means that they are natural and authentic. Therefore, this is an outstanding resource to help students acquire pragmatic competence in the target language.

While applications such as Yabla and TIL facilitate interpretive listening skills (and pragmatics), two applications that are useful for stimulating presentational speaking are PhotoStory 3 and VoiceThread. PhotoStory 3 is an application that is used for digital storytelling, which is the practice of telling stories through the use of computer-based tools. Similar to traditional storytelling, digital stories enable individuals to present their point of view

Figure 3.9 Overview of the capabilities of Photo Story 3.
Used with permission from Microsoft.

on a specific topic. Digital stories typically contain a mixture of computer-based images, text, recorded audio narration, video clips, and music. This application allows students to practice their presentational speaking within a meaningful cultural context through the use of authentic images and music. Figure 3.9 provides an overview of the capabilities of the Photo Story 3 application.

To create a digital story using this application, students would narrate ten to fifteen digital images in the target language with the option of playing target culture music in the background. The application also provides space for students to type their script, which can be used to assist the narration process. The Photo Story 3 application automatically adds effects to still images, such as panning and zooming, to help capture viewers' attention. Students may alter the preset panning and zooming effects to create their own effects. Furthermore, Photo Story 3 enables users to add text, such as titles and captions, as well as other graphics to images. It also allows users to save their digital stories as project files, which can be edited at a later time, or they may be saved as Windows Media Video (WMV) files, which can be stored on the user's computer or uploaded to the LMS. Digital stories may also be sent to others via e-mail if the file size is small enough. Photo Story 3 is available as a

free download. Students should also be encouraged to use their own personal
technologies, such as videos shot on their mobile phones, for creating digital
stories.

VoiceThread is another effective tool to stimulate presentational speaking.
It is a media player that contains a built-in online discussion space. Teachers
are able to upload media such as PowerPoint presentations, images, documents,
or videos to an online collection that has the appearance of a slide show. After
the media is added, both instructors and students are able to post comments
in which they engage in an on-going asynchronous discussion of the topic.
The discussions are asynchronous because students do not have to be on the
VoiceThread platform at the same time. Rather, they may post their comments
and replies during the days and times that are convenient for them prior to
the instructor's due date for the assignment. During these online discussions,
students may ask and answer each other's questions and critique each other's
comments. Moreover, comments may be made with video and audio (using a
web cam), with audio (using an external microphone or telephone), or via text
(using the computer's keyboard). If users opt to make their audio recordings
using a telephone, they are provided with a phone number and pin. Figure 3.10
demonstrates how to use VoiceThread to engage beginning-level learners in
presentational speaking.

Figure 3.10 Using VoiceThread to stimulate presentational speaking among beginning-level
Spanish language learners.

In online, blended, or flipped L2 classrooms, VoiceThread provides students with a space to engage in presentational speaking in the target language. In addition to using VoiceThread for interactive voice boards, students may create individual presentations by uploading and narrating a single image or slide, an entire PowerPoint presentation, or a video that they shoot with their cell phone or digital camera.

To promote interpersonal speaking in online and blended environments, conversation platforms enable students to engage in synchronous conversations with native speakers. Some conversation platforms that are available include LinguaMeeting (Wiley's En Vivo application uses this platform), Speaky, TalkAbroad, and WeSpeke. These applications allow individual students or small groups of students to interact with native speakers for up to 30 minutes at a time. The course instructor may add assignments, guiding questions, and/or instructions for the students' conversation partners. Some of the applications allow the conversations to be recorded and stored on the vendor's website. All of the platforms listed above, except for WeSpeke, have costs associated with them and they have a limited number of available languages. WeSpeke is a free conversation exchange platform that has 130 available languages; however, students must find their own conversation partner and they must take turns speaking in the target language and in English with their partners. Because many individuals around the world are engaged in learning English, it is relatively easy for students to locate partners who are native speakers of the target language. More information on free conversation tools is available in Chapter 2.

Conversation platforms have revolutionized online language course delivery because it is extremely difficult for one instructor to have extended conversations in the target language with each student. The one-on-one to small group synchronous interactions in the target language that occur on these platforms facilitate the negotiation of meaning, which is critical for the language acquisition process. Conversation platforms bring the language to life for online, blended, and flipped learners, and they help students understand the real-world applications of being able to communicate with native speakers of the target language.

There are also several platforms that allow students to practice interpersonal writing via text chat such as Bilingua, HelloTalk, HiNative, and Tandem. Most of these applications are free, but students must locate a conversation partner and take turns texting in the target language and in English. While the authors do not endorse any particular conversation platform, they do encourage online, blended, and flipped language instructors to explore all of the available options to determine which one(s) best meet the needs of their students and their own unique instructional contexts.

While several specific tools were mentioned above, it is important to note that any tool or application may be used provided that the following elements are present in the course: (1) learners receive ample comprehensible input in the target language, (2) learners have opportunities to produce output in the target language, and (3) learners have interactions with others in the target language. For online course delivery, it is often easier for instructors to use the technology tools and applications that are available at their institutions because then the institution, and not the instructor, is responsible for providing technical support to students in the event that they need it, which lifts some of the burden off of the instructor.

Authentic Materials

Guideline 8 from Table 3.1 is to integrate authentic materials, which are materials and resources that were created by and/or for native speakers of the target language. Infusing the course with authentic materials is of paramount importance in online, blended, or flipped language learning environments. Authentic materials allow students to read and/or listen to the language as it is used by native speakers in everyday situations. Galloway (1998) defined authentic texts as those that are "written by members of a language and culture group for members of the same language and culture group" (p. 133). Exposure to authentic texts and materials provides students with perspectives from the target language culture(s) on events, issues, themes, and concepts.

ACTFL advocates fostering students' understandings of cultural products, practices, and the perspectives that underpin them, and one way to do so is to expose students to authentic materials. The ACTFL World-Readiness Standards for Learning Languages (National Standards Collaborative Board, 2015) include two Cultures standards as follows: (1) "Learners use the language to investigate, explain, and reflect on the relationship between the practices and perspectives of the cultures studied" and (2) "Learners use the language to investigate, explain, and reflect on the relationship between the products and perspectives of the cultures studied" (p. 1).

With respect to the ACTFL Cultures standards, authentic reading materials help students learn about the daily practices and products of the target language cultures and the perspectives that inform them. There are numerous authentic materials available on the Internet that may be curated to create cultural lessons. For example, the Newseum website provides the front pages of more than 2,000 newspapers from around the world. While this website only offers the front page stories, it is possible for students to see different cultural perspectives on the same news story from different countries where the target language is spoken. Students may also compare perspectives on the same story between the target language country and their own country.

Front pages are available from various regions of the word including Africa, Asia, the Caribbean, Europe, the Middle East, North America, Oceania, and South America. Figure 3.11 depicts the landing page for Today's Front Pages. It is important for instructors to keep in mind that the newspapers are unedited and appear in their original "authentic" format. Therefore, L2 instructors, especially those who teach at the K-12 level, may wish to preview the materials to make sure that they are appropriate for younger learners before sharing the front page stories with students.

For Novice learners, simply pointing out the differences in the size and placement of the same headline that is covered in newspapers from different countries or regions is a good starting point. Some discussion in English on the cultural, political, and geographical similarities and differences between the two countries will promote the development ICC. Intermediate-level learners should be able to read the two articles with scaffolding from the instructor (e.g., providing background information and defining key vocabulary items), and Advanced-level learners should be able to discuss the similarities and differences between the perspectives of two different countries in the target language.

Figure 3.11 Today's front pages from the Newseum website.

Courtesy Newseum.

In addition to Today's Front Pages, there are numerous other websites that feature authentic materials that may be used for language learning, including several that were featured in this chapter (e.g., CARLA, COERLL, LangMedia, MERLOT, TIL, and Yabla). Authentic texts that are incorporated into lesson activities should be age appropriate, context appropriate, and at the appropriate level of difficulty for students' proficiency level with the assistance of scaffolding from the instructor. While it may take time for language instructors to search the Internet and to create activities that promote awareness of cultural products and practices and the perspectives that underpin them, exposure to authentic materials not only adds interest for language learners, but it also helps them recognize that there is a whole population of speakers of the target language in the world who have rich and diverse cultural perspectives (ACTFL, 2014).

Creating a Meaningful Cultural Context

Guideline 9 from Table 3.1 is to create a meaningful cultural context for language instruction. Perhaps the most straightforward way to do this is to incorporate ACTFL's two Communities standards: (1) "Learners use the language both within and beyond the classroom to interact and collaborate in their community and the globalized world," and (2) "Learners set goals and reflect on their progress in using languages for enjoyment, enrichment, and advancement" (National Standards Collaborative Board, 2015, p. 1). It should be noted that language instructors often find that these two standards are the most challenging to implement due to time constraints, a lack of resources, and other factors. However, there are a number of ways to implement them in the online environment that would facilitate Guideline 9 as described below.

One way to create a meaningful cultural context in online classes is to create a language partnership or exchange. This type of activity allows students to interact with their peers from the target language culture. Students will typically spend half of the time communicating in the target language and the other half of the time communicating in English (to help the conversation partner). Technology such as Skype or other video conferencing platforms may be used for these conversations. There are also several free websites such as Italki and The Mixxer that help students locate conversation exchange partners. However, it may be difficult to hold learners accountable and/or grade their work on free language exchange platforms such as these. Regardless of the platform used, instructors should provide guiding topics or questions to ensure that students maximize their linguistic and cultural exposure during conversations with their partners. If the platform has the capability to record and store conversations, then students should be required to listen to the recordings and to reflect on how they could improve their fluency and accuracy in subsequent conversations. See Chapter 2 for more information on developing language partnerships and exchanges.

Creating a language exchange may be time consuming, but it is a powerful way to connect students to the target language community beyond the walls of the classroom, whether those walls are virtual or traditional. This type of activity would also meet the first Communities standard listed above. Furthermore, by interacting with native speaker peers, language students will develop a deeper understanding of cultural products and practices as well as the perspectives that underpin them.

Another way of creating a meaningful cultural context is to have students curate the cultural artifacts that they find on the Internet, which they will then order and display using websites or blogs. During the curation process, students sort through a large amount of Internet-based content. After selecting the cultural artifacts that interest them, the students will organize the artifacts in a meaningful way that can be shared with their instructor and peers. Students may work either individually or in groups. When instructors require that students only curate authentic materials—those that are created by and/or for native speakers of the language—learners are exposed to the target language as it is used in its natural social and cultural context. Furthermore, when students select materials that are of interest or relevance to themselves, the lesson content becomes more meaningful to them. For example, the instructor may ask students to find examples of dance in Spain. While some students may opt to research traditional *flamenco* dancing, others may choose to research more modern dance such as *salsa*, which originated in Latin America, but is currently popular among young people in Spain. The curation of cultural artifacts is an excellent way for students to learn about the target language and culture simultaneously. In addition, this type of activity meets the second Communities standard above with respect to students' use of the language for enrichment and enjoyment. If instructors do not have access to an LMS with built-in blog or wiki tools, open-access websites such as Cool Tools for School, WordPress, and Wakelet are useful for student curations.

While language exchanges and student curations may take some time to implement, online instructors can also create a meaningful cultural context simply by engaging students in real-world communication. Placing students in pairs or small groups to discuss topics that are relevant to them—such as their daily lives, schedules, interests, and concerns—ensures that their communication is meaningful and authentic. As long as students are communicating real-world information, then instruction is occurring within a meaningful cultural context. Activities that promote real-world interactions should be employed in online, blended, and flipped learning environments.

Holistic Grading and Corrective Feedback

Guideline 10 from Table 3.1 (grade students holistically and provide appropriate corrective feedback) pertains to assessing student learning. All learners make mistakes during the language acquisition process and it is important to help students understand that it will be impossible for them to speak or write with perfect accuracy, even after studying the target language for many years. Language instructors also need to recognize that our goal is to foster students' development as "successful multicompetent speakers, not failed native speakers" (Cook, 1999, p. 204). Nonetheless, many students fear making mistakes, so it is necessary to create a learning environment that encourages all students to communicate in the target language, even when their language production is inaccurate. When instructors place emphasis on meaning rather than on form, students will likely feel less inhibited and less anxious about expressing themselves in the target language. To encourage students to speak in the target language despite their inaccuracies, instructors should not penalize them for each and every mistake that they make in their written and/or oral production. Rather than counting errors and tallying a score based on students' accuracy, rubrics may be used to evaluate specific criteria holistically, with grammatical accuracy being only one criterion among many. This type of grading focuses on the overall quality of students' work rather than on individual errors. When assessing students' production at the Novice through Intermediate levels, the most important thing to consider is whether they are able to get their meaning across so that a sympathetic native speaker could understand them. Therefore, certain types of errors— such as pronunciation—may be a more important factor than grammatical accuracy when students attempt to convey meaning in the target language. As students advance in their language learning, instructors could then begin to increase their expectations regarding students' fluency and accuracy. This increase in student expectations should accompany lesson tasks and activities that build in complexity over time.

The ACTFL Performance Descriptors for Language Learners (ACTFL, 2015) are useful for creating grading rubrics for online, blended, or flipped learning because they contain specific descriptions of the type of language that learners can produce as a result of explicit instruction at three main levels (Novice, Intermediate, and Advanced). The ACTFL Performance Descriptors were created to accompany the ACTFL Proficiency Guidelines (ACTFL, 2012), which are used to evaluate an individual's functional language ability irrespective of how a learner may have acquired the language (e.g., classroom-based learning, heritage language learning, immersion). See Chapter 5 for a detailed description of the ACTFL Performance Descriptors and the current research findings on using rubrics and performance-based assessments in the world language curriculum.

While proficiency and performance are related constructs, there is a key difference in how they are each assessed. In instructional settings, performance—rather than proficiency—is generally measured. For example, in educational contexts, instructors will set an instructional goal and write specific learning objectives for their lessons with the overall learning goal in mind. Students will then practice and rehearse the language functions and vocabulary items that pertain to the instructional goals and objectives (during class time and for homework). While students learn the new content, the instructor continually assesses student learning with formative assessments, which measure students' progress toward meeting the learning goals and objectives. Instructors may also determine whether certain content must be re-taught or if more or less time needs to be spent on specific topics based on the results of formative assessments. Finally, a summative assessment is administered that measures student mastery of the content that was taught in a learning segment or unit of instruction. An example of a summative performance-based assessment is a student giving an oral presentation on how to cook a specific dish from the target language culture after learning food/kitchen vocabulary, command forms, and cultural information surrounding cuisine in the target language culture.

Proficiency, on the other hand, is not tied to any specific course or curriculum. It measures a learner's ability to use the language in various contexts, with the linguistic content being very broad and touching on a wide range of real-world topics. An example of a proficiency assessment is the ACTFL OPI, which was described earlier in the chapter.

By using the ACTFL Performance Descriptors to create rubrics for both formative and summative assessments, language educators can help ensure that their instruction adheres to CLT. In online and blended courses, it is particularly important that students understand how they will be assessed on each assignment, assessment, and/or interaction. Online instructors should post the grading rubrics for all items of consequence in the course prior to the due dates. It is also a good practice to provide students with examples of target-level performance. For example, if Novice High students are expected to write a paragraph in the target language, the instructor could post a sample paragraph that uses simple sentences and structures. Often students who are adults or adolescents attempt to speak or write on a level that is much higher than their current proficiency level in the target language. This often results in production that is riddled with so many errors that it is not comprehensible. Students may then examine the rubrics, assessment criteria, and examples so that they have a solid understanding of exactly what is expected of them.

The ACTFL Performance Descriptors are a good starting point for the creation of rubrics because they provide clear language that addresses the three modes of communication (interpretive, interpersonal, and presentational) across seven domains as follows: functions, contexts and content, text type, language control, vocabulary, communication strategies, and cultural awareness (ACTFL, 2015). The first three address the parameters for language learning and the final four address how well a student is able to make and understand meaning in the target language. Each of these parameters is discussed in greater detail in Chapter 5 along with the research on assessment.

For those who teach ESL, the WIDA Performance Definitions (2018a, 2018b) for both Listening/Reading and Speaking/Writing are valuable resources for creating rubrics that are tied to each of the six levels of English language development. These documents provide specific language that describes target-level performance across three criteria: linguistic complexity, language forms and conventions, and vocabulary usage. The definitions are also well aligned with the WIDA (2012) ELD standards and the WIDA (2016) Can Do Descriptors.

While the ACTFL Performance Descriptors may be used for a rubric's content (e.g., mode of communication, domain, and evaluation criteria), there are several open-access websites that provide technology tools for creating customizable online rubrics. These include the following: Annenberg Learner, RubiStar, Teachnology, and RubricMaker. It is also helpful to include space for instructor comments/feedback as well as space for students to reflect on their own learning. Students may also be encouraged to rate themselves on the rubric and to compare their ratings with those of the instructor.

While it is not necessary to correct each and every mistake, language educators must provide their students with negative evidence, or what is not possible in a language, to facilitate the language acquisition process (Ellis, 1994; Long, 1996). Corrective feedback may be either written or oral in an online, blended, or flipped language class. There are several free tools that are useful for providing oral feedback for students including Audacity, Online Voice Recorder, and Vocaroo. Audacity is an application that enables users to create and edit audio files. Vocaroo and Online Voice Recorder are more simple tools that allow for audio recording but not editing. Audio feedback allows instructors to correct students' pronunciation errors. This is of particular importance in online classes that are asynchronous because the students do not have regular class meetings in which their pronunciation may be corrected. Audio feedback may also help students improve their listening skills in the target language. When providing audio feedback, it is important for the instructor to speak clearly, to have a tone that is motivating and positive rather than critical, and to give positive as well as negative feedback so that the learner is not discouraged.

There are numerous ways to provide written feedback for students in online, blended, or flipped classes. For example, instructors may use the track changes feature in Microsoft Word to leave comments; they may send written feedback via e-mail, text, or chat; or they may use an application such as Lino or Padlet, where instructors can leave feedback and communicate with students regarding their errors and/or answer their questions about their feedback in a collaborative whiteboard space. Google docs also allows instructors to edit and/or comment on their students' written work.

Regardless of the tool or application that is used to provide written corrective feedback, it is helpful for language instructors to use a correction code. With correction codes, symbols are used to indicate specific mistakes (e.g., w/o = incorrect word order). When students are allowed to re-write their written work after viewing the instructor feedback using a correction code, they not only improve their written production, but they also gain metalinguistic awareness about how the language works because they must look up each error and understand exactly why their production was inaccurate.

In summary, language instructors should focus on meaning rather than on form with respect to grading students' work and correcting their errors. If their production could be comprehensible to a sympathetic native speaker, even if they have inaccuracies, then students should be rewarded for making meaning in the target language. A benefit of online language learning is that students often submit recordings of their oral work and online instructors can correct students' production and pronunciation errors asynchronously using technology tools and applications. Therefore, online learners are likely to feel less embarrassment about their oral error corrections because these can be done in private—using the tools listed above—rather than in front of their peers. Finally, the ACTFL Performance Descriptors (2015), for those who teach a world language, or the WIDA (2018a, 2018b) Performance Definitions, for those who teach English as a second or foreign language, are useful resources for the development of rubrics that grade students holistically.

Conclusion

If language educators follow the ten guidelines listed above when delivering online, blended, or flipped language instruction, then they can rest assured that they are adhering to the major tenets of CLT and that the learning environments they create are communicative. It is possible to teach communicatively in online environments; however, it takes some forethought as well as the inclusion of instructional technologies that facilitate communication in the target language. As a final thought, technologies are always changing and evolving. Therefore, it is not the tool or application that makes online communicative language teaching happen; rather, it is the instructor's knowledge of online language pedagogy, which is knowledge of the pedagogy and technology for teaching language online—the focus of this chapter. Numerous resources for professional development in online language pedagogy are described in detail in Chapter 4. Readers who have little or no experience teaching in online, blended, or flipped learning environments are strongly encouraged to explore these resources and to plug into an online community of practice, several of which are listed in the next chapter.

Key Takeaways

- Language instructors need professional development, resources, and support to transition effectively from the traditional to the online, blended, or flipped learning environment.
- Students' development of communicative competence should be the overarching goal of every language course, irrespective of the delivery mode (traditional, online, blended, or flipped).

- Internet-based resources, such as authentic audio and video clips, show students how the target language is spoken among native speakers in natural sociocultural contexts. Therefore, these resources may be superior to language textbooks for facilitating learners' communicative competence.
- Following the guidelines listed in Table 3.1 will help ensure that online, blended, and flipped language courses are taught communicatively (using the CLT approach).

Discussion Questions

1. Many educators are tempted to teach the way that they were taught, even if those methods were ineffective or outdated. What methods did your language instructors use? Did they teach communicatively? Do you strive to teach communicatively? How will you enact CLT in online, blended, or flipped learning environments?

2. Do you facilitate your students' development of sociolinguistic and strategic competence? If so, how do you do this? How will you facilitate these competencies in online, blended, or flipped learning environments?

3. Do you agree with Glisan and Donato's (2017) core teaching practices? Why (not)? Are you able to enact all of these practices in the traditional brick-and-mortar environment? Do you think it will be more challenging to enact them in online, blended, or flipped learning environments? Why (not)?

4. Glisan and Donato (2017) advocate the PACE model. Do you agree that this is a good technique for teaching L2 grammar? Why (not)? Do you think it will be effective for instructing all grammatical forms (both simple and complex forms)? In your opinion, how difficult would it be to use the PACE/story-based approach for teaching grammar in traditional versus online environments?

5. Do you think it will be challenging to incorporate the ten guidelines for teaching communicatively in online, blended, and flipped learning environments? Why (not)? Which ones do you think will be easy to incorporate? Which ones will be difficult?

6. A number of online tools and resources were mentioned in this chapter. Which ones will you integrate into your online, blended, or flipped language classes? Can you think of any novel ways of using these resources that were not mentioned in the chapter?

Suggestions for Further Reading

Communicative Language Teaching:
Canale, M., & Swain, M. (1980). Theoretical bases of communicative approaches to second language teaching and testing. *Applied Linguistics*, *1*(1), 1–47.

Lee, J. F., & VanPatten, B. (2003). *Making communicative language teaching happen* (2nd ed.). New York, NY: McGraw Hill.

Richards, J. C. (2006). *Communicative language teaching today*. New York, NY: Cambridge University Press.

Wong, W., & VanPatten, B. (2003). The evidence is IN: Drills are OUT. *Foreign Language Annals, 36*(3), 403–423.

Core Practices for Language Instruction:
Glisan E. W., & Donato, R. (2017). *Enacting the work of language instruction: High leverage teaching practices*. Alexandria, VA: The American Council on the Teaching of Foreign Languages.

Learner Curation of Authentic Materials:
Mathieu, L., Murphy-Judy, K., Godwin-Jones, R., Middlebrooks, L., & Boykova, N. (2019). Learning in the open: Integrating language and culture through student curation, virtual exchange, and OER. In A. Comas-Quinn, A. Beaven, & B. Sawhill (Eds.), *New case studies of openness in and beyond the language classroom* (pp. 65–82). Research-publishing.net. https://doi.org/10.14705/rpnet.2019.37.967

PACE / Story-Based Approach:
Donato, R., & Adair-Hauck, B (2016). PACE: A story-based approach for dialogic inquiry about form and meaning. In J. Shrum & E. W. Glisan (Authors), *Teacher's handbook: Contextualized language instruction* 5th ed., (pp. 206–230). Boston, MA: Cengage Learning.

Project-Based Language Learning:
National Foreign Language Resource Center at the University of Hawaii at Manoa (2020). *Project-based language learning*. Retrieved from http://nflrc.hawaii.edu/projects/view/2014A/

Task-Based Teaching:
Ellis, R. (2003). *Task-based language learning and teaching*. Oxford, U.K.: Oxford University Press.

González-Lloret, M. (2016). *A practical guide to integrating technology into task-based language teaching.* Washington DC: Georgetown University Press.

Teaching Pragmatics:
Ishihara, N., & Cohen, A. D. (2010). *Teaching and learning pragmatics: Where language and culture meet.* New York, NY: Routledge.

Note

1   The LangMedia "Spanish in Mexico" videos were produced by the Five College Center for World Languages with funding from the National Security Education Program (NSEP) and the Fund for the Improvement of Post-Secondary Education (FIPSE) of the U.S. Department of Education. For more information and resources, visit https://langmedia.fivecolleges.edu/ or e-mail: fclang@fivecolleges.edu.

References

Adair-Hauck, B. (1993). *A descriptive analysis of whole language/guided participatory versus explicit teaching strategies in foreign language instruction* [Unpublished doctoral dissertation]. University of Pittsburgh, Pittsburgh, PA.

Allen, I. E., Seaman, J., Poulin, R., & Straut, T. T. (2016). *Online report card: Tracking online education in the United States* (Babson Survey Research Group Report), pp. 1–57. Retrieved from https://onlinelearningsurvey.com/reports/onlinereportcard.pdf

American Council on the Teaching of Foreign Languages (ACTFL). (2012). *ACTFL proficiency Guidelines.* Retrieved from https://www.actfl.org/resources/actfl-proficiency-guidelines-2012

American Council on the Teaching of Foreign Languages (ACTFL). (2014). *ACTFL board approved position statements: Global competence position statement.* Retrieved from https://www.actfl.org/list/position-statement/global-competence-position-statement

American Council on the Teaching of Foreign Languages (ACTFL). (2015). *Performance descriptors for language learners* (2nd ed.). Retrieved from https://cms.azed.gov/home/GetDocumentFile?id=5748a47daadebe04c0b66e64

American Council on the Teaching of Foreign Languages (ACTFL). (2017). *Use of the target language in language learning.* Retrieved from https://www.actfl.org/resources/guiding-principles-language-learning/use-target-language-language-learning

American Council on the Teaching of Foreign Languages, & Council for the Accreditation of Educator Preparation (ACTFL & CAEP). (2013). *Program standards for the preparation of foreign language teachers.* Retrieved from https://www.actfl.org/sites/default/files/caep/ACTFLCAEPStandards2013_v2015.pdf

Ball, D. L., & Forzani, F. M. (2009). The work of teaching and the challenge for teacher education. *Journal of Teacher Education, 60*(5), 497–511.

Bärenfänger, O., & Tschirner, E. (2008). Language educational policy and language learning quality management: The common European framework of reference. *Foreign Language Annals, 41*(1), 81–101.

Byram, M. (1997). *Teaching and assessing intercultural communicative competence.* Clevedon, UK: Multilingual Matters.

Canale, M. (1983). From communicative competence to communicative language pedagogy. In J. C. Richards & R. W. Schmidt (Eds.), *Language and Communication* (pp. 2–27). London, England: Longman.

Canale, M., & Swain, M. (1980). Theoretical bases of communicative approaches to second language teaching and testing. *Applied Linguistics, 1*(1), 1–47.

Cook, V. (1999). Going beyond the native speaker in language teaching. *TESOL Quarterly, 33*(2), 185–209.

Council of Europe. (2011). *Common European framework of reference for languages: Learning, teaching, assessment.* Cambridge, UK: Cambridge University Press.

Cowie, N., & Sakui, K. (2015). Assessment and e-learning: Current issues and future trends. *JALT CALL Journal, 11*(3), 271–281.

Cummins, J. (1984). *Bilingual education and special education: Issues in assessment and pedagogy.* San Diego, CA: College Hill.

Cummins, J. (1991). Language development and academic learning. In J. Cummins, L. Malave, & G. Duquette. *Language, culture and cognition* (pp. 161–175). Clevedon, England: Multilingual Matters.

Donato, R., & Adair-Hauck, B. (1992). Discourse perspectives on formal instruction. *Language Awareness, 1*(2), 73–89.

Donato, R., & Adair-Hauck, B. (1994, November). *PACE: A model to focus on form.* Paper presented at the annual meeting of the American Council on the Teaching of Foreign Languages, San Antonio, TX.

Donato, R., & Adair-Hauck, B. (2016). PACE: A story-based approach for dialogic inquiry about form and meaning. In J. Shrum & E. W. Glisan (Authors), *Teacher's handbook: Contextualized foreign language instruction* 5th ed., (pp. 206–230). Boston, MA: Cengage Learning.

Egbert, J., Herman, D., & Chang, A. (2014). To flip or not to flip? That's not the question: Exploring flipped instruction in technology supported language learning environments. *International Journal of Computer-Assisted Language Learning and Teaching, 4*(2), 1–10.

Ellis, R. (1994). *The study of second language acquisition.* Oxford, England: Oxford University Press.

Galloway, V. (1998). Constructing cultural realities: "Facts" and frameworks of association. In J. Harper, M. Lively, & M. Williams (Eds.), *The coming of age of the profession* (pp. 129–140). Boston, MA: Heinle.

Glisan E. W., & Donato, R. (2017). *Enacting the work of language instruction: High leverage teaching practices.* Alexandria, VA: The American Council on the Teaching of Foreign Languages.

Glisan, E. W., Swender, E., & Surface, E. (2013). Oral proficiency standards and foreign language teacher candidates: Current findings and future research directions. *Foreign Language Annals, 46*(2), 264–289.

Higher Education Academy. (2015). *Flipped learning.* Retrieved January 30, 2020, from https://www.heacademy.ac.uk/knowledge-hub/flipped-learning-0

Hymes, D. (1972). On communicative competence. In J. B. Pride & J. Holmes (Eds.), *Sociolinguistics: Selected readings* (pp. 269–293). Harmondsworth, England: Penguin.

Ishihara, N. (2010). Adapting textbooks for teaching pragmatics. In N. Ishihara & A. D. Cohen (Eds.), *Teaching and learning pragmatics: Where language and culture meet* (pp. 145–165). New York, NY: Routledge.

Johnshoy, M. (2006). *Competencies for effective online language teaching.* Retrieved from Center for Advanced Research on Language Acquisition website: http://carla.umn.edu/technology/tlo/

Johnson, K. (2018). *An introduction to foreign language learning and teaching* (3rd ed.). New York, NY: Routledge.

King, A. (1993). From sage on the stage to guide on the side. *College Teaching, 41*(1), 30–35.

Krashen, S. (1980). The input hypothesis. In J. Alatis (Ed.), *Current issues in bilingual education* (pp. 175–183). Washington, DC: Georgetown University Press.

Krashen, S. (1985). *The input hypothesis: Issues and implications.* New York, NY: Longman.

Lee, J. F., & VanPatten, B. (2003). *Making communicative language teaching happen* (2nd ed.). New York, NY: McGraw Hill.

Long, M. H. (1981). Input, interaction, and second language acquisition, In H. Winitz (Ed.), *Native language and foreign language acquisition* (pp. 259–278). New York, NY: Annals of the New York Academy of Sciences.

Long, M. H. (1983a). Native speaker/non-native speaker conversation and the negotiation of comprehensible input. *Applied Linguistics, 4*(2), 126–141. doi:10.1093/applin/4.2.126

Long, M. H. (1983b). Linguistic and conversational adjustments to non-native speakers. *Studies in Second Language Acquisition, 5*(2), 177–193. doi:10.1017/S0272263100004848

Long, M. H. (1996). The role of the linguistic environment in second language acquisition. In W. C. Ritchie & T. K. Bahtia (Eds.), *Handbook of second language acquisition* (pp. 413–468). San Diego, CA: Academic Press.

Mosher, A., Slagter, P., & Surface, E. (2010, November). *CEFR and ACTFL guidelines: Correlating the rubrics and descriptors.* Paper presented at the American Council on the Teaching of Foreign Languages Annual Convention and World Languages Expo, Boston, MA. http://static1.1.sqspcdn.com/static/f/272209/10229922/1295031592423/Mosher+Slagter++Surface+2010.pdf?token=4zstp9JhF754S8FC1ZnrZ3Yz6S4%3D

National Council of State Supervisors for Languages, & American Council on the Teaching of Foreign Languages (NCSSFL-ACTFL). (2017a). *NCSSFL-ACTFL can-do statements.* Retrieved from https://www.actfl.org/resources/ncssfl-actfl-can-do-statements

National Council of State Supervisors for Languages, & American Council on the Teaching of Foreign Languages (NCSSFL-ACTFL). (2017b). *NCSSFL-ACTFL intercultural communication novice-distinguished can-do statements.* Retrieved from https://www.actfl.org/sites/default/files/can-dos/Intercultural%20Can-Do_Statements.pdf

National Council of State Supervisors for Languages, & American Council on the Teaching of Foreign Languages (NCSSFL-ACTFL). (2017c). *NCSSFL-ACTFL intercultural reflection tool.* Retrieved from https://www.actfl.org/sites/default/files/can-dos/Intercultural%20Can-Dos_Reflections%20Scenarios.pdf

National Standards Collaborative Board. (2015). *World-readiness standards for learning languages* (4th ed.). Alexandria, VA: Author.

Paulston, C. B. (1972). Structural pattern drills. In H. B. Allen & R. N. Cambell (Eds.), *Teaching English as a second language* (pp. 129–138). New York, NY: McGraw-Hill.

Pinto, D. (2002). *Perdóname, ¿Llevas mucho esperando? Conventionalized language in L1 and L2 Spanish* [Unpublished doctoral dissertation]. University of California, Davis.

Richards, J. C. (2006). *Communicative language teaching today.* New York, NY: Cambridge University Press.

Russell, V. (2014). A closer look at the output hypothesis: The effect of pushed output on noticing and inductive learning of the Spanish future tense. *Foreign Language Annals, 47*(1), 25–47. doi:10.1111/flan.12077

Seaman, J. E., Allen, E., & Seaman, J. (2018). *Grade increase: Tracking distance education in the United States* (Babson Survey Research Group Report), pp. 1–57. Retrieved from http://onlinelearningsurvey.com/reports/gradeincrease.pdf

Sharwood Smith, M. (1991). Speaking to many minds: On the relevance of different types of language information for the L2 learner. *Second Language Research, 7*(2), 118–132. doi:10.1177/026765839100700204

Swain, M. (1985). Communicative competence: Some roles of comprehensible input and comprehensible output in its development. In S. Gass & C. Madden (Eds.), *Input and second language acquisition* (pp. 235–253). Rowley, MA: Newbury House.

Swain, M. (1993). The output hypothesis: Just speaking and writing aren't enough. *Canadian Modern Language Review, 50*(1), 158–164. doi:10.3138/cmlr.50.1.158

Swain, M. (1995). Three functions of output in second language learning. In G. Cook & B. Seidlhofer (Eds.), *Principle and practice in applied linguistics: Studies in honour of H. G. Widdowson* (pp. 125–144). Oxford, England: Oxford University Press.

Swain, M. (1998). Focus on form through conscious reflection. In C. Doughty & J. Williams (Eds.), *Focus on form in classroom second language acquisition* (pp. 85–113). Cambridge, UK: Cambridge University Press.

VanPatten, B. (1993). Grammar teaching for the acquisition rich classroom. *Foreign Language Annals, 26*(4), 435–450. doi:10.1111/j.1944-9720.1993.tb01179.x

VanPatten, B. (1996). *Input processing and grammar instruction: Theory and research.* Norwood, NJ: Ablex.

VanPatten, B. (2002). Processing instruction: An update. *Language Learning, 52*(4), 755–803. doi:10.1111/1467-9922.00203

VanPatten, B. (2004). Input processing in SLA. In B. VanPatten (Ed.), *Processing instruction: Theory, research, and commentary* (pp. 5–31). Mahwah, NJ: Erlbaum.

Wong, W., & VanPatten, B. (2003). The evidence is IN: Drills are OUT. *Foreign Language Annals, 36*(3), 403–423. doi:10.1111/j.1944-9720.2003.tb02123.x

World-Class Instructional Design and Assessment (WIDA). (2012). *Amplification of the English language development standards kindergarten–grade 12.* Retrieved from https://wida.wisc.edu/sites/default/files/resource/2012-ELD-Standards.pdf

World-Class Instructional Design and Assessment (WIDA). (2016). *K–12 can do descriptors, key uses edition.* Retrieved from https://wida.wisc.edu/teach/can-do/descriptors

World-Class Instructional Design and Assessment (WIDA). (2018a). *Performance definitions: Listening and reading grades K–12.* Retrieved from https://wida.wisc.edu/sites/default/files/resource/Performance-Definitions-Receptive-Domains.pdf

World-Class Instructional Design and Assessment (WIDA). (2018b). *Performance definitions: Speaking and writing grades K–12.* Retrieved from https://wida.wisc.edu/sites/default/files/resource/Performance-Definitions-Expressive-Domains.pdf

Chapter 4

Online Professional Development: What Resources Are Available and Who Can Help?

Introduction

One of the most challenging aspects of teaching online can be the loneliness associated with it. It takes hundreds of hours to design and develop a new online language course and those hours are often spent working alone. However, once an online course has been created, it may be recycled in future semesters; moreover, updating and improving future iterations of a course are usually not as time consuming as initially creating it. Unfortunately, each time that a course textbook is changed, learning resources are updated, or a learning management system changes or evolves, online instructors often have to redevelop certain aspects of the course, spending many more hours working alone.

Furthermore, many online language courses adhere to the asynchronous delivery model, meaning that there are few or no required synchronous class meetings. While students have the benefit of learning anytime/anywhere, real-time communication between the instructor and the students is often limited and the lack of synchronous interaction can lead to feelings of loneliness and isolation on the part of both the students and the instructor.

While instructors can design a number of activities to increase learners' social engagement in the course, such as pair or small-group work, conversation exchanges, and peer connections through social media and/or virtual worlds (see Chapter 2 to learn how to foster social presence in an online course), online instructors must also attend to their own needs. One way to combat their feelings of loneliness or isolation is to engage with other online language educators through professional development activities that take place either online or in person (e.g., at conferences, seminars, and/or workshops). Joining a community of online language practitioners comes with many benefits, such as sharing resources and materials, collaborating with others, and/or participating in a mentoring relationship.

In this chapter, the authors will share how to connect with other online language instructors, and they will also explain where to find open-access resources for online professional development. The chapter begins with an overview of the American Council on the Teaching of Foreign Languages (ACTFL) Distance Learning (DL) Special Interest Group (SIG)/National Foreign Language Resource Center (NFLRC) Mentoring Program for Online Language Teachers as well as how to become involved in the program. Following this, the authors share information on several language resource centers (LRCs) that provide open-access professional development materials for language teachers.

Information on STARTALK programs and Basic Online Language Design and Delivery (BOLDD) workshops for teaching languages online are also included in this chapter—the former focuses on critical languages while the latter is appropriate for instructing any second or foreign language online. Professional organizations that support online language teaching and learning are also highlighted in this chapter. Finally, the chapter concludes with an overview of non-discipline-specific resources for learning general online pedagogy.

Online Mentoring Program for Language Teachers

The ACTFL DL SIG/NFLRC Mentoring Program for Online Language Teachers was designed to help language teachers who are new or less experienced in the online teaching environment gain the knowledge, skills, and dispositions that they need to become effective online language practitioners. With this program, mentees are paired with a mentor who has three or more years of experience teaching language online. However, it is necessary to be a member of ACTFL to participate in the program as either a mentee or a mentor. All ACTFL members receive at least one free ACTFL SIG membership. Therefore, after joining ACTFL, there is no additional cost to join the DL SIG.

Regarding the mentoring program, online language mentees may opt to participate for one semester or for a full academic year, depending upon their own professional development needs. For the half-year program, the mentee will complete nine online lessons and have five interactions with the mentor, two of which must be synchronous (e.g., a phone call or online meeting). Mentors and mentees are encouraged to engage in course sharing, which enables the mentees to see in practice the principles of sound instructional design, development, and delivery that they learn about in the online lessons. The full-year program is similar, but the mentee will complete 18 online lessons and have eight interactions with the mentor. At the final synchronous meeting (for either the half or full-year program), the mentor will complete a checklist on behalf of the mentee, and they will each receive an online badge from ACTFL.

The open-access online lessons used for the mentoring program were designed as part of the NFLRC project Online Language Pedagogy (OLP), the purpose of which is to produce much needed open resources for professional learning on online language pedagogy. The NFLRC's OLP project responds to a real need, which is the lack of attention to online learning in second and foreign language teacher preparation programs at many universities in the United States and abroad. This problem was highlighted in Chapter 3, which focuses on online language pedagogy (see Chapter 3 for guidelines and examples of teaching language communicatively online). All of the online lessons are hosted on the NFLRC website; and at present, there are five modules: (1) Introduction to Online Language Teaching, (2) Designing Interaction for Online Language Learning, (3) Materials Development for Online Language Courses, (4) Assessment in Online Language Courses, and (5) Selecting and Adapting Materials for Online Language Learning and Teaching.

The first module (Introduction to Online Language Teaching) contains the core lessons for the mentoring program and they are recommended for mentees who have little to no experience teaching language online. These lessons were informed by materials that were created by the BOLDD Collaboratory and have been used successfully in BOLDD workshops for more than ten years. The lessons for the remaining topics were conceptualized and designed by the NFLRC and are part of the OLP project. The purpose of the ongoing OLP project is to provide pedagogical resources for language instructors who are already teaching online. The NFLRC surveyed online language instructors nationwide to prioritize the pedagogical aspects of online teaching that the survey respondents deemed to be the most deserving of attention. Once a topic was selected, the NFLRC conducted a review of the professional literature to identify subtopics and invited individuals that had experience or expertise in those areas to give webinars on the selected topics. The experts also created online professional learning lessons based on the instructional design guidelines created by the NFLRC. The first pilot of this professional learning series was implemented through a collaboration with the North Carolina Virtual Public School (NCVPS) and an NCVPS instructor, who was contracted by the NFLRC, served as a moderator for the series. The resulting materials (webinars with supplemental professional learning lessons) are available as open access resources on the NFLRC website. Moreover, the NFLRC provided logistical, pedagogical, and technical support for the creation of all of the online lessons that are used for the mentoring program. It is important to note that the mentoring resources are openly available for all language educators to use, regardless of whether they participate in the mentoring program.

ACTFL typically opens the applications for mentees each spring and for mentors each summer (all ACTFL members can participate free of charge). The program begins in September at the start of the new academic year. Those who complete the half-year program will finish in December and those who complete the full-year program will finish in May. Language educators who are interested in participating in the program should consult the ACTFL website for more details as well as specific enrollment dates.

National Foreign Language Resource Center (NFLRC) Resources

The NFLRC, located at the University of Hawai'i at Mānoa, is a federally funded (Title VI) LRC whose purpose is to increase the capacity to teach and learn foreign languages effectively within the United States (NFLRC, 2020a). It achieves its mission by developing and disseminating research-based materials and resources. It should be noted that the NFLRC faculty and staff have a high level of expertise in language education, teacher development, and technology integration, which enables them to create appropriate and highly relevant research-based materials and programs for language educators. While the NFLRC is physically located in Hawai'i, many of its products are openly available on its website. NFLRC activities and resources address a wide range of interests (teaching and professional learning materials, research journals, professional conferences, etc.) and when they are language specific, they focus on the less commonly taught languages such as Chinese, Filipino, Hindi, Korean, Indonesian, Japanese, Persian, Portuguese, Vietnamese, etc. The NFLRC also offers numerous online materials that address a diversity of world language education topics, such as assessment, curriculum development, literacy, heritage language education, online language pedagogy, online professional development, pragmatics, task-based teaching, and technology integration to name a few. Moreover, many of the resources that are available on the NFLRC website fall under a creative commons license.

There are approximately 60 different projects available for language educators to explore on the NFLRC Projects page. Although several current NFLRC projects focus on blended, online, and project-based learning, many past projects have focused on aspects of distance and online learning—starting as early as 1992—and have resulted in resources that are still relevant today. All of these projects, past and present, are openly available for language educators and other stakeholders to explore. Table 4.1 displays a list of NFLRC's online and blended learning projects.

Table 4.1 NFLRC Projects for online and blended learning

National Foreign Language Resource Center Projects for Online and Blended Learning	
Title of Project	*Years Active*
Blended Learning	2014 – Present
Online Language Pedagogy	2014 – Present
Project-Based Language Learning	2014 – Present
Online Professional Development	2014 – Present
Online Learning Communities for Less Commonly Taught Languages	2010 – 2014
Online Cafes for Heritage Learners of Chinese, Filipino, Japanese, and Samoan	2006 – 2010
Online Certificate Courses in Chinese, Japanese, and Korean	2006 – 2010
Distance Education, Distributed Learning, and Introductory Language Instruction	2002 – 2006
Distance Education	1996 – 1999
Teacher Training via Interactive Television and Internet	1993 – 1996
Disseminating Technology-Based Models for Distance Education in Critical Languages	1992 – 2002

In addition to the projects listed above, online language educators may also be interested in the journals that are hosted by the NFLRC: *Language Documentation and Conservation, Reading in a Foreign Language,* and *Second Language Research and Practice.* The highly acclaimed journal, *Language Learning & Technology,* is published by the NFLRC with funding from these sources: (1) the NFLRC, (2) the Center for Open Educational Resources and Language Learning (COERLL) at the University of Texas at Austin, and (3) the Center for Language & Technology (CLT) at the University of Hawai'i at Mānoa. The following section will focus on two recent NFLRC projects: OLP and Project-Based Language Learning (PBLL).

Online Professional Development

NFLRC's OLP project is part of a broader initiative on online professional development. For the OLP project, the NFLRC collaborated with the NCVPS to create online professional learning opportunities that focused on online language pedagogy. NCVPS is one of the largest state-led virtual schools in the United States, with 51,000 student enrollments across disciplines for the 2018–2019 academic year (NCVPS, 2020). They currently offer secondary-level online language courses in Arabic, French, German, Japanese, Latin, Mandarin Chinese, Russian, and Spanish. It is often difficult for individual middle and high schools to offer less commonly taught languages due to low enrollments; however, NCVPS is able to fill the gap by combining students from across the state and country to learn these languages online. They also employ language teachers who hold state certi- fication in North Carolina.

As part of the OLP project, the NFLRC created and delivered online professional learning for the NCVPS foreign language teachers. Participants met once per week synchronously for lectures and discussions on specific topics for a period of 14 weeks. The synchronous meetings were facilitated and recorded by NFLRC staff (an explanation of how the content was selected and developed by the NFLRC was described above). Scholars in online language pedagogy who were invited by the NFLRC gave the webinar lectures and created TED Ed lessons based on their webinars. The webinar and lesson activities for each topic consisted of 10 professional development hours. After the facilitated instruction series ended, the NFLRC continued to offer the TED Ed lessons as self-paced learning modules. The TED Ed lessons remain openly available to all language educators who want to learn more about online language pedagogy. Participants in both the facilitated and self-paced modules are able to

Figure 4.1 Screenshot of NFLRC's Online Language Pedagogy landing page.
Used with permission.

earn an online badge from the NFLRC. A screenshot of some of NFLRC's resources for online language pedagogy is presented in Figure 4.1

The most recent module to be added—Selecting and Adapting Materials for Online Language Learning and Teaching—is part of the NFLRC's new grant funding cycle that runs through 2022. Therefore, language educators should be on the lookout for new modules, resources, and materials from the NFLRC's OLP project over the next few years.

Project-Based Language Learning (PBLL)

Project-based learning, in general, is a type of pedagogy that requires students to actively engage in solving complex, real-world problems. It is a student-centered approach where learners organize and manage their own work while the teacher acts as a facilitator. The students typically collaborate with their peers to create artifacts that represent their learning (Crane, 2009). According to Markham (2011), students who participate in project-based learning engage in two types of learning: (1) developing knowledge and skills associated with the curriculum, and (2) applying new knowledge to solve an authentic problem. Markham also asserted that online tools and resources help students create high-quality artifacts to showcase their learning; therefore, project-based learning could be applied to online, blended, or flipped language courses where students have access to digital media and content. Furthermore, students can showcase their projects with ePortfolios, which were discussed extensively in Chapter 2.

Within the context of language learning, the NFLRC defines PBLL as "a transformative learning experience designed to engage language learners with real-world issues and meaningful target language use through the construction of products that have an authentic purpose and that are shared with an audience that extends beyond the instructional setting. PBLL can be conceived as a series of language learning tasks that are articulated toward a common goal: the construction of a public product" (NFLRC, 2020b). This definition is relevant for language educators who wish to incorporate PBLL into the world language curriculum.

In 2014, the NFLRC launched an initiative to create professional learning resources for world language instructors interested in developing and implementing quality projects. As part of this initiative, the NFLRC has created online institutes, short courses, and MOOCs to help language educators understand how existing principles of quality project-based learning could be applied to language teaching and learning. Language instructors who have taken advantage of NFRLC PBLL opportunities have created and shared project design and implementation information through an online repository called Pebbles.

The following modules on PBLL are openly available on the NFLRC website: (1) PBLL in Action (2015), (2) PBLL and Interculturality (2016), (3) Pathways to PBLL (2017), and (4) Pragmatics in PBLL (2018). In addition to the online modules, the NFLRC has offered PBLL symposia and, more recently, short courses on the connections between PBLL and relevant pedagogical practices, such as the 2019 short course on intersections between PBLL and high-leverage teaching practices. Figure 4.2 presents the landing page for NFLRC's PBLL materials and resources.

The NFLRC has also developed an entire lower division online curriculum for learning Vietnamese (Vietnamese 101–202) at the college level through PBLL. This is a valuable resource, not only for those who teach less commonly taught languages online, but for all language schools and departments who wish to incorporate PBLL into their curriculum. More information on PBLL is available on the NFLRC website. Readers are encouraged to explore the NFLRC website to locate the content that is most relevant for their instructional needs.

Figure 4.2 Screenshot of NFLRC's Project-Based Language Learning landing page.

Used with permission.

Center for Advanced Research on Language Acquisition (CARLA) Resources

CARLA is a research and resource center that is housed at the University of Minnesota, which provides funding and infrastructure support. Many of its resources and materials were created with federal grants, as CARLA was an LRC from its inception in 1993 through 2018. CARLA's current mission is "to study multilingualism and multiculturalism, to develop knowledge of second language acquisition, and to advance the quality of second language teaching, learning, and assessment in the U.S." (CARLA, 2020). This is achieved by engaging in research projects (including action research), disseminating research findings, and applying the knowledge gleaned from research across the United States in educational and other settings. Table 4.2 shows CARLA's research and programs.

While CARLA offers a wide range of materials and resources, the focus of this chapter is on online language professional development. Therefore, the following topics from the CARLA website will be explored here: Content-Based Language Teaching with Technology (CoBaLTT), Technology and Second Language Learning, and Language Teacher Education. CARLA's summer institutes and other professional development opportunities for online language teachers will also be described in this chapter.

Table 4.2 Description of CARLA's research and programs

CARLA Research or Program	Description
Articulation of Language Instruction	Projects that focus on the articulation of proficiency-based language instruction and assessment.
Assessment of Second Language	Resources that promote and assess the development of second language proficiency.
Content-Based Language Teaching with Technology (CoBaLTT)	Online resources to help teachers create content-based lessons/units using technology.
Culture and Language Learning	Interdisciplinary initiatives that explore the connections between language and culture.
Cultures and Languages across the Curriculum (CLAC)	Projects that promote transformational learning through the integration of content, language, and culture.
Foreign Languages and Literacies	Tools and resources that foster the application of literacies pedagogy and the use of authentic texts.
Immersion Education	Research and professional development to support immersion education.
Language Program Direction	Resources and support for language program directors.
Language Teacher Education	Research and professional development for language teacher educators.
Learner Language	Research and professional development for analyzing learner language.
Lesson Commonly Taught Languages (LCTL)	Resources to support the instruction of less commonly taught languages.
Maximizing Study Abroad	A series of guidebooks for students, instructors, and program directors to maximize learners' linguistic and cultural experiences abroad.
Pragmatics/Speech Acts	Research and information on how to teach pragmatics and speech acts to language learners.
Strategies for Language Learning	Research and resources for strategy-based language instruction.
Technology and Second Language Learning	Professional development and resources for technology integration and online teaching.

Note. The research and programs highlighted above are from the Center for Advanced Research on Language Acquisition (CARLA), University of Minnesota. See: https://carla.umn.edu.

Content-Based Language Teaching with Technology (CoBaLTT)

According to Crandall and Tucker (1990), content-based instruction (CBI) is "an approach to language instruction that integrates the presentation of topics or tasks from subject-matter classes (e.g. math, social studies) within the context of teaching a second or foreign language" (p. 187). Because language courses incorporate many cross-disciplinary fields such as literature, history, social studies, and geography, instruction on topics from these disciplines could be delivered through the vehicle of the target language. In addition, adding cross-disciplinary material that is related to the target language and culture will enrich an online language course.

Research from other disciplines has shown that CBI is highly effective (Genesee, 1994; Grabe & Stoller, 1997); therefore, online language instructors should consider incorporating it into their curriculum. CoBaLTT includes both CBI and technology integration. CARLA provides a wealth of resources for incorporating CoBaLTT, including lesson and unit plans by language and level. CoBaLTT resources also include development materials, instructional strategies, assessment, and technology tools for using this instructional technique.

Technology and Second Language Learning

With respect to technology and second language learning, CARLA offers several technology integration modules. They also provide research and information regarding the knowledge, skills, and other competencies required to teach language online effectively. Language educators are able to use this information as a form of self-assessment to determine if they are ready to teach in the online environment. CARLA's Technology and Second Language Learning area also offers a wiki with links to numerous online tools and resources. The wiki not only contains links for accessing these tools, but it also provides descriptions of the tools as well as online tutorials regarding how to use them effectively. This type of support information is extremely valuable for those who are new to online language teaching.

Moreover, CARLA's technology integration modules provide instruction on topics such as digital storytelling, telecollaboration, and webquests. Digital storytelling, which can be used to elicit presentational speaking in online classes, was described in detail in Chapter 3. The CARLA website provides practical information on how to use several tools for creating digital stories. They also provide examples, readings, and activities related to digital stories.

CARLA's technology integration modules include the topic of telecollaboration (also known as teletandem or virtual exchanges), which refers to linguistic and cultural exchanges that can take place through any medium that allows students to see and hear each other in real time. The main feature of telecollaboration is students' ability to interact with their peers from the target language culture. Students typically spend half of the time interacting in the target language and half of the time speaking in English to help their conversation partners build their English language proficiency. Telecollaboration is a powerful way to incorporate ACTFL's Connections and Communities standards into online language courses (National Standards Collaborative Board, 2015). "Connections" refer to helping learners access and evaluate diverse perspectives by examining topics through the lens of other languages and cultures and "Communities" refer to helping learners use the language in the local community and beyond by collaborating and connecting with native speakers of the language throughout the world (National Standards Collaborative Board, 2015). Furthermore, incorporating telecollaboration into online language courses may help students feel more connected and less isolated in their online language learning experience. CARLA provides readings, examples, activities, and resources on telecollaboration.

CARLA also disseminates materials and resources for integrating webquests into the foreign and second language curriculum. Webquests are Internet-based group activities that are designed to stimulate higher order thinking among students. They were first proposed by Bernie Dodge in the mid-1990s; and since then, webquests have evolved to contain six essential parts (Concept to Classroom, 2004; Dodge, 1995a, Dodge, 1995b). Table 4.3 depicts the six essential parts of a webquest.

Table 4.3 The six essential parts of a webquest activity

Essential Parts of a Webquest	Description
Introduction	Background information on the task.
Task	What the students will do and produce.
Process	The steps that students will take to complete the task.
Resources	Preselected links so that students focus on learning information rather than locating it.
Evaluation	An explanation of how students' work will be graded, which may include peer evaluations.
Conclusion	Student reflection, discussion, and/or extension of the topic.

Dodge (1995b) suggested providing examples and an evaluation rubric to students before they get started on the task. In addition, many instructors assign students specific roles and they may also require students to evaluate each other's contribution to the project. In online classes, webquests can be used to help students learn about cultural products, practices, and perspectives.

Language Teacher Education

CARLA offers a number of workshops, workshop series, and summer institutes each year. While most of the instruction that they provide is offered onsite—on the University of Minnesota's campus—they also offer several online institutes each summer for those who are unable to travel. CARLA accepts instructors of every language and level, including teachers of English as a second or foreign language. They also accept administrators, curriculum specialists, and methods instructors from the United States and abroad into their workshops and institutes. CARLA's summer institutes are offered in June and July to accommodate teachers' academic schedules. Thus far, over 6,000 educators have participated in CARLA's summer institutes, which have registration fees that range between $250 and $500. For those who do not need academic credit, the registration fee and books are their only expenses. For those seeking academic credit, there are addition credit hour charges from the University of Minnesota. CARLA also provides affordable lodging options on or near campus for institute participants.

Many of CARLA's online summer institutes are designed primarily for online language teachers. For the summer of 2019, they offered the following online institutes: Transitioning to Teaching Language Online, Using the Web for Communicative Language Learning, and Teaching Linguistic Politeness and Intercultural Awareness. While the topics will vary from summer to summer, CARLA will continue to offer online institutes that are appropriate for both beginners and for those with some experience in online language design, development, and delivery.

One of CARLA's premier initiatives is the Transitioning to Teaching Language Online (TTLO) course, which is typically offered as a four-week course that is delivered fully online. Participants gain valuable experience as online students while they learn about online course design, best practices for online teaching, and technology integration among other relevant topics. Figure 4.3 shows the landing page for CARLA's TTLO course.

By the end of the course, each participant will have developed a portfolio of online activities that are ready to be implemented into their online courses. The cost of the course is $500 plus books for those who register early and all participants will receive a certificate of completion from CARLA. Registration is available on a first-come, first-served basis on the CARLA website.

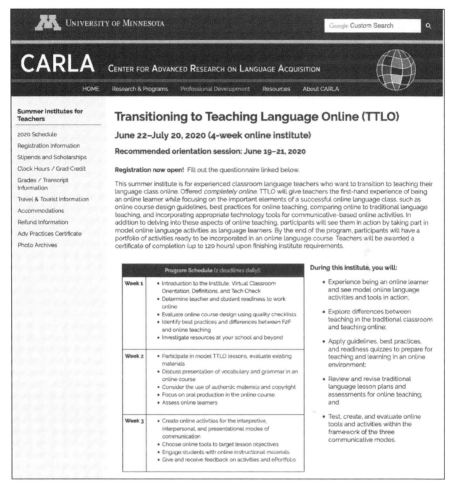

Figure 4.3 CARLA's Transitioning to Teaching Language Online program, Center for Advanced Research on Language Acquisition, University of Minnesota.

Used with permission.

The Center for Open Educational Resources and Language Learning (COERLL) Resources

COERLL, pronounced like coral, is an LRC that focuses on the following areas: "applied linguistic research, teaching materials, language assessment, teacher development, less commonly taught languages, K-12 initiatives, and outreach and dissemination" (COERLL, 2020). COERLL has funding from the Department of Education (Title VI) and is located at the University of Texas at Austin. Its primary mission is to create and distribute open educational Internet-based resources for the public. Individual users are free to download

Figure 4.4 Screenshot of COERLL's main page.

The Center for Open Educational Resources and Language Learning, The University of Texas at Austin. https://www.coerll.utexas.edu/coerll/. Used with permission.

and use COERLL's open access resources; however, permissions must be granted by COERLL for altering and/or redistributing them. Furthermore, the heart of COERLL's mission is to situate foreign language education within the fields of bilingualism and multilingualism, with a focus on language development along proficiency and dialectal continua (COERLL, 2020). A screenshot of COERLL's main page is presented in Figure 4.4. Given that this chapter is dedicated to online professional development, three areas from the COERLL website will be explored here: Language Learning Materials, Teaching Methods, and Open Education.

Language Learning Materials

One of the most time-consuming aspects of teaching language online is developing high-quality materials that are effective for online delivery. One way to help ease this burden is to use and/or modify open educational resources (OER) that are available online. COERLL offers a wide array of high-quality resources for the following languages: Arabic, Bangla, Chinese, Czech, English, French, German, Hebrew, Hindi, Italian, Japanese, K'iche', Malayalam, Persian, Portuguese, Russian, Sanskrit, Spanish, Tamil, Turkish, Urdu, and Yoruba. The number of critical and less commonly taught languages that they address with their online materials is impressive. COERLL language learning materials include video-based resources, online textbooks (for French), open-access courses, podcasts, websites, online activities, dictionaries, flash cards, and more. Furthermore, online instructors may opt to use OER in place of language textbooks that are available from publishers to reduce costs for their students. Moreover, language textbooks are typically only available for commonly taught languages such as French, German, Latin, and Spanish in the United States, with very few publisher-created materials available for less commonly taught languages. Online teachers of less commonly taught languages are encouraged to explore open-access resources, such as COERLL's offerings, to determine which of their language learning materials are appropriate for their instructional contexts and learners.

Teaching Methods

The Teaching Methods area of their website contains materials and resources that are relevant to foreign language educators. Table 4.4 presents that topics that are available on COERLL's website for professional development in language pedagogy.

The foreign language teaching methods self-paced course contains 12 interactive modules that are primarily geared for secondary and postsecondary world language educators. This content may be of interest to anyone who wants to refresh their knowledge of foreign language pedagogy. While this resource was not designed specifically for online language educators, much of the information that it contains is still relevant for them.

The Tadriis website is a valuable resource for those who teach Arabic, either in a traditional classroom or in blended or online environments. It

Table 4.4 Overview of COERLL's resources for language pedagogy

COERLL OER Material	Description
Foreign Language Teaching Methods	A video-based foreign language teaching methods self-paced course
Tadriis	An Arabic teaching methods website
Introduction to Oral Proficiency Levels (Spanish)	Practice modules for assessing Spanish language learners' oral proficiency levels
Spanish Proficiency Training Website and Learner Corpus	Activities and videos for assessing Spanish language learners' oral proficiency levels

Note. The research and programs highlighted above are from the Center for Open Educational Resources and Language Learning, The University of Texas at Austin. https://www.coerll.utexas.edu/coerll/

contains samples of student-teacher interactions, samples of student production, teaching tips, pedagogical demonstrations, a glossary of key terms, and suggestions for further reading. All of the material are presented in Arabic and all of the content is OER.

COERLL's Introduction to Oral Proficiency Levels contains OER materials and resources for all levels of Spanish language learners. This resource contains 17 video-based practice modules that facilitate Spanish language educators' understanding of ACTFL's Proficiency Guidelines (ACTFL, 2012) and how to assess students' oral proficiency using them. The practice materials are also available on Google drive, which enables educators to edit and share them with others. Furthermore, COERLL provides guidance and instructions for conducting oral interviews to assess students' oral proficiency in Spanish.

The Spanish Proficiency Training Website and Learner Corpus provides videos of Spanish language learners—from Novice through Advanced proficiency—answering questions in the target language. This content also includes a written transcript of the video recordings as well as activities that guide Spanish language educators to notice specific features of learner language and what learner language looks like at different levels of proficiency. Answers to the activities are also included.

While the majority of COERLL's language pedagogy materials were designed for instructors of Spanish or Arabic, the video-based teaching methods course is appropriate for instructors of all foreign and second languages. The resources in the Teaching Methods area may also be particularly useful for methods instructors and the learner corpus may be of interest to researchers who investigate learner language.

Open Education

 The Open Education area of COERLL's website would be helpful for all online language educators who wish to use and/or modify OER resources. COERLL offers two websites as well as self-paced learning modules on how to use OER effectively. One of the two websites provides information on how to use and create online badges within the world language curriculum. The other website presents voices from the classroom, which show how students, teachers, and developers use and/or create OER for language teaching and learning.

Perhaps COERLL's most powerful resource is the online, self-paced course for learning about OER. The course contains six modules as follows: (1) introduction to OER, (2) searching for OER, (3) licensing and attribution, (4) remixing and revising OER, (5) creating OER, and (6) publishing and sharing OER. It is not uncommon for educators to be confused about what content from the Internet they are allowed to use, modify, and/or distribute to their students without infringing on copyright laws; therefore, COERLL's online OER course is a valuable resource on this topic.

COERLL also offers presentations and workshops throughout the academic year at the University of Texas at Austin campus. While their presentations are free of charge, their workshops have a nominal fee. In addition to these professional development opportunities, COERLL also publishes an online newsletter twice per year that contains issues that are relevant to language educators.

STARTALK Summer Programs

These are federally funded summer programs for K-12 students and teachers, as well as university professors of eight critical languages including: Arabic, Chinese, Hindi, Korean, Persian, Russian, Turkish, and Urdu (STARTALK, 2020). The funding source is the National Security Agency and the purpose of the STARTALK grant program is to increase the number of students and effective teachers of critical languages in the United States and to increase the number of materials and curricula available for the instruction of critical languages. In addition, programs that are geared for teachers of critical languages may provide pathways to state certification.

Funding is provided to STARTALK programs on a yearly basis and those who wish to administer a program must apply each year during their annual grant cycle. All types of institutions may offer STARTALK programs, including school districts, universities, community colleges, nonprofit organizations, and libraries (STARTALK, 2020). The STARTALK website also has information on how to apply for a STARTALK grant.

The majority of STARTALK summer programs take place on location at institutions across the United States, but some of the programs are offered online. For the nonresidential programs, participants travel to the location each day to receive instruction. For the residential programs, participants live onsite for the duration of the program. STARTALK programs vary in length from one to four weeks and they each allow a fixed number of participants, depending upon the amount of funding that was received. The summer programs for both students and teachers of critical languages are either free or have a nominal fee for participants.

Online STARTALK Programs for Teachers

While the topics for online summer STARTALK programs will vary by year with each new funding cycle; for the summer of 2019, two online programs were available: (1) Planning for Authentic, Interactive Language Experiences and (2) Online Korean Teacher Training. The former included 80 contact hours and was designed for instructors of Arabic, Chinese, and Persian, and the latter provided 45 contact hours and it targeted instructors of Korean exclusively. The online program for teachers of Arabic, Chinese, and Persian focused on technology-enhanced language learning and backward design, while the online program for Korean teachers focused on how to design standards-based language instruction as well as how to use educational technologies effectively. Due to the global pandemic caused by COVID-19, all 2020 summer STARTALK programs were deferred to 2021.

Furthermore, online summer STARTALK programs may provide a combination of synchronous and asynchronous instruction. From the main page, it 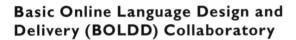 is possible to search all available STARTALK programs that are delivered both online and onsite for the summer of 2021 and beyond.

Basic Online Language Design and Delivery (BOLDD) Collaboratory

The BOLDD Collaboratory is a group of online practitioners and scholars who are involved with the design, development, and delivery of online language courses and programs. According to Wulf (1993), a collaboratory is a space in which researchers can interact, perform research, and share data without the barriers of a physical location. Therefore, members of the BOLDD Collaboratory interact and collaborate online through digital media to collect, review, and share best practices and resources for online language teaching and learning. The collaboratory also performs important research in the field by delivering a national survey to take the pulse of online language teaching and learning in the United States. They also summarize the data and disseminate the findings of the survey through publications in academic journals and presentations at professional conferences. Murphy-Judy and Johnshoy (2017) published the most recent analysis of the survey findings. The data that they reported is useful for online language practitioners, program coordinators, administrators, teacher educators, and policy makers. Murphy-Judy and Johnshoy's article is listed as recommended reading at the end of this chapter.

Furthermore, the work of the BOLDD Collaboratory informed the first set of pedagogical materials and resources that are used for the ACTFL DL SIG/NFLRC Mentoring Program for Online Language Teachers. Members of the ACTFL DL SIG and faculty from the NFLRC created online modules for those who are completely new or less experienced in online teaching. These modules were described in detail earlier in the chapter.

BOLDD Workshops

The BOLDD Collaboratory also regularly holds workshops at national, regional, and state professional conferences across the United States. In recent years, collaboratory members have been offering pre-conference workshops at the annual Computer-Assisted Language Instruction Consortium (CALICO) conference. These workshops are intended for those with little or no experience teaching language online and there is a nominal fee paid to CALICO. Attendees are typically K–16 language teachers, teacher educators, government employees, and/or other stakeholders who are responsible for creating, delivering, and/or administering online language courses and programs. BOLDD workshops provide attendees with the knowledge, tools, and resources that they need to create synchronous or asynchronous basic online language classes and programs. The CALICO website includes information on how to enroll in a BOLDD workshop.

Professional Development Organizations for Online Language Teachers

In addition to the BOLDD Collaboratory, there are a number of professional organizations that provide support for online language educators. While they are listed with a brief description here, links to each organization are available in the book's eResources and readers are encouraged to explore them to determine which organizations are of the greatest interest and benefit to themselves.

ACTFL Distance Learning (DL) Special Interest Group (SIG)

DL SIG members must be ACTFL members to participate in the DL SIG. Each ACTFL membership includes free membership to one SIG. Therefore, ACTFL members only need to select the DL SIG as their free SIG. If they are already members of another ACTFL SIG, they may join for $5 annually. The DL SIG has five main goals as follows:

- To provide a forum for world language teachers who are engaged in distance learning to share experiences and concerns
- To promote the exchange of information about distance learning in the interest of developing best-practice principles
- To bring issues related to distance learning in world languages to all ACTFL members
- To encourage and support the dissemination of research and best practices
- To cooperate and to collaborate with other ACTFL special interest groups (e.g., technology, teacher development, language learning for children) on projects of mutual concern (ACTFL, 2020).

To meet the goals listed above, the ACTFL DL SIG co-created the ACTFL DL SIG/NFLRC Mentoring Program for Online Language Teachers, which was presented at the beginning of this chapter. They also host two or three webinars each year on topics of interest to online language educators. All members may attend the webinars live or they may view recordings of them at their convenience. Furthermore, in order to connect members with each other, the ACTFL DL SIG hosts an online community that is delivered through the main ACTFL website. All members have access to the DL SIG online community where they can ask and answer questions as well as post concerns, research data, and/or other information. This online community allows members to stay abreast of new developments in online teaching and learning in the United States. Members may also reach out to their colleagues via the online community if they need help or support.

The DL SIG also holds an annual business meeting at the ACTFL conference where members are encouraged to network and collaborate. The ACTFL DL SIG partners with CALICO to present annual online teaching awards in Higher Education and K-12 each year at the DL SIG business meeting. All members of the ACTFL DL SIG are eligible to submit an application for an online teaching award. Therefore, the DL SIG and CALICO strive to recognize the achievements of those engaged in online teaching and learning.

Computer-Assisted Language Instruction Consortium (CALICO)

This is an international professional organization with a focus on computer-assisted language learning; therefore, its membership includes both language educators and those involved with language learning technologies.

CALICO holds an annual conference either in the United States or in Canada each year. CALICO members may also become involved with the following SIGs:

- Computer-Mediated Communication (CMC) SIG
- Gaming SIG
- Graduate Student SIG
- Intelligent Computer-Assisted Language Learning (ICALL) SIG
- Language Teaching and Learning Technologies (LTLT) SIG
- Second Language Acquisition and Technology (SLAT) SIG
- Teacher Education SIG
- Virtual Worlds SIG

CALICO's mission includes disseminating research on the application of technology to language teaching and learning. This is achieved in two ways, first through the quarterly publication of the *CALICO Journal*, and second, through CALICO's edited book series. Access to the journal is available to members through the CALICO website. The latest edition of each book in the CALICO series is provided to attendees of the CALICO conference. Books may also be purchased on CALICO's website.

CALICO recognizes those who make an impact on the field by sponsoring annual awards. In addition to partnering with the ACTFL DL SIG to co-sponsor online teaching awards in K-12 and higher education each year, CALICO also sponsors annual awards for an outstanding graduate student in computer-assisted language learning, a language learning website award, an outstanding *CALICO Journal* article award, and a lifetime achievement award.

European Association of Computer-Assisted Language Learning (EUROCALL)

This is a sister organization of CALICO that provides a European lens on the use of technology for the teaching and learning of language and culture. EUROCALL and CALICO offer discounted memberships for those who wish to join both organizations. Similar to CALICO, EUROCALL offers annual conferences in Europe, SIG memberships, as well as two scholarly journals to disseminate research findings in the field: *ReCALL* and *EUROCALL Review*. The former is available to members on the EUROCALL website and the latter is an open-access scholarly journal.

International Association for Language Learning Technology (IALLT)

IALLT is another sister organization of CALICO that has a large presence at the annual CALICO conference. IALLT's mission is to provide a community for its members who are leaders in developing, integrating, evaluating, and managing instructional technologies for the teaching and learning of world languages, cultures, and literatures. IALLT began as an organization to support language lab directors; but today, its members are also comprised of language educators, librarians, software developers, and computer programmers among others. In addition to their annual conference, IALLT also makes webinars and publications available to its members. Their open-access publications include *The IALTT Journal* and *FLTMAG*. IALLT creates a sense of community through its eight regional groups that provide professional development and networking opportunities. The regional groups also host conferences.

Non-Discipline-Specific Resources

EDUCAUSE

This is a nonprofit association dedicated to advancing higher education through the use of instructional technologies; it is the largest organization with this mission in the United States. In addition to providing conferences and networking opportunities, EDUCAUSE also makes a Core Data Service (CDS) application available to its members. The CDS tool allows members to contribute data, to analyze and use data to measure their own institution's information technology spending and resources, and to compare their institution's data with that of other peer institutions. The CDS tool is a unique feature of this association. EDUCAUSE also provides a research database that contains scholarly publications related to instructional technologies and higher education. Those who work in higher education and who are stakeholders in the acquisition of instructional technologies may be particularly interested in joining this organization. More information on EDUCAUSE is available in the eResources.

The Online Learning Consortium (OLC)

The OLC is a nonprofit organization that serves online instructors, instructional designers, administrators, and other stakeholders in higher education across all disciplines. Their mission is to advance the quality of modern online learning and teaching. The OLC provides online instructor-led and self-paced professional development workshops, online teaching certificate programs, summer institutes on site at the University of Central Florida, online webinars, and resources for best practices in online teaching. The OLC also offers two conferences annually, Accelerate and Innovate. The former focuses on networking and research in the field of online teaching and learning, while the latter emphasizes personalized conversations, collaborative learning, and hands-on activities. Although this organization is geared toward higher education, those who teach language online at the secondary level may also benefit from the OLC's online programs, conferences, and resources.

Multimedia Educational Resource for Learning and Online Teaching (MERLOT)

MERLOT is on online collection of discipline-specific materials, exercises, webpages, bookmark collections, and other resources that are openly available on the Internet. MERLOT was created and is managed by the California State University System in collaboration with other institutions/systems of higher education, partners from industry and professional organizations, as well as individual users. MERLOT has a number of discipline-specific communities, including the World Language Community, where thousands of learning materials and resources are available both for commonly and less commonly taught languages. In addition, over 600 resources are available in the World Language Community for instructing English as a second or foreign language. Moreover, learning materials and resources are available for every level of learner and language teachers and students may download, copy, and use the open-access materials that are posted on MERLOT's World Language Community free of charge. Furthermore, language instructors may share their own resources with others on the MERLOT website. The philosophy behind the open-access movement is that when individuals connect and share resources, then the whole community advances. All online language instructors should explore MERLOT's World Language Community for useful materials that may be incorporated into their online courses. The authors also encourage language educators to share their resources with others via MERLOT's World Language Community.

Conclusion

This chapter provided an overview of professional development opportunities and resources for online foreign and second language teachers. Three LRCs were highlighted: NFLRC, CARLA, and COERLL. While it is beyond the scope of this chapter to describe all of the LRCs that exist across the United States, those that were presented in this chapter provide materials and resources that are specific for online language education. While the Center for Applied Second Language Studies (CASLS) also provides many valuable resources for online language educators, their materials and applications were discussed thoroughly in Chapters 1 and 2. Links to the other federally funded LRCs are available in the book's eResources. It should be noted that many LRCs are geared for certain language groups and regions (e.g., Asian Studies) and they specialize in creating materials and resources for less commonly taught languages. Therefore, teachers of Asian, East Asian, Eastern European, Eurasian, and Slavic languages will find those LRCs of particular interest.

While many materials, resources, and professional development opportunities were presented in this chapter, online instructors will need to determine which ones will be the most beneficial for their instructional context, their specific learners, and their current skill level with respect to delivering language instruction online. Online language educators should also keep in mind that they do not have to design, develop, and deliver their courses in isolation. Many professional organizations, programs, workshops, and symposia—as described in this chapter—are available to meet the needs of online language educators. Furthermore, the authors would like to encourage everyone who teaches a language online to reach out and plug into at least one of the communities of practice that were presented in this chapter.

Key Takeaways

- There are many LRCs that have a wide array of OER materials and resources that could be implemented in flipped, blended, or online language courses.
- The ACTFL DL SIG/NFLRC has an online mentoring program for those who are new or less experienced in online language teaching. Participation in the program is free to all ACTFL members.
- Non-discipline-specific organizations, such as MERLOT, OLC, and EDU-CAUSE, have many resources that could be employed by language educators.

Discussion Questions

1. Which of the professional organizations is the most appropriate for the language and level that you teach?

2. Would the ACTFL DL SIG/NFLRC Mentoring Program for Online Language Teachers or the open-access mentoring resources be helpful for you? Why (not)?
3. Would you consider using PBLL or CoBaLTT in your online language courses? Why (not)?
4. Is there a specific tool or resource that you would like to explore further? How could you incorporate this tool or resource into your online language class?
5. If you had the time and the resources, would you be interested in attending a summer STARTALK program or a CARLA summer institute? If so, which one appears to be the most beneficial for your particular professional development needs?

Suggestions for Further Reading

Content-Based Language Instruction:
Cammarata, L. (Ed.). (2016). *Content-based foreign language teaching.* New York, NY: Routledge.
Grabe, W., & Stoller, F. L. (1997). Content-based instruction: Research foundations. In M. A. Snow & D. M. Brinton (Eds.), *The content-based classroom: Perspectives on integrating language and content* (pp. 5–21). New York, NY: Longman.

Online Learning National Survey Results:
Murphy-Judy, K., & Johnshoy, M. (2017). Who's teaching which languages online? A report based on national surveys. *IALLT Journal, 47*(1), 137–167.
Seaman, J. E., Allen, I. E., & Seaman, J. (2018). *Grade increase: Tracking distance education in the United States* (Babson Survey Research Group Report). Retrieved from http://onlinelearningsurvey.com/reports/gradeincrease.pdf

Project-Based Learning:
Beckett, G., & Slater, T. (Eds.). (2019). *Global perspectives on project-based language learning, teaching, and assessment: Key approaches, technology tools, and frameworks.* New York, NY: Routledge.
Markham, T. (2011). Project-based learning: A bridge just far enough. *Teacher Librarian, 39*(2), 38–42.

Telecollaboration:
O'Dowd, R., & Lewis, T. (Eds). (2018). *Online intercultural exchange: Policy, pedagogy, practice.* New York, NY: Routledge.

Harris, J. (2000). Taboo topic no longer: Why telecollaborative projects sometimes fail. *Learning and Leading with Technology*, *27*(5), 58–61. Retrieved from https://scholarworks.wm.edu/educationpubs/21/

Note

1 The National Foreign Language Resource Center (NFLRC) at the University of Hawai'i at Mānoa is partially funded by a grant from the U. S. Department of Education (CFDA 84.229, P220A180026). However, the contents produced by the NFLRC do not necessarily represent the policy of the Department of Education, and one should not assume endorsement by the Federal Government. Dr. Julio C. Rodríguez is the Director of the NFLRC at the University of Hawai'i at Mānoa.

References

American Council on the Teaching of Foreign Languages (ACTFL). (2012). *ACTFL proficiency guidelines.* Retrieved from https://www.actfl.org/resources/actfl-proficiency-guidelines-2012

American Council on the Teaching of Foreign Languages (ACTFL). (2020). *Distance learning.* Retrieved from https://www.actfl.org/connect/special-interest-groups/distance-learning

Center for Advanced Research on Language Acquisition (CARLA). (2020). *Mission statement.* Retrieved from https://carla.umn.edu/about/mission.html

Center for Open Educational Resources and Language Learning (COERLL). (2020). *About COERLL.* Retrieved from https://www.coerll.utexas.edu/coerll/about-coerll

Concept to Classroom. (2004). *What are the essential parts of a webquest?* Retrieved from https://www.thirteen.org/edonline/concept2class/webquests/index_sub3.html

Crandall, J., & Tucker, G. R. (1990). Content-based instruction in second and foreign languages. In A. Padilla, H. H. Fairchild, & C. Valadez (Eds.), *Foreign language education: Issues and strategies* (pp. 187–200). Newbury Park, CA: Sage.

Crane, B. (2009). *Using web 2.0 tools in the K–12 classroom.* New York: Neal-Schuman.

Dodge, B. (1995a). *Some thoughts about webquests.* Retrieved from http://webquest.org/sdsu/about_webquests.html

Dodge, B. (1995b). WebQuests: A technique for Internet-based learning. *Distance Educator, 1*(2), 10–13.

Genesee, F. (1994). *Integrating language and content: Lessons from immersion* (Educational Practice Report 11). Santa Cruz, CA: National Center for Research on Cultural Diversity and Second Language Learning.

Grabe, W., & Stoller, F. L. (1997). Content-based instruction: Research foundations. In M. A. Snow & D. M. Brinton (Eds.), *The content-based classroom: Perspectives on integrating language and content* (pp. 5–21). New York, NY: Longman.

Markham, T. (2011). Project based learning. *Teacher Librarian, 39*(2), 38–42.

Murphy-Judy, K., & Johnshoy, M. (2017). Who's teaching which languages online? A report based on national surveys. *IALLT Journal, 47*(1), 137–167.

National Foreign Language Center University of Maryland (2020). *STARTALK.* Retrieved from https://startalk.umd.edu/public/

National Foreign Language Resource Center University of Hawai'i at Mānoa (2020a). *About the NFLRC.* Retrieved from http://nflrc.hawaii.edu/about/

National Foreign Language Resource Center University of Hawai'i at Mānoa (2020b). *Project-based language learning.* Retrieved from http://www.nflrc.hawaii.edu/projects/view/2014A/

National Standards Collaborative Board. (2015). *World-readiness standards for learning languages* (4th ed.). Alexandria, VA: Author.

North Carolina Virtual Public School. (2020). *NCVPS annual report 2018–2019.* Retrieved from https://ncvps.org/annual-report-2018-19/

Wulf, W. (1993). The collaboratory opportunity. *Science, 261*, 854–855.

Chapter 5

A Review of Relevant Research on Online Language Teaching: What Works and Why?

Introduction

This chapter introduces research on online language teaching and learning. The overarching purpose of this chapter is to help language educators apply the findings of research to their online course design, development, and delivery. While most K-12 practitioners do not have time to read research articles extensively, the findings of research can yield many practical applications for their practice. Moreover, incorporating research-based practices may help improve learning outcomes, promote teacher and learner satisfaction, increase learners' perceptions of presence and connectedness, and reduce students' levels of perceived foreign language anxiety. This chapter examines themes that are relevant to online course and program design, development, and delivery through the lens of empirical research. Furthermore, the authors describe the research findings and the practical implications that can be drawn from them in a way that is free from jargon and easily accessible to those who are unaccustomed to reading empirical research studies. To that end, the authors set out to answer the following questions in this chapter:

- Are online language teachers and learners more or less satisfied than their peers who teach or learn in traditional classrooms?
- What is the optimal class size for an online language class?
- Do online language learners have more or less language anxiety than their peers in traditional (brick-and-mortar) language classrooms?
- What are the best practices for online language course delivery? How can language instructors incorporate best practices into their online courses?
- How can online language instructors facilitate teacher, social, and cognitive presence?
- What is connectedness and how can online language teachers promote it?
- What types of assessments are effective for online language teaching and learning and what types of outcomes should be measured?

Research on Online Teacher and Learner Satisfaction

Are online language teachers and learners more or less satisfied than their peers who teach or learn in traditional classrooms? The brief answer to this question is: it depends! Some language educators who teach in traditional, brick-and-mortar classrooms and who have never taught language online believe that online language teaching is extremely burdensome, impersonal, boring, and perhaps even ineffective for language learning. The authors of this textbook have come across many language instructors—and even some administrators—who feel this way. Some language instructors have even expressed concerns to the authors that their end-of-course evaluations would be lower if they were to teach in the online environment; therefore, they firmly resist teaching language online. Unfortunately, there are many negative perceptions about online courses in general—on the part of students, instructors, and administrators—that are simply false. Most of these negative perceptions stem from those who have never taken and/or taught an online course. According to a large-scale national survey of stakeholders across disciplines in higher education in the United States, less than 30% of faculty "accept the value and legitimacy of online education" (Allen, J. Seaman, Poulin, & Straut, 2016, p. 26). The survey found a strong correlation between the level of acceptance of online learning and the number of online students at the institution; for example, at institutions with a high number of online students (over 10,000), the majority of faculty (60.1%) reported valuing online learning (Allen et al., 2016, p. 26). However, at institutions with fewer than 5,000 online enrollments, only 34.6% of faculty reported that they accepted the value of online education, while at institutions with no online enrollments, only 11.6% of faculty accepted the legitimacy of online learning (Allen et al., 2016, p. 26). It is important to note that the survey was not discipline specific, although foreign languages were included as an academic discipline. There is also a misconception that online students are located far away from campus, perhaps in another state or country. While some online students are physically located far from the institution where the course is delivered, a large-scale national survey by the Babson Survey Research Group (J. E. Seaman, Allen, & J. Seaman, 2018) found that the majority of online students (52.8%) took at least one course on campus (p. 16). This indicates that many students in higher education opt to take an online course for convenience. J. E. Seaman et al. (2018) found that most students who took all of their courses online (84.2%) were located in the same state as the higher education institution; therefore, the results of this survey indicate that online education is becoming more localized (p. 17). Moreover, enrollment patterns reveal that institutions of higher education are more likely to focus their recruiting efforts and online program offerings on local students (J. E. Seaman et al., 2018).

With respect to online language learning, Murphy-Judy and Johnshoy (2017) found that in postsecondary settings, the most commonly taught languages online were Spanish, English as a second language, French, and German; however, they also found that many less commonly taught languages such as Arabic, Chinese, Portuguese, and Russian were also widely taught online in higher education. They noted that the majority of online language courses were offered at the first or the second year of language instruction, which is important because these courses feed into the higher-level courses that are required for language minors or majors, with most of the upper-level coursework being offered in traditional, brick-and-mortar settings. Therefore, with respect to first and second year online language learners, both student satisfaction and positive learning outcomes are essential for the success of language programs across the United States.

While the findings of research demonstrate that there is a perception among some instructors who do not teach online that online education is not as effective as delivering instruction in a traditional classroom (Allen et al., 2016), the results of recent research in online language education are in stark contrast to these negative perceptions. For example, a common misperception is that student satisfaction is higher in traditional, brick-and-mortar classes than in online classes. However, research studies that have compared student satisfaction between online language courses and face-to-face courses have found that students who take language classes online have higher levels of satisfaction over time compared to their peers in traditional, face-to-face classes (Chenoweth, Ushida, & Murday, 2006; Harker & Koutsantoni, 2005; Young, 2008). Regarding learning outcomes, some research has shown that students' oral proficiency gains are similar in both online and traditional language classes (Blake, Wilson, Cetto, & Pardo-Ballester, 2008; Chenoweth & Murday, 2003). Other studies have found that online language students outperform their counterparts in traditional classes in written production (Chenoweth & Murday, 2003) and in oral proficiency gains (Moneypenny & Aldrich, 2016). According to Young (2008), the effectiveness of an online language class is largely dependent upon the instructor's pedagogical effectiveness. Therefore, it is vitally important that online language educators receive sufficient professional development in online language pedagogy, which is the overarching purpose of this book. Chapter 4, in particular, provides a wealth of resources for obtaining online professional development for online language teaching and learning. Moreover, the resources outlined in Chapter 4 are mostly open and available (free of charge) to the public.

Factors That Affect Teacher and Learner Satisfaction

Russell and Curtis (2013) found that student and teacher satisfaction are largely dependent on factors such as institutional support, class size, teacher preferences/characteristics, and student beliefs and expectations. According to Russell and Curtis, both teacher and learner satisfaction are dependent upon whether instructors receive the institutional support that they need, which includes an environment where they have both the time and the resources to make use of their knowledge of online language pedagogy. Conversely, when instructors do not receive sufficient institutional support, even if they have ample knowledge of online pedagogy and technology, then both student and teacher satisfaction with online learning suffers. Russell and Curtis compared levels of student and teacher satisfaction between online, second-semester Spanish language courses at two different universities. One of the instructors had a class size in excess of 100 students per section, while the other instructor had a maximum of 20 students per section. It is not surprising that both the students and the instructor in the large-scale class were much less satisfied than their counterparts in the course with fewer than

20 students enrolled. Unfortunately, some administrators believe that online teaching is less burdensome than teaching in a traditional classroom; therefore, they view online offerings as a way to make a larger profit by enrolling more students per section. In Russell and Curtis' study, the instructor with over 100 students reported that her delivery of online language instruction was far less than optimal because she simply did not have the time to adhere to all of the pedagogically sound principles that she knew to be effective. For example, she was unable to provide students with sufficient opportunities for student-student interaction and student-teacher interaction due to the time constraints involved with grading assignments for so many students. Similarly, the students themselves expressed their concerns. One student stated, "I have to try and teach myself a language and the explanations were in Spanish. The homework was just lengthy and helped little. The instructor could be a little more involved in the subject" (Russell & Curtis, 2013, p. 9). This response shows the student's frustration with the course as well as her perceptions of a lack of support from her instructor. The student's low level of satisfaction with the class was likely a result of the administrative decision to enroll over 100 students per online course section and thus overburden the teacher. Any instructor who is contemplating creating an online course or program should pay careful attention to Russell and Curtis' findings regarding teacher and student satisfaction and online class size.

Russell and Curtis's (2013) findings with respect to student satisfaction in the small-scale class support the results of previous research in this area (Chenoweth, Ushida, & Murday, 2006; Harker & Koutsantoni, 2005; Young, 2008); namely, students who are enrolled in small online class sections with instructors who are experts in online language pedagogy have reported high levels of satisfaction with their online language learning experiences, even higher than those of their peers in traditional, face-to-face, language classes. Therefore, the research on student and teacher satisfaction points to the need for smaller online language class sizes. More research on online class size is available in the next section of this chapter.

Revisiting the question: Are online language teachers and learners more or less satisfied than their peers who teach or learn in traditional classrooms? The research that was reviewed above indicates that online language classes can yield even higher levels of satisfaction than traditional, face-to-face classes provided that instructors have, at a minimum, the following criteria: a reasonable class size (see the next section for specific recommendations on online language class size), institutional, administrative, and technical support, as well as sufficient knowledge of online language pedagogy to design, develop, and deliver an effective course. The research findings with respect to learning outcomes are also very promising for online language delivery, especially when gains in oral proficiency were compared between online and traditional language learners (Blake, Wilson, Cetto, & Pardo-Ballester, 2008; Moneypenny & Aldrich, 2016).

Research on Online Class Size

What is the optimal class size for an online language class? There has been very little research on class size in the fields of second and foreign language education—whether in traditional or in online environments—even though class size has been the subject of much debate since 1956 when the Modern Language Association recommended that foreign language class sizes should not exceed 20 students. Horne, who conducted research in 1970 at the Defense Language Institute, suggested a maximum class size of 12 for effective language learning. However, for intensive language courses, Horne (1970) recommended a class size of five to nine students. Other scholars in language education have also made claims regarding optimal language class sizes; for example, Alatis (1992) asserted that "class size directly affects the quality of language instruction: the smaller the class, the more intensive the exposure to the language and the better the results" (p. 13). Similarly, Morgan (2000) advocated for small language class sizes due to affective factors, such as anxiety, that come into play with language learning. In addition, Yi (2008) found that learners in smaller language classes outperformed their peers in larger classes in the areas of listening, reading, and writing.

Orellana (2006) asserted that online class sizes should depend on the level of interactivity needed for students to complete the course; she claimed that there is no one-size-fits-all approach to determining an optimal online class size. While some disciplines may be delivered via massive open online courses (MOOCs), which are open-access online courses that are generally self-paced and delivered on a large scale, the MOOC model would not work well for online language courses where a high level of interaction (both student-student and student-teacher) is needed to develop language skills in the three modes of communication. With respect to research on online class size in other disciplines, Taft, Kesten, and El-Banna (2019) reviewed 58 journal articles on optimal online class size in higher education across disciplines and found that the content that is taught should dictate the online class size. For example, they found that courses that focus on the acquisition of facts and foundational content can have larger class sizes—of 40 or higher—and still be effective, especially when little student-instructor contact is needed (Taft et al., 2019). Conversely, their results indicated that courses that require mastery of complex topics, higher order thinking, and/or students' development of skill are better suited to small class sizes of 15 or fewer students (Taft et al., 2019). Their research supports the assertions of previous scholars regarding class size (Alatis, 1992; Horne, 1970; Morgan, 2000; Orellana, 2006; Yi, 2008).

Similar to Taft et al. (2019), Goertler's (2011) findings stress the importance of student interaction—among peers, with the materials, and with the instructor—in online language classes. She asserted that language students can easily become lost without ample opportunities for interaction. In order for language instructors to build sufficient interaction into an online course, it is imperative that the class size be relatively small.

Recommendations from Professional Organizations on Class Size

The American Council on the Teaching of Foreign Languages (ACTFL) issued a position statement in 2010 on class size, recommending that language classes be capped at 15 students—whether in traditional or in online environments. When drafting this position statement, ACTFL took into account the recommendations on class size that were set forth by the National Education Association (NEA) and the Association of Departments of Foreign Languages (ADFL) (ADFL, 2009; NEA, 2008). ACTFL asserted that a small class size is necessary for language learning, where frequent student-student and student-teacher interaction is necessary for students to develop oral and written proficiency within standards-based language programs (ACTFL, 2010). ACTFL made no distinction between online and traditional language classrooms regarding class size recommendations. It should be noted that ACTFL is currently reviewing their position statement on class size and the update was not yet available at the time of this publication.

In summary, what is the optimal class size for an online language class? The answer to this question is that online language class sizes should be small, with a cap of 15 students per the recommendations of research and professional organizations. While this might not be feasible in every educational setting, online language instructors should continually advocate for small class sizes. The research and recommendations that are presented in this chapter should help them to do so.

Research on Online Language Learner Anxiety

Do online language learners have more or less language anxiety than their peers in traditional, face-to-face language classrooms? To answer this question, it is important to understand the concept of foreign language classroom anxiety. Krashen set forth the Affective Filter Hypothesis (1981, 1982), which states that stress and anxiety create a filter in the learner's mind that blocks linguistic input from entering. Since comprehensible input is the most important element for learners to build an internal grammar, otherwise known as an implicit linguistic system, anything that prevents input from reaching the learner is problematic and can impede language learning (Krashen, 1980, 1981, 1982, 1985).

Foreign Language Classroom Anxiety Scale (FLCAS)

In 1986, E. K. Horwitz, M. Horwitz, and Cope introduced the Foreign Language Classroom Anxiety Scale (FLCAS), which is intended to measure learners' perceptions, beliefs, and behaviors related to learning language in a classroom setting (E. K. Horwitz et al., 1986). According to the researchers, language anxiety is debilitating and can have a highly negative impact on the language acquisition process. The FLCAS incorporates three types of anxiety that may be felt by classroom learners: (1) communication apprehension, (2) fear of negative evaluation, and (3) test anxiety. There are 33 items on the FLCAS survey that learners rate on a 5-pont Likert scale (ranging from strongly agree to strongly disagree). Scores from the 33 items are added together to arrive at an anxiety score, which ranges from 33 to 165, with 33 being a very low score (reflecting low levels of perceived anxiety) and 165 being a very high score (reflecting high levels of perceived anxiety). The authors of the FLCAS invite language educators to use it for classroom purposes; however, if individuals wish to use the FLCAS for research purposes, they must obtain permission from its primary creator, Elaine Horwitz. The FLCAS is available in Horwitz, Horwitz, and Cope's 1986 article, which is published in the *Modern Language Journal.*

Research Using the FLCAS with Online Language Learners

It may seem logical that students in online classes would have lower levels of perceived foreign language anxiety than their counterparts who take face-to-face language classes—especially if students are required to stand up in class and speak in front of their peers. Pichette (2009) asserted that some students have so much language anxiety that they "resort to distance learning for that particular reason and to seek security in anonymity" (p. 78). However, the results of recent research show that online learners have equal amounts of anxiety as their peers who take face-to-face language courses at the beginning levels of language study (Pichette, 2009; Ushida, 2005). This may be due to the fact that online students may also have anxiety related to the online learning platform and/or the instructional technologies that they are required to use in the online course (Ushida, 2005), or it may be due to the fact that online learners are typically expected to interact with their peers in the target language using audio and video tools, which may also be a source of foreign language anxiety (Pichette, 2009).

Pichette (2009) conducted a large-scale study with 186 French speakers who were learning either English or Spanish in Canada. He examined students' general foreign language anxiety as measured by the FLCAS, which focuses primarily on oral communication. He also measured their writing anxiety with the Daly-Miller Writing Apprehension Test and their reading anxiety with the Foreign Language Reading Anxiety Scale. Therefore, Pichette used three different instruments to measure students' speaking, reading, and writing anxiety in the target language. While Pichette found no difference in anxiety levels between online and face-to-face language learners at the beginning levels of language study, he did find that anxiety tended to drop off in online language classes among more experienced language learners. In contrast, he found equally high levels of perceived foreign language anxiety between beginning-level and experienced students in traditional, brick-and-mortar classrooms. Consequently, online language learning seems to have the advantage over classroom-based learning with respect to perceived levels of language anxiety among more experienced language students (Pichette, 2009). In other words, Pichette (2009) found that more advanced online language learners experience less foreign language anxiety than their counterparts in traditional classrooms. Conversely, beginning-level language learners in both brick-and-mortar and online environments experience equally high levels of language anxiety.

A study by Russell (2016, 2018) supports Pichette's findings. She examined third semester university students of Spanish who were using a synchronous conversation platform for the first time. At the beginning of the semester, her students' perceived anxiety levels (as measured by the FLCAS) were very high, but by the end of the course and after completing four, 30-minute conversations with native speakers using a conversation platform, their anxiety levels were significantly lower. Russell's students were asked to describe their feelings about the synchronous conversations on a discussion board at the beginning of the semester. One student stated the following, "I feel very anxious when it comes to foreign language. I feel less anxious with an online class, but when I learned we have the TalkAbroad conversations, I became more anxious" (Russell, 2016). This student's comment revealed that she believed that online language learning would be less stressful than classroom-based language learning. However, after enrolling in the online course, she became even more anxious when she learned that she had to interact with native speakers online. Another student commented, "As far as the TalkAbroad goes, I am so scared of it that I didn't even DO the first one" (Russell, 2016). From this comment, it appears that this student's perceived levels of foreign language anxiety were so high at the beginning of the term that he did not even complete the first assigned conversation. As the semester moved forward, he did complete the subsequent conversations and his reported anxiety levels diminished with each one. One of the students experienced very high levels of perceived foreign language anxiety; he stated, "I do not like posting oral work for the course in Spanish. Speaking in front of others is definitely one of my biggest fears. Even just imagining someone watching me speak in Spanish (even like posting a video of myself to get graded) makes me nervous. I have experienced a lot of foreign language anxiety while in college" (Russell, 2016). This comment illustrates the high level of language anxiety that may be felt by online language learners.

Students' high levels of language anxiety at the beginning of the term in Russell's study were likely attributed to a combination of fears related to the new technology (the conversation platform), fears regarding speaking in the target language in front of native speakers, as well as fears about having their conversations recorded. However, with time and experience using the conversation platform, Russell (2018) found that "students' anxiety levels were significantly lower at the end of the course compared to the beginning of the semester" (p. 62).

The research on foreign language anxiety in online learning environments indicates that online learners do experience language anxiety, especially at the beginning levels of language learning. Therefore, online instructors should be aware of their students' foreign language anxiety and take steps to help alleviate it. For example, the instructor may post encouraging messages on the course discussion board and/or send individual messages to students reassuring them and letting them know that their feelings of anxiety will diminish over time and with practice using the language. Instructors should also consider using the same types of technologies and platforms throughout the semester so that students can become accustomed to them, which should also help decrease their perceived anxiety levels over time. Providing technical and language learning support up front may also help decrease students' language anxiety. With respect to technical support, instructors should create a technical help module that outlines all of the technologies that will be used in the course with help contact details for each technology tool or application that is employed. Goertler (2011) also suggested that instructors analyze their students' language development and computer literacy at the beginning of the course to determine what types of assistance and resources are needed; she also suggested that online learners require course navigation help, immediate feedback, and consistency in learner and teacher roles. Incorporating Goertler's (2011) recommendations should help reduce learners' language anxiety at the beginning of the course. With respect to language support, online tutoring (furnished by the institution, the department, or the instructor), peer support discussion groups, and virtual office hours may help meet students' language learning needs and therefore help diminish their perceptions of language anxiety.

Revisiting the question: Do online learners have more or less language anxiety than their peers in traditional, face-to-face language classrooms? After reviewing the research above, it appears that both online and classroom-based language learners can experience significant levels of foreign language anxiety at the early stages of language learning. While anxiety appears to diminish with experience for online learners, classroom-based learners seem to maintain high levels of anxiety when speaking in the target language in front of their peers at all levels of instruction. Therefore, the online environment appears to have the advantage over the traditional, face-to-face environment after students complete their first semester of language study (Pichette, 2009).

Research on Best Practices for Online Language Teaching

What are the best practices for online language course delivery? How can language instructors incorporate best practices into their online courses? Thus far, only a handful of research studies have focused on best practices for online language teaching, which the authors review below. Given that there is scant research on best practices for instructing language online, the research on general best practices for online teaching across disciplines will also be highlighted in this section; however, the authors examine these findings through the lens of language teaching and make recommendations for incorporating them in online, blended, and flipped language classes.

Research on Best Practices in Online Language Teaching Contexts

With respect to best practices, Don (2005) surveyed a pool of Spanish language teaching experts, Spanish language course developers, and online Spanish language students to determine the characteristics of effective online language courses. Don's findings are presented in Table 5.1.

Among the items listed in Table 5.1, the first five were found to be of paramount importance and Items 6–12 were found to be of secondary importance for effective online language courses. In terms of design, development, and delivery, it is noteworthy that the first nine of the twelve items in Table 5.1 pertain to online course design and development, including all five of the characteristics found to be of primary importance. This should underscore the necessity of putting forth the time and effort up front to create a solid online course design and to develop each component carefully. Therefore, online language course developers should strongly consider engaging in alpha testing (having colleagues and other stakeholders evaluate the course design as it is being developed) and beta testing (having actual students

Table 5.1 Don's (2005) characteristics of effective online language courses

Features of Primary Importance in Rank Order	Features of Secondary Importance in Rank Order
(1) Clear instructions from the teacher	(6) Infusing culture into the curriculum
(2) Opportunities for student-teacher interaction	(7) Providing clear expectations of students
(3) The incorporation of all four skills (reading, writing, listening, and speaking) into the curriculum	(8) Having a strong course organization
(4) The inclusion of audio-based content	(9) Furnishing sample assignments and assessments
(5) Opportunities for student-student interaction	(10) Having a competent language instructor in place
	(11) Providing a prompt student response time
	(12) Having one-on-one contact with students (e.g., phone calls, virtual meetings)

evaluate these items to check for clarity of expression, ease of navigation, and whether the course design is intuitive among other items). See Chapter 1 for a deeper explanation of online course design and alpha/beta testing.

Items 1, 7, and 8 from Table 5.1 pertain to being clear in the instructions and expectations provided to students as well as in the overall course design. A good place to post these expectations is in the "Getting Started" module. In addition to a well-developed "Getting Started" module (See Chapter 1, Learner Orientation, for more details), it is also a good idea to provide either a synchronous or a recorded course orientation presentation that highlights the course expectations regarding communication (e.g., how often students should sign on to the online course and where and how often they should check their course e-mail, course discussion posts, announcements, etc.). Expectations regarding workload should also be clear (e.g., how much time they should spend on the course each week, how many assignments they are expected to complete each week, what days and times assignments are due, etc.). Item 9, furnishing sample assignments and assessments, is likely a best practice whether the course is face-to-face or online. However, with online classes, these items may help clarify student expectations.

Items 2 through 6 from Table 5.1 should be built into the course at the design phase and then executed at the development and delivery phases. Items 2 and 5 deal specifically with interaction, both student-teacher and student-student. While it could be argued that interaction is instrumental in online courses across disciplines, it is of paramount importance in online language courses, as learners must listen to comprehensible input in the target language, produce target language output, and interact with their teacher and their peers in the target language in order to negotiate meaning and build proficiency (Krashen 1980, 1981, 1982, 1985; Swain, 1985, 1993, 1995, 1998; Long, 1985, 1996).

Item 3 (incorporating all four skills) and Item 6 (teaching culture) from Table 5.1 are specific to language course development. While ESL instruction still focuses on instructing the four skills, world language education has moved to the three modes of communication (interpretive, interpersonal, and pre-sentational). Interpretive communication occurs in the reading, viewing, and listening modalities, while presentational and interpersonal communication occurs in the spoken and written modalities. The difference between presentational and interpersonal communication is whether students have time to practice and rehearse their production, which they do in the former but not in the latter. While Item 4, using audio-based content, is a good idea for any online course, it is essential in an online language course. Students need to hear the language as it is spoken by native speakers, they need opportunities to produce the language (orally and in writing), and they must interact with others to negotiate meaning, all of which must be done through audio- or video-based tools and content. See Chapter 3 for a review of the modes of communication and Chapter 2 for a review of audio-based tools.

Teaching culture, Item 6 from Table 5.1, was covered in Chapter 3. It is impossible to divorce language and culture while teaching an effective online language course and Don's (2005) research underscores this. Moreover, the infusion of culture into the course can increase students' interest and motivation to learn the content. One way to teach language and culture simultaneously is to incorporate pragmatics-focused instruction, which is also covered in Chapter 3.

Item 10 from Table 5.1, having a competent language instructor in place, is key for the success of any course. However, in an online language course, the instructor needs to be not only a content expert in the target language (with a minimum proficiency of Advanced Low for the most commonly taught languages in the United States), but also an expert in instructional technology and online pedagogy. As was discussed in Chapter 3, most initial language teacher preparation programs do not incorporate online language teaching into their curricula. Therefore, language teachers who deliver online language courses must seek out professional development in technology and in online language pedagogy to be successful. The authors hope that this book, in particular the professional development opportunities described in Chapter 4, will help fill this need.

The final item from Table 5.1, Item 12, highlights the importance of having one-on-one contact with students. While student-teacher interaction (Item 2) can include interactions between one teacher and many students, Don's (2005) findings indicate that building a personal relationship with each student through one-on-one communication is a key factor in an effective online language course. This recommendation resonates with the authors of this book who are experienced online language instructors. At the end of a course, it is not unusual for students to express that they got to know their online language teacher better than their teachers in their face-to-face courses. This is likely because there are often more frequent, and/or longer, one-on-one interactions in online language classes than in traditional, brick-and-mortar classes. In a traditional classroom, students can easily ask their peers for help and few students linger after class or visit their instructor during office hours. Conversely, whenever online students need help, whether with the language content or with the instructional technologies used to deliver the course, they must reach out to their instructor. These recurrent, one-on-one interactions build rapport between the teacher and student.

While the recommendations from Don's study make sense and they are aligned with the principles of sound instructional design, they are not all inclusive. Moreover, the study had a small number of participants and the research took place over a decade ago. More research is urgently needed in this area, especially studies that query a large number of stakeholders who teach both commonly and less commonly taught languages online across various contexts and levels. Vorobel and Kim (2012) reviewed the empirical research on distance language education between 2005 and 2010 and they found that most studies focused on the instruction of ESL, Spanish, and German at the graduate or undergraduate level, with only one study at the high school level. They stated that more research is urgently needed across a variety of languages and, most importantly, in K-12 settings. Vorobel and Kim (2012) also claimed that there was insufficient research on student engagement and student-teacher interaction in online language courses. Future research in these areas will help scholars make recommendations regarding best practices for online language course delivery.

Research on Best Practices in Online Teaching Across Disciplines

Given that there has been scant research conducted on best practices that are specific for online language course delivery, it is useful to look to examples from other discipline areas. Boettcher and Conrad (2016) reviewed the literature across disciplines in higher education with respect to online course design, development, and delivery and they asserted that there are 14 best practices as shown in Table 5.2.

Interestingly, only Practice 3 from Table 5.2 (set explicit expectations) overlaps with Don's (2005) findings. Therefore, it will be helpful for online language instructors to be familiar with Boettcher and Conrad's (2016) best practices, which the authors of this book present through the lens of online language teaching. While some of their recommendations are self-explanatory, others may require a bit of unpacking, which will be done with examples that are relevant to online language teaching and learning. The first, and most important, best practice on the list—to be present in the course—will be covered extensively in the next section of this chapter (research on teaching, social, and cognitive presence). The concept of presence was also introduced and described in detail in Chapter 1.

Creating a supportive online community, Practice 2, could be achieved in an online language course in several ways. One way is to create a help discussion board where students can ask questions and receive help and support both

Table 5.2 Best practices for eLearning: Boettcher and Conrad's 10 plus 4

Best Practices for Teaching Online	
Best Practice	*Description*
Best practice 1	Be present at the course site.
Best practice 2	Create a supportive online course community.
Best practice 3	Develop a set of explicit expectations for your learners and yourself as to how you will communicate and how much time students should be working on the course each week.
Best practice 4	Use a variety of large group, small group, and individual work experiences.
Best practice 5	Use synchronous and asynchronous activities.
Best practice 6	Ask for informal feedback early in the term.
Best practice 7	Prepare discussion posts that invite responses, questions, discussions, and reflections.
Best practice 8	Search out and use content resources that are available in digital format.
Best practice 9	Combine core concept learning with customized and personalized learning.
Best practice 10	Plan a good closing and wrap activity for the course.
Best practice 11	Assess as you go by gathering evidences of learning.
Best practice 12	Rigorously connect content to core concepts and learning outcomes.
Best practice 13	Develop and use a content frame for your course.
Best practice 14	Design experiences to help learners make progress on their novice-to-expert journey.

from both the teacher and from their peers. When online language teachers encourage peers to answer each other's questions on the help discussion board, then all students can feel more supported in the course. It is quite possible that students will be working on the course at all hours of the day and night. While it is not possible for one instructor to be online and available 24/7, it is highly likely that other students will also be online and working at the same time as those who need help. Therefore, students can help and support each other in real time. Online teachers can encourage this by praising those who help their peers or by giving them extra credit. Another, more subtle way of creating a supportive online community is to take care when answering students' questions via e-mail. It is very easy to interpret a negative tone in e-mails. Online language instructors need to remember that their students are alone in cyberspace and they may be lost and confused in the language learning process or they may require technical help to complete their assignments. Therefore, online instructors should explicitly state that they care for and are concerned about their students' success and well-being when answering students' e-mails—this can go a long way in creating a supportive environment. For example, online students often begin e-mail messages stating, "I am so sorry to bother you." It is important for learners to know that they are not a bother and that their questions and concerns are important to the instructor. Therefore, a response such as, "You are no bother, I am here to help you!" can put students at ease right away so that they feel comfortable reaching out to the instructor when help is needed. Another way to support online language learners is to place them in peer support groups. These small groups can be used not only for course projects and assignments, but also as a place where peers can help each other with the online language learning process. Students in peer support groups could be encouraged to contact each other for help with assignments as well as for peer tutoring. Peer support groups could have their own private discussion board as well as their own online meeting space to connect and collaborate with each other when needed.

Practice 3, developing a set of explicit workload and communication expectations for learners and instructors, overlaps with Don's (2005) recommendation of providing clear expectations of students. However, Boettcher and Conrad (2016) take it step further by stating that clear expectations should be made not only for the students but also for the instructor. Therefore, instructors should provide information up front on their availability (e.g., office hours, whether on campus or online), what days and times they will be working online, and when students should expect to have their assignments and assessments graded (e.g., grades will be posted within one week of the due date). Online instructors are advised to be available online at set times and to hold virtual office hours. This can be achieved either through the learning management system (LMS) where the course is delivered or through other applications such as Skype, Zoom, Google Meet, or GoToMeeting to name a few. Students could then seek assistance during the days and times that are convenient for the teacher. Instructors may not wish to work over the weekend; if so, they should state this explicitly up front. They should also let students know how long it will take to receive a response to their e-mail inquiries (e.g., students will receive a reply within 24 hours, Monday through Friday).

The fourth best practice—using a variety of large group, small group, and individual work experiences—could also be achieved through the use of peer support groups, as described above. In addition, students could be assigned a course partner who is also part of their peer support group. Having a partner and a small peer support group would also help combat the loneliness that students may feel when taking an online language course. Moreover, the interaction in the target language that students have with their partner and/or their peer group is also highly conducive to language learning, as even Novice students who interact with each other will need to negotiate meaning, which is an essential factor for second language acquisition (Long, 1985, 1996). Large-group activities could take place during whole class discussions, synchronous class sessions, and/or during course projects where students are required to review their peers' work.

Using both synchronous and asynchronous activities is the fifth best practice and it is of paramount importance for online language learning. Language students must engage in the three modes of communication (interpretive, interpersonal, and presentational) and it is extremely challenging to engage in interpersonal—or person to person—communication asynchronously because it is impossible to determine whether learners have consulted outside resources in the formulation of their responses. Conversely, it is not difficult for online language instructors to curate interpretive listening and reading materials that are authentic, such as electronic newspapers and magazines, podcasts, and blogs. Authentic materials are those that were created by and/or for native speakers of the language. For presentational speaking, students can make audio or video recordings in the target language, which allows them to practice, rehearse, and re-record as needed. However, when engaging in the interpersonal mode, it is easiest to do this in real time. This may be achieved in a number of ways; for example, instructors may pair students up for synchronous conversations, they may use a conversation platform such as TalkAbroad, LinguaMeeting, or WeSpeke, where learners have conversations with native speakers in real time, or they may take part in a language exchange where they interact with their peers from the target language country (links to conversation and language exchange platforms are available in the eResources for Chapter 3).

Teachers may also engage with their students synchronously on an individual basis or in small groups. A number of tools such as Zoom, Skype, Blackboard Collaborate, or any other online meeting tool may be used to facilitate synchronous interpersonal communication (see Chapter 2 for more information on online meeting tools). Interpersonal communication can also occur in the written modality asynchronously through virtual chat bots that simulate real-time communication (students view the input once and they have a set amount of time to reply using a timer) and synchronously through applications such as text chat and Twitter where students interact with their peers in real time. It should be noted that some online programs only offer asynchronous delivery of instruction; therefore, students' engagement in the interpersonal mode of communication must rely on technology tools and applications.

Asking for informal feedback early on, the sixth best practice, allows instructors to take the pulse of the online class. Most learning management platforms have a survey tool. If instructors do not have access to one, then a free tool such as Google Forms or SurveyMonkey may be used. Online language instructors should ask students their perceptions regarding the workload and whether it is manageable, how well they are able to navigate the online content (e.g., the location of online assignments, assessments, and interactions), how well they are able to comprehend the online target language input, how supported they feel in the course by the instructor, how timely the instructor's responses to their questions are, and whether the assessments adequately measure learners' knowledge, skills, and understandings of the target language and cultures. If student feedback is provided prior to the middle of the semester, then the instructor will have time to make adjustments to the course to better meet students' needs. This practice will likely result in higher student evaluations at the end of the course.

Boettcher and Conrad's (2016) seventh best practice is to create discussion board posts that promote student reflections, responses, questions, and discussions. In an online language class, this recommendation could be combined with their fourth recommendation of using a variety of large group, small group, and individual work experiences. Separate discussion boards could be set up for paired and small group work in the target language. Instructors could even differentiate their instruction by creating flexible groupings—or groupings that continually change based on student background knowledge, needs, or interests. If students are grouped by ability on discussion boards, then instructors could provide additional challenge for advanced students as well as additional support for those who struggle to grasp concepts. With respect to an online language class, discussions should not merely focus on the technical aspects of language (e.g., grammar and vocabulary); rather, students should be encouraged to make cultural comparisons, connections to other disciplines, and connections to their everyday lives. By connecting language content to other disciplines such as history, geography, and English/Language Arts, students' understandings of both the target language and other disciplines are strengthened. Moreover, teaching language through content is a powerful way to facilitate the language acquisition process.

In addition, instructors should stimulate cultural comparisons on discussion boards, with students examining cultural products and practices as well as the perspectives that underpin them. By focusing on rich cultural content, course discussion posts will be more interesting for students, thus promoting deeper student reflections. At the early stages of language learning, cultural instruction and subsequent discussions may need to occur in English to promote students' cultural awareness. Language instructors should also keep in mind that students will be able to understand what they hear and read in the target language at a higher level than they can speak and write. Therefore, online language teachers may provide authentic audio or video clips for Novice Low through Intermediate Low students in the target language, while allowing their oral or written discussions of cultural topics to take place in English.

In their book, Boettcher and Conrad (2016) provide a number of tips on how to create rich discussion posts as well as how to create rubrics for course discussions that facilitate deeper reflection and student engagement (Chapter 2 also covers this content). They also advocate the use of staggered due dates for discussion posts so that students are encouraged to communicate with and connect to each other on a regular basis throughout the course. Their 2016 book is a suggestion for further reading for those who wish to delve further into the topic of best practices for eLearning.

Thinking digital for all course content, the eighth best practice, refers to using content that is available digitally (Boettcher & Conrad, 2016). It may seem self-evident that online courses should use eBooks, online materials, and digital resources, but many language instructors who teach in traditional classrooms may be accustomed to using a printed textbook. It should be noted that using print materials only is not an effective practice for online course delivery. Most language textbooks that are available on the secondary and post-secondary markets have online versions. Many of them also have additional online resources available, such as online workbooks and online lab manuals. However, some online students will still want to have printed versions of the course materials in addition to their eBooks and online resources; this is acceptable provided that students understand that they must access the course and submit their assignments online. Having printed versions of the course texts allows students to study in different locations and it may ease the eye strain that can occur from spending numerous hours reading online; to that end, some publishers provide loose-leaf copies of their books that students can place in a three ring binder—these cost less than hardcover texts and are more portable.

Thinking digitally also refers to taking advantage of the capabilities of the online language learning environment by employing audio, video, animation, and/or other multimedia tools and resources that facilitate language learning. It is also important to ensure that course content is accessible via mobile devices. As today's students often access their online courses via their mobile phones, it is increasingly important that textbooks, platforms, and other resources are able to be displayed and accessed via mobile devices.

The ninth best practice, according to Boettcher and Conrad (2016), is to combine core concept learning with customized and personalized learning. The first step in this process is to have well-developed core concepts that are linked to the course learning objectives during the online language course design and development process (See Chapters 1 and 2). The second step includes personalizing the learning for each student, which can be achieved when students set their own language learning goals that are tied to the course learning objectives. While it may seem daunting to personalize learning for each student in the online class, there are some important resources available that can help instructors to do so; namely, the National Council of State Supervisors for Languages (NCSSFL) and ACTFL created the NCSSFL-ACTFL (2017) Can-Do Statements that describe what language learners can do at each stage of proficiency (Novice, Intermediate, and Advanced) across the three modes of communication. The NCSSFL-ACTFL (2017) Can-Do Statements also encompass students' development of intercultural communicative competence (ICC) with specific statements that focus on intercultural communication.

Speakers who attain ICC, according to Byram (1997), not only gain an inside view of another culture, they also attempt to understand their own culture from another cultural perspective. Similarly, the World-Class Instructional Design and Assessment (WIDA) consortium developed the WIDA (2016) Can-Do Descriptors, Key Uses Edition, Grades K-12 for English language learners at six levels of English language proficiency (Entering, Emerging, Developing, Expanding, Bridging, and Reaching). These Can-Do Statements and Descriptors may be used by students to set their own language and culture learning goals. In online language classrooms, learners could be encouraged to examine the learning outcomes that are listed in the weekly modules as well as a list of the relevant Can-Do Statements or Descriptors. Students could then select the Can-Do Statements/Descriptors that reflect their own language learning goals in relation to the course and/or module learning outcomes. This is a powerful way to connect the core concepts that are covered in the course to students' customized and personalized learning. Instructors could also ask students to self-reflect at the end of each module to determine whether or not their own learning goals were met. This reflection tool would enable instructors to identify when remediation is needed on a particular topic for individual learners.

Boettcher and Conrad's (2016) tenth best practice is to create a good closing/ wrap activity for the online course. This is an opportunity for students to reflect on their learning and to summarize the key takeaways that they have gleaned from the course. In an online language course, students may reflect on all of the NCSSFL-ACTFL (2017) Can-Do Statements or WIDA (2016) Can Do Descriptors that they have met. This type of activity can provide language students with a sense of accomplishment. They may also wrap up the course with a role-play or presentation in the target language using the language forms, structures, and cultural knowledge that they mastered throughout the weekly learning modules. The closing activity should require students to engage in target language communication within a meaningful cultural context. In other words, learners should use language in authentic, real-world contexts that focus on the notions and functions of language (See Chapter 3 for a review of communicative competence and language notions/functions).

Best Practice 11 is to engage in continual assessment and data gathering to provide evidence of student learning (Boettcher & Conrad, 2016). Because assessment is such an important part of an online language course, the research on effective assessment practices for language learning is discussed at length a bit later in this chapter. With online courses, each module will have module learning objectives that are tied to the overall course learning objectives and goals. A good practice is to assess each module's learning objectives before students are able to move on to the next module. It is also important to use assessment data to modify future instruction. For example, if the majority of the class performs poorly on a module assessment, then additional instruction may be needed before students are allowed to move on in the course. This is especially important in a language course where the grammatical forms and structures build upon each other and where students are expected to create with language using increasingly complex knowledge and understandings. Because language learning is different from other types of learning, special attention must be paid to how language learning is assessed. The forthcoming section on assessment delves deep into this process by providing the findings from research on effective assessment practices for language teaching and learning.

According to Boettcher and Conrad (2016), Best Practice 12 is to connect course content to core concepts and learning outcomes. This practice is directly related to the concepts of backward design (see Chapter 1) and lesson alignment, which refers to the connection between learning outcomes, learning activities, and lesson assessments. When a lesson is aligned, then the objectives, activities, and assessments reinforce one another such that the lesson activities facilitate mastery of the learning objectives and the assessments measure what the students are actually learning. For online language classes, one way to ensure that the core concepts are covered is to base each lesson on professional standards. Language educators can tie their course content to core concepts and learning outcomes if they base their lessons on professional standards, write realistic learning objectives regarding what learners can do at each level of proficiency, and tie their learning objectives, lesson activities, and lesson assessments to their selected standards. Creating lessons that are well aligned is of paramount importance for effective language instruction in every type of learning environment, whether traditional, blended, flipped, or online. See Chapter 3 for a review of lesson design, professional standards, and student proficiency level.

Best Practice 13 is to create and implement a content frame for the online course (Boettcher & Conrad, 2016). A content frame is a graphic or concept map that provides a visual overview of the course. One way to create a simple content frame for the course is to create a storyboard, which is a sequence of panels in which the instructor lays out the framework of the course. For example, if the course is taught over a period of eight weeks, then the instructor would create eight panels, one for each weekly module. Each panel would contain a visual image that depicts that core content that is covered in that module. The instructor can also provide an overview of the key assignments, assessments and interactions that will be completed in the module. Figure 5.1 depicts an example of a simple content frame for an eight-week introductory Spanish course using the storyboard approach. Concept maps, or wireframes, often use a set of images to depict the functionality and navigation of the course. Therefore, instructors could create a storyboard to visually depict the content and a wireframe to show the course navigation. See Chapter 1, which covers concept maps/wireframes in greater detail.

By viewing the content frame, students will gain an understanding of both the core content that is covered in the course as well as how the course is laid out. Furthermore, content frames that incorporate images provide an anticipatory set for students, which is a way to pique students' interest and prime them for the lesson content. Content frames could be placed either on the syllabus, in the Start Here module, or both. In addition, each image from the storyboard could be embedded in the weekly modules as a visual representation of the lesson content. See Figure 5.2 for an example of how an image from the content frame could be used to introduce a weekly module.

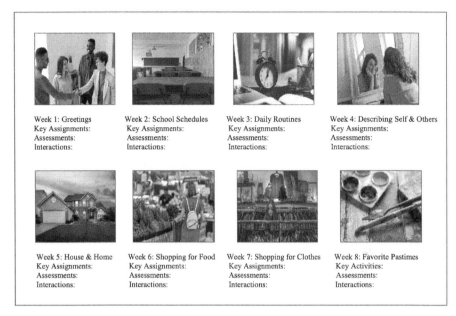

Figure 5.1 Content frame for an eight-week Spanish course.

Using a content frame and then repeating the images to introduce the weekly modules facilitates a cohesive course structure and design. Moreover, images can provide a powerful representation of key content, while the content frame allows students to gain a holistic sense of a course (Boettcher & Conrad, 2016).

Figure 5.2 Introduction to a module in an online Spanish course on D2L's Brightspace platform.

D2L product screenshot reprinted with permission from D2L Corporation.

Infusing the online course with images is also a helpful way to personalize the course. However, instructors need to keep in mind that images must be free from copyright protections before embedding them into their courses. The photos that were used above were obtained from Pexels, which is a website that provides openly available stock photos and videos on hundreds of topics. Authors and course designers are free to use Pexels' images in their creative works, but they are not allowed to sell the images to others.

Boettcher and Conrad's (2016) final best practice, Best Practice 14, is to create learning experiences that help students move forward on their novice-to-expert journey. With respect to language learning, students are often exposed to mixed messages in the media regarding how long it takes to become an expert (or to achieve Advanced proficiency) in a second language. Some products claim that a language can be learned in a few days, or in a few weeks, or even while the learner sleeps! Therefore, it is not surprising that many students enter beginning-level language courses with unrealistic expectations regarding what is possible, or even probable, at the end of one semester of language study. Perhaps the best thing that online language instructors can do with respect to this final best practice is to let students know exactly how long it takes to become conversationally fluent in another language. This will help learners not to feel discouraged about the slow pace of their own language learning. It is also important to explain to students that conversational fluency is different than near-native fluency, which could take a lifetime to achieve. With conversational fluency, learners can understand most of what they read and hear with respect to everyday topics; however, they may not understand more complex, technical topics. Regarding speaking skills, learners with conversational fluency have clear pronunciation and their production is mostly accurate; moreover, they are easily understood by sympathetic native speakers.

The context of language learning is also a key factor in how long it will take to achieve conversational fluency. Those learning a foreign language without the benefit of immersion in the second language context will take longer to achieve conversational fluency compared to those studying language with full immersion in the second language context. In other words, students who take formal coursework while being immersed in the second language context—such as studying Spanish in Spain or learning English while living in the United States—will typically learn at a quicker pace than those studying a foreign language without the benefit of immersion in the second language context (Lafford, 2006). Dual immersion students are also likely to learn a second language more quickly than their peers in traditional schools (where they are only exposed to the target language a few hours per week). With dual immersion schools, students spend half of their day learning content through the vehicle of the first language and the other half of their day learning content through the vehicle of the second language (e.g., a U.S. history class taught in Spanish).

The Foreign Service Institute (FSI) has set forth parameters on how many classroom hours it takes for native English speakers, on average, to achieve professional working proficiency in various foreign languages based on the level of difficulty of the target language. It is important to note that professional working proficiency is a higher level of proficiency than conversational fluency; it is classified as level 3 on the Interagency Language Roundtable (ILR) scale, which is the proficiency scale used by the FSI. According to North (2006), an ILR score of 3 corresponds to Superior according to the ACTFL Proficiency Guidelines (ACTFL, 2012) or to C1 according to the Common European Framework of Reference (CEFR) for Languages: Learning, Teaching, and Assessment scale (Council of Europe, 2011). The FSI parameters do not reflect how long it would take to achieve near-native fluency in the foreign language nor do they reflect how long it would take to achieve professional working proficiency through immersion. See Chapter 1 for a cross walk of the ACTFL, ILR, and CEFR scales.

The FSI has classified languages into four categories from the easiest to the most difficult for native English speakers to learn. They also provide estimates of the number of classroom hours required to learn a wide array of languages in each of the four categories (U.S. Department of State, Foreign Service Institute, n.d.). Table 5.3 below presents FSI's language categories and the

Table 5.3 FSI's language leaning timelines

Category	Number of Classroom Hours	Language
I	600–750	Danish, Dutch, French, Italian, Norwegian, Portuguese, Romanian, Spanish, Swedish
II	900	German, Haitian Creole, Indonesian, Malay, Swahili
III	1,100	Albanian, Amharic, Armenian, Azerbaijani, Bengali, Bulgarian, Burmese, Czech, Dari, Estonian, Farsi, Finnish, Georgian, Greek, Hebrew, Hindi, Hungarian, Icelandic, Kazakh, Khmer, Kyrgyz, Kurdish, Lao, Latvian, Lithuanian, Macedonian, Mongolian, Nepali, Polish, Russian, Serbo-Croatian, Sinhala, Slovak, Slovenian, Somali, Tagalog, Tajiki, Tamil, Telugu, Thai, Tibetan, Turkish, Turkmen, Ukrainian, Uzbek, Urdu, Vietnamese
IV	2,200	Arabic, Chinese (Cantonese), Chinese (Mandarin), Japanese, Korean

Note. Data obtained from U.S. State Department, Foreign Service Institute, n.d.

required number of classroom hours to learn each language in a given category. Category I and II languages are similar to English, while Category III and IV languages have significant differences—both linguistically and culturally—from English. Category IV languages are noted for being exceptionally difficult for native speakers of English to learn.

It is important to understand that the estimated number of classroom hours presented on the table above does not include the hours that learners must spend studying and completing assignments on their own outside of class; therefore, including the additional self-study hours would essentially triple the number of hours required to learn each language that is listed in Table 5.3. The FSI notes on their website that the list of Category III languages in the table above is not exhaustive.

By providing students with information on how long it really takes to achieve Advanced proficiency in another language, they will have a better understanding of their novice-to-expert journey. Boettcher and Conrad's Best Practice 14 could be applied to overall program design, with undergraduate students beginning at the Novice Low or A1 level of proficiency and moving through a series of articulated and sequenced language courses over the span of four years so that they could potentially reach Advanced Low or B2 proficiency by graduation. In order to reach higher levels of proficiency, students may need to seek immersion experiences through study abroad and/or pursue further language study in graduate school.

Revisiting the questions: What are the best practices for online language course delivery? How can language instructors incorporate best practices into their online courses? The research reviewed above provides clear guidance as well as practical advice for language educators to follow with respect to the integration of best practices. While it would be extremely difficult to incorporate all of the best practices listed in this chapter with the first iteration of an online language class; over time, instructors could continually strive to improve by adding in one or two new best practices with each subsequent delivery of the course. If faculty are required to set annual goals at their institutions, then adding in a new best practice to each online course each year would not only satisfy the goal-setting requirement, but it would also likely result in more effective, efficient, and satisfying online experiences for both the students and the instructor. Moreover, as was discussed in Chapter 1, online instructors should continually evaluate their instructional design, development, and delivery in order to improve their courses, and in turn their learners' experiences.

In this chapter, Boettcher and Conrad's (2016) 14 best practices for online course delivery were presented with specific examples from foreign and second language teaching contexts. The authors recognize the important work that Boettcher and Conrad have done to synthesize the relevant literature in general online course design, development, and delivery to create their list of best practices, and they hope that their interpretation of the practices through the lens of online language teaching builds upon their important work.

Research on Teaching, Social, and Cognitive Presence

How can online language instructors facilitate teaching, social, and cognitive presence? Presence is perhaps one of the most important facets of a successful online course across all disciplines. Shin (2003) asserted that success rates in online courses are positively impacted by the psychological presence of the institution, the instructor, and the learner's peers. Similarly, Angelino, Williams, and Natvig (2007) claimed that building relationships among peers and/or cohorts is essential for the successful completion of online courses or programs. Boettcher and Conrad (2016) asserted that the first best practice to follow for online course delivery is "Be present at the course site" (p. 45). According to Garrison, Anderson, and Archer (2000), there are three types of presence—social, teaching, and cognitive presence—with each of them being necessary to ensure that both instructors and students have efficient, effective, and satisfying experiences in the online teaching and learning environment. Social presence refers to the connection between individuals that is based on their unique backgrounds and personal interests, which includes their lifestyles, hobbies, and family relationships; teaching presence includes all of the behaviors in which faculty engage to design, direct, mentor, and guide students' online learning experiences throughout the course; and cognitive presence refers to the support that students receive regarding their intellectual growth and their development of knowledge, skills, and understandings (Boettcher & Conrad, 2016).

Rourke, Anderson, Garrison, and Archer (2001) proposed that instructors create a community of inquiry in their online courses by fostering the three types of presence. Given that instructors are typically content experts in their fields and that they are accustomed to supporting student learning, it is often much less difficult for them to cultivate teaching and cognitive presence than social presence. Moreover, some research has shown that social presence, which is sometimes overlooked in the online environment, may be the mediating factor between cognitive and teaching presence (Garrison, Cleveland-Innes & Fung, 2010;

Shea & Bidjerano, 2009). Garrison et al. (2000) asserted that learners' social and emotional interactions are of paramount importance for the development of their social connections and for the creation of an online community of inquiry, where students actively explore, create, and develop understandings collaboratively. In other words, when social, teaching, and cognitive presence overlap, meaningful collaboration occurs and a community of inquiry exists (Garrison et al., 2000).

Indicators of Social Presence

Certain types of behaviors in the online environment are indicators of social presence, and these indicators can be broken down into three categories: affective, interactive, and cohesive (Garrison et al., 2000). Affective indicators are related to students' emotions, such as expressing humor and sharing personal information. Some examples of interactive indicators include replying to a discussion thread, asking questions of peers, or quoting others. Cohesive indicators relate to social functions, such as greetings, using inclusive pronouns (e.g., we, us, our), and addressing the class or a small group (Garrison et al., 2000). Instructors can create online learning environments that foster indicators of social presence in a number of ways, such as creating introduction discussion boards, dividing students into small groups to work collaboratively, and encouraging peer feedback and support through course assignments, assessments, and interactions.

Given that social presence is the more difficult presence to cultivate in online courses (Boettcher & Conrad, 2016; Garrison et al., 2010; Shea & Bidjerano, 2009; Shin, 2003), the research on social presence is highlighted below. The following tools or applications have been shown to stimulate social presence among online language learners: (1) desktop video/audio conferencing (Satar, 2015; Yamada & Akahori, 2007), (2) Instagram (Fornara & Lomicka, 2019), (3) microblogs (Dunlap & Lowenthal, 2009; Lomicka & Lord, 2012; Lord & Lomicka, 2012), and (4) virtual worlds (Cooke-Plagwitz, 2008; Peterson, 2011).

Research Findings on Social Presence

Satar (2015) examined whether engaging in desktop video or audio conferencing enables learners to build social presence. The participants were Turkish learners of English as a foreign language and they communicated in pairs via desktop video conferencing. Satar (2015) focused on the interactive indicators, which typically include behaviors such as quoting from their classmates' messages, expressing agreement, complimenting or expressing appreciation, and asking questions. Given that participants could see and hear each other via desktop conferencing, Satar also examined their non-verbal communication for evidence of interactive indicators. These non-verbal cues, also known as backchannels, included head nods, smiles, facial expressions, and/or the raising of an eyebrow. Satar's findings demonstrated that there are three powerful ways for students to build social presence during video conferencing: (1) asking questions and providing appropriate responses (indicating that the partners were paying attention to each other), (2) providing verbal and non-verbal cues that express friendliness and warmth, and (3) having an appropriate response time with respect to turn taking and silences. Satar asserted that students must believe that their classmates are involved with and attending to the conversation. This can be achieved by providing responses that refer back to previous interactions and by demonstrating non-verbal signals, such as facial expressions and head nods. Moreover, paralinguistic cues, such as smiling, and verbal cues, such as sharing humor, enable participants to express warmth and friendliness during video conferencing. Regarding response time, Satar claimed that students need to distinguish when silences and slow turns are caused by technical or linguistic problems and when they indicate an actual unwillingness to communicate.

Satar (2015) set forth some guidelines for teachers to help language learners build social presence during video conferencing; namely, teachers should encourage their students "incorporate their feelings, experiences, examples, and ideas in task completion" and "initiate new topics, ask follow-up questions, and ... provide quick, and above all, non-verbal backchannels" (p. 498). She also suggested that teachers give students ample time for "off task" talk so that they can build rapport and establish social presence. Satar also stressed the importance of making students aware of potential silences in their interactions via video conferencing, which can occur due to technical issues or due to the limited linguistic knowledge of the participants. Students should be advised not to interpret silences as an unwillingness to communicate, but rather as an opportunity to help their conversation partner with respect to problems that they may be experiencing with their technology or language skills.

Similar to Satar's (2015) study, Fornara and Lomicka (2019) investigated Intermediate-level university students of French and Spanish and their use of Instagram to build social presence online. The researchers examined affective (e.g., students' emotions), interactive (e.g., replying to peers), and cohesive (e.g., social functions such as greetings) indicators and quantified them in students' messages and visual representations on Instagram.

They found that for both languages, students mostly displayed affective and interactive indicators. Examples of their affective indicators included self-disclosure, or telling personal information about themselves, and expressions of emotion, such as the use of exclamation points, emojis, or caps. Interactive indicators included quoting others, asking questions, or continuing a conversation or thread. Of note, the least common indicators were the cohesive ones, with learners rarely or never using inclusive pronouns (i.e., we, us, our). In summary, Fornara and Lomicka (2019) found that students were able to build social presence online through the use of Instagram in Intermediate-level language classes. The most important finding of their study was that visual information, such as pictures and videos, can help learners build social presence online.

Lomicka and Lord (2012) examined the role of Twitter among 13 Intermediate-level university learners of French. Participants tweeted among themselves and with 12 university students in France who were studying English. Twitter was used as a medium for short communications, as messages were limited to 140 characters; furthermore, the messages were directed toward one person, were privately viewed, or were shared with others via retweeting.

The study participants were asked to tweet twice per week in French and once per week in English. The researchers examined participants' tweets for indicators of social presence, which they classified as affective (e.g., humor, emotion), interactive (e.g., replies, retweets), and cohesive (e.g., inclusive pronouns, salutations). The researchers found more affective indicators than interactive ones. Although participants were not required to reply to others, they often did so, which indicated that they had built a community of inquiry. According to Lomicka and Lord (2012), over time, "students became more interested in talking with each other and sharing opinions, comments, and information" (p. 56). The researchers concluded that Twitter enabled the participants in their study to create a community and to build social presence (Lomicka & Lord, 2012). The findings of this study indicate that Twitter is an effective tool for building social presence in an online course.

Peterson (2011) conducted a review of the literature on how social presence may be facilitated in virtual words, which are defined as "persistent virtual environments in which people experience others as being there with them and where they interact with them" (Schroeder, 2008, p. 2). According to Peterson, the two most popular platforms for virtual worlds are Active Worlds and Second Life. Unlike chatrooms or other temporary virtual environments, virtual worlds provide permanent venues for interaction and they typically have a common theme, such as a specific location or country. A key benefit of using a virtual world is the multimodal nature of communication, including visual, text, and audio-based interactions. Users can create their own personalized avatars, which are icons or images that represent the user. Some research has shown that learners become emotionally attached to their avatars and the use of avatars can strengthen learners' perceptions of presence (Cooke-Plagwitz, 2008; Lombard & Ditton, 1997; Schroeder, 2002). After reviewing key studies on the use of virtual worlds for language learning, Peterson (2011) concluded that virtual worlds increased learners' sense of their own presence as well as the presence of their classmates (co-presence). However, the use of Second Life, in particular, led to feelings of frustration and stress among some students due to the steep learning curve to master the online platform. Moreover, some students did not perceive the game-like nature of virtual worlds to be appropriate for formal coursework. While virtual worlds can be a powerful tool to foster social presence in online classes, instructors should be aware that they will need to provide ample technology training for their students if they wish to incorporate them. Therefore, instructors would need to determine whether they have sufficient time and technical expertise to employ virtual worlds in their online courses.

Revisiting the question: How can online language instructors facilitate presence? There are likely numerous online tools and applications that have the potential to stimulate social presence among learners; however, there has been scant research on how technology tools and applications can help build social presence in the context of online language learning. More research is needed in this area, especially given that social presence can make a significant, positive impact on students' experiences in online language courses. The research studies that were reviewed above indicate that desktop conferencing, Instagram, microblogs/Twitter, and virtual worlds have the potential to increase social presence in online language courses. However, instructors should keep in mind that while virtual words—such as Second Life and Active Worlds—can foster presence, sufficient training for students and faculty would be necessary to incorporate them smoothly. Other tools—such as desktop conferencing, Instagram, and Twitter—may be easier to incorporate into online courses to help build students' perceptions of social presence. See Chapters 1 and 2 for more information on building social presence online.

Research on Learner Connectedness

Closely tied to the constructs of teaching, social, and cognitive presence is the concept of learner connectedness. According to Liu, Magjuka, Bonk, and Lee (2007), learner connectedness is the perception that members of an online group have a shared commitment and that they matter to one another. In other words, connectedness refers to a sense of virtual community (Blanchard, 2007). A number of researchers have documented that online learning may lead to feelings of social isolation (Haythornthwaite, Kazmer, Robins, & Shoemaker, 2000; Kanuka & Jugdev, 2006; Rovai, 2002; Shieh, Gummer & Niess, 2008). In addition, online students may experience both physical (space and time) and psychological (emotional) isolation from their peers. Online courses tend to have higher dropout rates than traditional, brick-and-mortar classes across disciplines (Herbert, 2006; Heyman, 2010) and some researchers have speculated that the higher attrition rates in online courses may be due to learners' feelings of disconnectedness in the online environment (Angelino, Williams, & Natvig, 2007; Kanuka & Jugdev, 2006). One way to combat feelings of social isolation is to foster students' perceptions of connectedness, which may also decrease attrition in online courses.

Bolliger and Inan (2012) asserted that learners who feel connected to their peers are more likely to engage with others and to participate in course tasks and activities; they also claimed that connectedness refers to learners' perceptions of belonging, acceptance, and a belief that they have a relationship with at least one other person in the online course. Furthermore, Bolliger and Inan (2012) asserted that connectedness is comprised of four measurable domains as follows: (1) comfort, (2) community, (3) facilitation, and (4) interaction and collaboration. Each of these constructs is measured by Bolliger and Inan's (2012) Online Student Connectedness Survey (OSCS), which is described below.

Evaluating Learner Connectedness

The OSCS is a summative evaluation instrument for online courses or programs and it is comprised of 25 items that are rated on a 5-point Likert scale ranging from 1 (strongly disagree) to 5 (strongly agree). The survey items are broken down as follows: (1) eight items measure comfort, or learners' feelings of contentment, security, and ease with the learning environment and course technologies, (2) six items measure community, which refers to students' emotional attachments to their peers in the online course, (3) six items measure facilitation, or learners' perceptions of the level of teacher presence in the course, and (4) five items measure interaction and collaboration, which refer to learners' perceptions of the depth of their interactions with their instructor and with their peers to complete course tasks. It should be noted that the OSCS is not intended to be used as a pre-assessment. Rather, it is a summative assessment that must be delivered at the end of an online course or program; furthermore, it has been found to be a valid and reliable instrument (Bolliger & Inan, 2012; Zimmerman & Nimon, 2017). The OSCS items are listed in Table 5.4.

Table 5.4 Bolliger & Inan's (2012) Online Student Connectedness Survey (OSCS)

Subscale	Statement
Comfort	1. I feel comfortable in the online learning environment provided by my program. 2. I feel my instructors have created a safe online environment in which I can freely express myself. 3. I feel comfortable asking other students in online courses for help. 4. I feel comfortable expressing my opinions and feelings in online courses. 5. I feel comfortable introducing myself in online courses. 6. If I need to, I will ask for help from my classmates. 7. I have no difficulties with expressing my thoughts in my online courses. 8. I can effectively communicate in online courses.
Community	1. I have gotten to know some of the faculty members and classmates well. 2. I feel emotionally attached to other students in my online courses. 3. I can easily make acquaintances in my online courses. 4. I spend a lot of time with my online course peers. 5. My peers have gotten to know me quite well in my online courses. 6. I feel that students in my online courses depend on me.
Facilitation	1. Instructors promote collaboration between students in my online courses. 2. Instructors integrate collaboration tools (e.g., chat rooms, wikis, and group areas) into online course activities. 3. My online instructors are responsive to my questions. 4. I receive frequent feedback from my online instructors. 5. My instructors participate in online discussions. 6. In my online courses, instructors promote interaction between learners.
Interaction and Collaboration	1. I work with others in my online courses. 2. I relate my work to others' work in my online courses. 3. I share information with other students in my online courses. 4. I discuss my ideas with other students in my online courses. 5. I collaborate with other students in my online courses.

While there has been some research in other disciplines using the OSCS (Bowers & Kumar, 2015; Croxton, 2015: Ford & Inan, 2013; Zimmerman & Nimon, 2017); thus far, there has been very little research using this instrument in online language learning contexts. Russell (2018) investigated learner connectedness among 33 university students who were enrolled in an Intermediate-level online Spanish course. The instructor created seven peer support groups with five or six students in each group. Students were required to engage in biweekly discussions in their native language (English). The peer support discussion board was intended to provide an outlet for students to discuss their fears and anxieties related to the online language learning process, to create a forum where students could share their strategies for successful online language learning, as well as a venue to help combat students' false beliefs about language learning (e.g., the false belief that a language can be learned while sleeping). The OSCS was delivered at the end of the course and the results showed that the subscales with the highest mean scores were facilitation and comfort, while the subscale the lowest mean score was community. The mean score for interaction and collaboration was slightly above average.

These results showed that the students perceived the instructor to be present and highly responsive to their needs; in addition, they felt comfortable with the course technologies and with the online learning environment (Russell, 2018). The high score for comfort also indicated that students felt at ease asking their instructor and their peers for help and they also felt comfortable expressing their opinions and thoughts; conversely, the low score in the area of community demonstrated that students did not feel an emotional connection with their peers, nor did they feel that they got to know their peers well in the course (Russell, 2018). These results indicate that students may have desired a deeper level of connection and social presence in the online course. This finding supports the assertions of several scholars who claimed that social presence may be the most difficult type of presence to stimulate in an online course or program (Angelino et al., 2007, Boettcher & Conrad, 2016; Shin, 2003). In Russell's 2018 study, it appears that the peer support discussions may have stimulated cognitive presence, but they failed to foster social presence, as the students may have viewed these discussions as another course task rather than an as opportunity to get to know their peers more deeply. It should be noted that the sample size in Russell's study was small; therefore, the results should be interpreted with caution. Future studies should examine pedagogical interventions using social media tools to determine if students' perceptions of community, as measured by the OSCS, are positively impacted. Given the importance of connectedness in online courses and the negative outcomes— such as high attrition rates—associated with a lack of social presence, this is a rich area for future research.

Using the OSCS as a summative evaluation for an online course or program is an easy way to measure students' perceptions of connectedness. Because the OSCS only contains 25 Likert-scale items, it only takes students a few minutes to complete it. Bolliger and Inan's (2012) OSCS instrument is available in Table 5.4. If instructors wish to use the OSCS to measure perceptions of connectedness among students in their courses or programs, they simply have to contact the authors to request permission. Other instruments that are designed to measure connectedness are the Classroom Community Scale (Rovai, 2002) and the Community of Inquiry Scale (Arbaugh et al., 2008), which is openly available for all users. An article that contains the Community of Inquiry Scale is listed in the suggestions for further reading at the end of this chapter. The OSCS, the Classroom Community Scale, and the Community of Inquiry Scale all measure related constructs.

Revisiting the question: What is connectedness and how can online language educators promote it? In this chapter, the concept of connectedness was defined as students' perceptions of a virtual community (Blanchard, 2007) or the perception that they share a common goal and matter to one another (Liu et al, 2007). While it is relatively easy to define connectedness; in practice, it is quite difficult to stimulate in an online course. As was described previously, the construct of social presence is closely tied to connectedness, and while it is challenging to promote social presence and connectedness in online courses, learners' perceptions of them are likely to make a significant impact on both attrition rates and learning outcomes. More research is urgently needed in this area and the OSCS could be a useful tool to measure connectedness in future studies. Online language instructors would benefit greatly from research that yields better techniques for stimulating social presence and connectedness in their courses.

Research on Assessment in Online Language Education

After designing, developing, and delivering online language instruction, it is important to understand how to assess language learning outcomes appropriately in the online environment. The key questions that the authors examine in this chapter include: What types of assessments are effective for online language teaching and learning and what types of outcomes should be measured? Assessment is an integral part of all online language courses and programs and testing is necessary to evaluate mastery of student learning outcomes, which is typically achieved through formative and summative assessments. Formative assessments are intended to measure students' developing knowledge, skills, and understandings as new learning takes place. These are the frequent small checks, formal or informal, that teachers do to assess whether their students understand new concepts. The results of formative assessments enable teachers to evaluate whether their instruction needs to be modified, if content needs to be re-taught, or if students are ready to move on to the next concept. Summative assessments occur at the end of a unit of instruction and measure how well students have mastered the course learning objectives.

Performance-Based Assessments

In traditional language classrooms, summative assessments are typically paper-and-pencil tests that measure students' mastery of grammar, vocabulary, and cultural content. Most traditional tests contain discrete-point items that focus on form. Discrete-point assessments are those that focus on one aspect of language at a time, often via multiple choice, true/false, and fill-in-the-blank items. According to Adair-Hauck, Glisan, Koda, Swender, and Sandrock (2006), these types of tests are not able to capture fully the outcomes of standards-based instruction in which "learners develop the ability to communicate in another language, gain knowledge and understanding of other cultures, connect with other disciplines and … participate in multilingual communities at home and around the world" (p. 360). Similarly, VanPatten, Trego, and Hopkins (2015) asserted that communicative and proficiency-based instruction is advancing very slowly because of the washback effect of traditional exams. The washback effect refers to the impact that testing has on teaching. If tests are well designed, then the washback is positive; however, if tests are poorly designed, then the washback is negative. VanPatten et al. (2015) asserted that a large part of the problem with traditional language testing is due to, "instructors and students seeing traditional testing as a means of evaluating student progress for the purpose of providing a formal grade. Yet such tests normally do not reflect the constructs underlying either communication or proficiency" (p. 660). In other words, language instructors who attempt to engage in communicative, standards-based language instruction should also strive to assess what students can accomplish with the language in meaningful contexts across the three modes of communication (interpretive, interpersonal, and presentational). The meaningful context is the communication that takes place within the classroom (e.g., student-student and student-teacher interaction), within real-world scenarios that are designed by the teacher and/or the students, or with native speakers of the language outside of the classroom (e.g., within a language exchange or on a conversation platform). Assessments that measure what students can do with language within a meaningful or authentic context are known as performance-based assessments. These types of assessments are effective for measuring learning outcomes within standards-based, communicative language courses and programs. However, many language educators are often unsure about how to design assessments that measure their students' performance in the target language and it is often more straightforward and easier to assess grammatical concepts, vocabulary items, and cultural facts.

Moreover, if language instructors employ a textbook from a commercial publisher, then the publisher typically provides a testing program for both pencil-and-paper and online delivery. The authors have reviewed publisher-created assessments from a wide array of companies and the majority of them are traditional, discrete-point assessments that focus on vocabulary, grammar, and cultural facts. While it is easy to make use of publisher-created testing materials, language instructors need to examine their assessments carefully to determine whether they fit into a communicative, standards-based curriculum. Grammar-based, discrete-point exams are not only a poor fit for communicative classrooms, they also have the potential to create a negative washback on instruction. For example, instructors typically feel pressure to focus their instruction on grammar so that students can succeed on the grammar-based tests. Conversely, performance-based assessments are a good fit for communicative classrooms because students are required to produce goal-directed language using multiple-skills and modes of communication while integrating the course content (Liskin-Gasparro, 1996; Wiggins, 1994, 1998). Liskin-Gasparro (1996) and Wiggins (1998) asserted that performance-based assessments require learners to respond to prompts or tasks, which can reflect authentic, real-world challenges; moreover, students are able to create with language and more than one correct response is possible. Examples of performance-based assessments include presentations, debates, role-plays, and the creation of portfolios, including digital portfolios—see Chapters 1 and 2 for more information on using LinguaFolio for digital portfolios. LinguaFolio is an open-access, e-portfolio tool where language students can create and upload text, audio, and video content; therefore, this tool is ideal for performance-based assessments across the three modes of communication. Moreover, performance-based assessments, using platforms such as LinguaFolio, allow students to express their innovation and creativity, engage in critical thinking and problem-solving, and collaborate and communicate with their peers in the target language.

When using performance-based assessments, it is of the upmost importance to ensure that students understand what is expected of them and how they will be assessed. One way to do this is by using rubrics that describe a range of performance characteristics and the degree to which learners have approached, met, or exceeded the standard of performance. Moreover, rubrics enable instructors to supply feedback for future improvement and they can even provide clues for students about what a strong performance looks like (Shrum & Glisan, 2005). Providing examples and models of the expected performance along with clear rubrics demystifies performance-based assessments for learners (Adair-Hauck et al., 2006).

The ACTFL Performance Descriptors for Language Learners (2015) describe the targeted outcomes of students' language performance at the Novice, Intermediate, and Advanced levels of proficiency across the three modes of communication. The descriptors are applicable to the standards-based language instruction that occurs in traditional, flipped, online, and blended learning environments. They also provide the specific language necessary to assess student performance across the following domains: functions, contexts/content, text type, language control, vocabulary, communication strategies, and cultural awareness. Functions refer to the various tasks that students can perform in the language, such as asking or responding to questions, naming, identifying, narrating, describing, expressing thoughts and preferences, and telling/retelling a story to name a few. Context describes the circumstances in which learners can function (e.g., in a classroom, in a department store, in a restaurant) and content refers to the specific topics that students can both understand and discuss. Text type refers both to the length (e.g., word, sentence, or discourse level) as well as the breadth (e.g., authentic texts supported by visual cues, simple stories, correspondence, reports, or literary texts) of language, while language control describes learners' level of accuracy in the target language. Vocabulary refers to appropriate word choice as well as whether learners have sufficient breadth of vocabulary for the communicative context. Communication strategies describe how well learners are able to maintain conversations and make meaning (see Chapter 3 for a review of circumlocution, word coinage, gesture, and back-channeling cues). Cultural awareness refers to whether the learners' cultural knowledge is reflected in their language use.

Instructors can select the domains that apply to their particular assessment. The descriptors would then need to be adjusted up or down to create a rubric where learners approach, meet, or exceed expectations. For example, the descriptor for presentational speaking or writing at the Novice level under the domain "vocabulary" is the following:

> Produces a number of high frequency words and formulaic expressions; able to use a limited variety of vocabulary on familiar topics
>
> (ACTFL, 2015).

The language listed above describes "target-level performance" (or meets expectations) for Novice learners in presentational speaking or writing regarding learners' use of vocabulary. The following is an example of how the descriptor could be modified to describe the performance of a learner who approaches expectations:

Produces **some** high frequency words **and at least one** formulaic expression; able to use a limited variety of vocabulary on **highly** familiar topics.

Similarly, the descriptor could be adjusted up to describe the performance of a learner who exceeds expectations:

Produces **a large number** of high frequency words and formulaic expressions; able to use **a variety** of vocabulary on familiar topics **and on topics of personal interest.**

Perhaps the most valuable aspect of the ACTFL Performance Descriptors for Language Learners (ACTFL, 2015) is that they help language educators understand what target-level performance should look like at three levels of proficiency—Novice, Intermediate, and Advanced—across the three modes of communication. The descriptors were designed to work hand-in-hand with the ACTFL World-Readiness Standards for Learning Languages (National Standards Collaborative Board, 2015); therefore, using the ACTFL Performance Descriptors (ACTFL, 2015) to create assessment rubrics should help ensure that instructors are engaging in standards-based language instruction. Moreover, if instructors use the backward design model that was described in Chapter 1, then they would create their summative assessment rubrics using the ACTFL Performance Descriptors after selecting their learning objectives, which will facilitate lesson alignment between the standards, objectives, and assessments.

For those teaching English as a second or foreign language, there are WIDA (2018a, 2018b) Performance Definitions for both listening/reading and speaking/writing. These definitions are tied to the WIDA (2012) ELD standards and they provide a description of the language acquisition process from Level 1 (Entering) though Level 6 (Reaching) in the areas of linguistic complexity, language forms and conventions, and vocabulary usage. These definitions can be used to create rubrics for assessing students' language production across the four skills (reading, writing, listening, and speaking). Links for the ACTFL Performance Descriptors for Language Learners (ACTFL, 2015) and the WIDA (2018a, 2018b) Performance Definitions are available in the eResources for this book.

The Integrated Performance Assessment (IPA)

The sections above explained why performance-based assessments are superior to discrete-point assessments as well as how to create rubrics for performance-based assessments that are tied to professional standards. This section of the chapter explores the integrated performance assessment (IPA), which is the gold standard of performance-based assessments for language classrooms. The IPA is an assessment template that was designed by ACTFL with federal grant funding. The purpose of the IPA is to measure learners' attainment of the ACTFL World-Readiness Standards (National Standards Collaborative Board, 2015) while connecting language instruction with assessments (Adair-Hauck et al., 2006). In other words, the IPA is a performance-based assessment template that integrates students' language learning experiences in the classroom with the assessment of their knowledge, skills, and understandings across three modes of communication. Therefore, IPAs are well suited to communicative language classrooms and proficiency-based language programs. Adair-Hauck, Glisan, & Troyan (2015) asserted that the IPA is a multi-task assessment that incorporates three tasks, with each task focusing on one of the modes of communication (interpretive, interpersonal, and presentational). Moreover, all of the tasks are interrelated on a common theme and the tasks build upon each other. Several prominent scholars in the field of world language education have claimed that the IPA design is consistent with how students naturally acquire and use language both in the classroom and in the real world (Glisan, Adair-Hauck, Koda, Sandrock, & Swender, 2003).

The IPA takes a cyclical approach to assessing student learning and it has three distinct phases:

- Phase I is the Interpretive Communication Phase. In this phase, learners read or listen to an authentic text, such as a newspaper article or a radio broadcast. After reading or listening, the students answer interpretive questions that assess their comprehension. To conclude Phase I, the teacher provides students with specific feedback regarding how well they did as well as guidance regarding how they may be able to improve in the future.
- Phase II is the Interpersonal Phase. In this phase, students engage in interpersonal communication that is related to a topic from an authentic text or listening passage from Phase I. It is recommended that Phase II be audio or video recorded. To conclude Phase II, the teacher provides specific feedback and guidance regarding what was done well and what needs to be improved.

- In Phase III, students present their opinions, ideas, and/or research. Students' presentations may take many forms, such as skits, speeches, dramas, essays, brochures, and/or the creation of websites to name a few (Glisan et al., 2003; Glisan, Uribe, & Adair-Hauck, 2007).

IPAs have been shown to have a positive washback on teaching and learning (Adair-Hauck et al., 2006). They also encourage teachers to provide detailed feedback; namely, feedback that explains to students what they did well, what still needs improvement, and what steps they should take to advance their language learning. According to Adair-Hauck and Troyan (2013), simply providing students with a letter grade and a comment such as "well done" are insufficient to help language learners improve their performance (p. 24). Moreover, several studies found that students do not receive sufficient feedback regarding their performance in the target language (Muñoz & Álvarez, 2010; Shohamy, 1992; Shohamy, Donesta-Schmidt, & Ferman, 1996; Wall & Anderson, 1993). Given that the provision of detailed feedback is a key component of each of the three phases of the IPA, language teachers' practices related to the provision of feedback as well as students' understandings of their performance are likely to improve with the use of this assessment template.

Moreover, research at the elementary (Davin, Troyan, Donato, & Hellman, 2011), secondary (Kissau & Adams, 2016), and postsecondary (Glisan et al., 2007; Zapata, 2016) levels indicate that the implementation of IPAs into the second language curriculum has many benefits, such as the provision of detailed descriptions of student performance, the promotion of standards-based language instruction, and the integration of teaching, learning, and assessment. Zapata (2016) also found that postsecondary students were able to make connections between the instruction that they received prior to the IPA and what they learned while using the IPA as an assessment tool.

Davin et al. (2011) asserted that implementing the IPA also has the potential to identify the strengths and weaknesses of language courses and programs; the researchers focused on elementary-level language learners and the findings indicated that students performed the least well on the interpretive phase of the IPA. Interestingly, Glisan et al. (2007) focused on postsecondary students and they had the same findings: students' weakest performance was in the interpretive mode. Davin et al. asserted that students' lack of familiarity with the vocabulary and their lack of exposure to authentic audio, video, and text-based materials may have resulted in lower scores on the interpretive tasks (Davin et al., 2011). Given these results, language educators should strive to include more spoken and written texts into their daily instructional activities.

See Chapter 4 for open-access authentic resources that can be used to engage students in the interpretive mode.

In addition, research studies conducted by Davin et al. (2011) and Kissau and Adams (2016) indicate that teachers may not address each of the three modes of communication equally. Kissau and Adams (2016) found that teachers placed greater emphasis on presentational writing and interpretive reading and paid less attention to presentational speaking, interpersonal speaking, and interpretive listening. The researchers noted that there was a disconnect between teachers' beliefs and their practices because their participants (who were language teachers) expressed a belief that "developing interpretive listening and interpersonal modes of communication should be the focus of introductory language classrooms" and that "presentational writing was the most challenging skill and one that should be introduced later" (Kissau & Adams, 2016, p. 119). However, in practice, the researchers found that one-third to one-half of all assessments in the introductory language classes focused exclusively on presentational writing. This finding indicates that language educators who teach Novice-level learners should strive to teach and assess more in the interpretive and interpersonal modes of communication and less in the presentational writing mode.

Other issues have emerged with respect to implementing the IPA into the world language curriculum, including locating authentic texts that are age appropriate for elementary- and secondary-level students (Adair-Hauck et al, 2006; Kissau & Adams, 2016) and selecting topics and materials that interest and motivate postsecondary students (Martel & Bailey, 2016). Moreover, Martel and Bailey (2016) found that some postsecondary instructors had negative perceptions with respect to implementing IPAs into the curriculum, especially regarding the rubrics that were used in the IPAs for their study. Moreover, some participants expressed the need for more sophisticated IPAs that honor adult learners' intellectual capacities (Martel & Bailey, 2016). Given these findings, university instructors should use caution with IPAs that were developed for secondary-level classrooms, as they may not be appropriate for postsecondary students. Martel and Bailey also point out that in order for IPAs to become implemented widely across postsecondary language courses and programs, a wide array of IPAs need to be developed and openly shared.

Revisiting the question: What types of assessments are effective for online language teaching and learning? The research above indicates that performance-based assessments are appropriate for communicative language instruction, whether it is delivered in traditional, blended, flipped, or online environments. While there are many types of performance-based assessments from which to choose, such as role-plays, skits, and dialogues, the IPA is a performance-based assessment that provides a research-based approach to assessing learning outcomes in language courses across the three modes of communication. IPAs are also able to connect classroom activities and practices with assessment of student learning; in addition, they have a positive washback on instruction and they can help promote standards-based language instruction (Adair-Hauck et al., 2006). While it may be time consuming to design IPAs, the Center for Advanced Research on Language Acquisition (known as CARLA) has published some open-access IPAs that teachers may employ for both commonly and less commonly taught languages. However, for students to be successful on IPAs, language educators should strive to incorporate more interpretive listening and reading activities, as the research studies reviewed above found this to be the weakest area among language students of every age and proficiency level.

Revisiting the question: What types of outcomes should be measured? Language educators should reject discrete-point exams that focus on form in favor of assessing students' performance in the interpretive, interpersonal, and presentational modes of communication. Assessing students' knowledge of grammatical forms, structures, and vocabulary does not ensure that they can actually use the language to communicate. In order to assess communication within a meaningful cultural context, instructors need to assess students' ability to comprehend the authentic texts that they hear or read, their ability to engage in person-to-person communication in real time, and their ability to present topics or ideas in the spoken and written modalities.

Furthermore, language instructors should strive to strike a balance between assessing each of the three modes of communication, but they should take students' proficiency level into account when doing so. The research that was reviewed above suggests that teachers tend to focus on assessing presentational writing, even at the Novice level. Language instructors should place greater emphasis on assessing interpretive listening and interpretive reading among Novice language learners, while emphasizing the assessment of presentational writing among more advanced learners. However, Novice learners should still engage in all three modes of communication during lesson tasks and activities, but it may be more helpful to focus on presentational speaking—rather than on presentational writing—for their assessments until they gain more experience with the language.

The research reviewed above also indicates that students are not receiving enough practice in the interpretive mode with authentic materials. Instructors should strive to include ample instructional activities that focus on the

interpretive mode using authentic materials and resources, which will provide students with sufficient practice prior to assessing their performance on
interpretive listening and reading tasks. Moreover, instructors can ensure that
they are assessing each of the three modes by engaging in backward design
(See Chapter 1) in which the assessments are created first, followed by the
instructional tasks and activities. By creating an equal balance of assessments
across three modes of communication, there should be a positive washback on
instruction. Finally, the LinguaFolio e-portfolio tool enables online language
learners to engage in performance-based assessments, such as IPAs, in a digital environment. The link to this online assessment resource, which is made
available through the Center for Applied Second Language Studies (known as
 CASLS) at the University of Oregon in partnership with NCSSFL, is available
as an eResource.

Conclusion

A wide array of research was reviewed in this chapter on themes such as student
and teacher satisfaction, class size, language anxiety, best practices, social presence, learner connectedness, and assessment. While it was beyond the scope of
this chapter to include all of the research topics that are available on language
learning in blended, flipped, and online learning environments, the authors
chose the topics that they felt were the most relevant for the implementation
of quality instruction in these environments. The studies that were presented in
this chapter and their implications can help online language instructors create
more meaningful, effective, and enjoyable learning experiences for their students and for themselves. Furthermore, recommendations from research were
presented for stimulating social presence and learner connectedness, which
may help decrease attrition rates in online language classes. Implementing the
research findings on best practices also has the potential to decrease attrition
rates and to ensure a smooth delivery of instruction. Moreover, the research
that was reviewed in this chapter may be useful for making administrative
decisions such as setting course caps and determining who is qualified to teach
in online environments, where knowledge of online language pedagogy is
of paramount importance. Finally, research-based assessment techniques were
presented in this chapter. By creating and implementing performance-based
assessments across the three modes of communication, there will be a positive
washback on instruction because these assessments will foster the use of communicative approaches among language instructors in online, blended, and
flipped learning environments.

Key Takeaways

- Online language education can be satisfying for both instructors and students provided that they have appropriate institutional support in terms of technology, infrastructure, and resources and that instructors have academic freedom to design courses using their unique knowledge and expertise in online language pedagogy (Russell & Curtis, 2013).
- Due to the high level of interaction that is needed, online language class sizes should be as small as traditional language class sizes. World language classes should not exceed 15 students, regardless of delivery mode (ACTFL, 2010). While this may not be possible in every instructional context, online language educators should advocate for smaller class sizes and they may do so using the research that was presented in this chapter.
- Online language instructors should be aware that their Novice-level students have equally high levels of foreign language anxiety as their counterparts in face-to-face language courses; however, foreign language anxiety tends to decrease among Intermediate- and Advanced-level learners in the online environment, while remaining equally high across all levels in the traditional, face-to-face environment (Pichette, 2009).
- Online instructors should attempt to include one or two new best practices into their courses with each subsequent iteration after the initial development. They should continually evaluate their course design, development, and delivery and strive for continuous improvement to make their courses more effective, efficient, and enjoyable for both the students and the instructor.
- Social presence is the most difficult presence to foster in the online language learning environment (Boettcher & Conrad, 2016; Garrison et al., 2010; Shea & Bidjerano, 2009; Shin, 2003) and social media tools should be explored to determine if they are able to increase students' perceptions of social presence and connectedness, which can be measured by the OSCS (Bolliger & Inan, 2012).
- Online language instructors should reject discrete-point exams that focus on form in favor of performance-based assessments such as the IPA (Adair-Hauck et al., 2006; VanPatten et al., 2015). This practice will have a positive washback effect on instruction.

Discussion Questions

1. Have you ever taken an online course? If so, was it a satisfying experience? Why (not)? Which aspects of the online course did you find enjoyable and which did you find to be less so? The authors recommend that

everyone who plans to teach an online course should first take a course as an online student. If you have not taken an online course, would you consider doing so? What do you think you would learn from being an online student that could be translated into your online teaching?

2. What is the course cap for language classes at your institution? Do you find this number to be reasonable? If necessary, what could you do to advocate for smaller language class sizes at your institution or in your district, state, or region?

3. Which of the best practices would you incorporate into your online classes? Why did you select them? Do you think it is necessary to incorporate all of the best practices into your online course design for it to be successful? Are there any best practices that you disagree with; and if so, why do you disagree with them?

4. Have you attempted to use any social media tools to facilitate social presence in your online courses? If so, did you measure their effectiveness? Which social media tools do you think would foster your students' perceptions of connectedness? Why do you think that social presence is the most difficult presence to stimulate among online learners across disciplines? Would you be interested in using the OSCS, or another instrument, to measure connectedness in your online courses?

5. Do you use discrete point, focus-on-form tests? After reading this chapter, have you changed your opinion regarding the effectiveness of these types of tests? Have you used performance-based assessments in your traditional or online classes? If so, how effective did you perceive them to be? Have you attempted to assess language learning with an IPA? If not, would you consider implementing IPAs in your classes? Do you think it would be more or less difficult to implement IPAs with online students compared to traditional language students?

Suggestions for Further Reading

Assessment:

Adair-Hauck, B., Glisan, E. W., & Troyan, F. J. (2015). *Implementing integrated performance assessment*. Fairfax, VA: The American Council on the Teaching of Foreign Languages.

Link, S., & Li, J. (Eds). (2018). *Assessment across online language education*. Sheffield, UK: Equinox. CALICO Series: Advances in CALL Research and Practice.

Sandrock, P. (2015). *The keys to assessing language performance*. Fairfax, VA: The American Council on the Teaching of Foreign Languages.

Best Practices:
Boettcher, J., & Conrad, R. M. (2016). *The online teaching survival guide (2ⁿᵈ): Simple and practical pedagogical tips.* San Francisco: Jossey-Bass.
Don, M. R. (2005). An investigation of the fundamental characteristics in quality online Spanish instruction. *CALICO Journal, 22*(2), 285–306.

Social Presence and Connectedness:
Arbaugh, J. B., Cleveland-Innes, M., Diaz, S. R., Garrison, D.R., Ice, P., Richardson, J., & Swan, K.P. (2008). Developing a community of inquiry instrument: Testing a measure of the community of inquiry framework using a multi-institutional sample. *The Internet and Higher Education, 11*(3–4), 133–136.
Bolliger, D. U., & Inan, F. A. (2012). Development and validation of the Online Student Connectedness Survey (OSCS). *International Review of Research in Open and Distance Learning, 13*(3), 41–65.
Rovai, A. P. (2002). Development of an instrument to measure classroom community. *The Internet and Higher Education, 5*(3), 197–211.

References

Adair-Hauck, B., Glisan, E. W., Koda, K, Swender, E. B., & Sandrock, P. (2006). The integrated performance assessment (IPA): Connecting assessment to instruction and learning. *Foreign Language Annals, 39*(3), 359–382. doi: https://doi.org/10.1111/j.1944-9720.2006.tb02894.x
Adair-Hauck, B., Glisan, E. W., & Troyan, F. J. (2015). *Implementing integrated performance assessment.* Alexandria, VA: The American Council on the Teaching of Foreign Languages.
Adair-Hauck, B., & Troyan, F. J. (2013). A descriptive and co-constructive approach to integrated performance assessment feedback. *Foreign Language Annals, 46*(1), 23–44. doi: https://doi.org/10.1111/flan.12017
Alatis, J. (1992). *State university system of Florida foreign language and linguistics program review.* (Report No. FL020250). Tallahassee, FL: Florida State University.
Allen, I. E., Seaman, J., Poulin, R., & Straut, T. T. (2016). *Online report card: Tracking online education in the United States* (Babson Survey Research Group Report), pp. 1–57. Retrieved from http://onlinelearningsurvey.com/reports/onlinereportcard.pdf
American Council on the Teaching of Foreign Languages (ACTFL). (2010). *ACTFL board approved position statements: Maximum class size.* Retrieved from https://www.actfl.org/advocacy/position-statements/maximum-class-size

American Council on the Teaching of Foreign Languages (ACTFL). (2012). *ACTFL proficiency guidelines*. Retrieved from https://www.actfl.org/resources/ actfl-proficiency-guidelines-2012

American Council on the Teaching of Foreign Languages (ACTFL). (2015). *Performance descriptors for language learners* (2nd ed.). Retrieved from https:// cms.azed.gov/home/GetDocumentFile?id=5748a47daadebe04c0b66e64

Angelino, L. M., Williams, F. K., & Natvig, D. (2007). Strategies to engage online students and reduce attrition rates. *Journal of Educators Online, 4*(2), 1–14.

Arbaugh, J. B., Cleveland-Innes, M., Diaz, S. R., Garrison, D. R., Ice, P., Richardson, J., & Swan, K.P. (2008). Developing a community of inquiry instrument: Testing a measure of the community of inquiry framework using a multi-institutional sample. *The Internet and Higher Education, 11*(3–4), 133–136. doi: https://doi.org/10.1016/j.iheduc.2008.06.003

Association of Departments of Foreign Languages (ADFL) (2009). ADFL guidelines for class size and workload for college and university teachers of foreign languages. *ADFL Bulletin, 40*(2–3), 92.

Blake, R., Wilson, N. L., Cetto, M., & Pardo-Ballester, C. (2008). Measuring oral proficiency in distance, face-to-face, and blended classrooms. *Language Learning & Technology, 12*(3), 114–127.

Blanchard, A. L. (2007). Developing a sense of virtual community measure. *Cyberpsychology and Behavior, 10*(6), 827–830. doi: 10.1089/cpb.2007.9946

Boettcher, J., & Conrad, R. M. (2016). *The online teaching survival guide (2ⁿᵈ): Simple and practical pedagogical tips*. San Francisco, CA: Jossey-Bass.

Bolliger, D. U., & Inan, F. A. (2012). Development and validation of the Online Student Connectedness Survey (OSCS). *International Review of Research in Open and Distance Learning, 13*(3), 41–65. doi: https://doi.org/10.19173/ irrodl.v13i3.1171

Bowers, J., & Kumar, P. (2015). Students' perceptions of teaching and social presence: A comparative analysis of face-to-face and online learning environments. *International Journal of Web-Based Learning and Teaching Technologies, 10*(1), 27–44. doi: 10.4018/ijwltt.2015010103

Byram, M. (1997). *Teaching and assessing intercultural communicative competence*. Clevedon, UK: Multilingual Matters.

Chenoweth, N. A., & Murday, K. (2003). Measuring student learning in an online French course. *CALICO Journal, 20*(2), 285–314.

Chenoweth, N. A., Ushida, E., & Murday, K. (2006). Student learning in hybrid French and Spanish Courses: An overview of language online. *CALICO Journal, 24*(1), 115–145.

Cooke-Plagwitz, J. (2008). New directions in CALL: An objective introduction to Second Life. *CALICO Journal, 25*(3), 547–557.

Council of Europe. (2011). *Common European framework of reference for languages: Learning, teaching, assessment.* Cambridge, UK: Cambridge University Press.

Croxton, R. (2015). Professional identity development among graduate library and information studies online learners: A mixed methods study. *Journal of Community and Junior College Libraries, 21*(3–4), 125–141.

Davin, K., Troyan, F. J., Donato, R., & Hellman, A. (2011). Research on the integrated performance assessment in an early foreign language learning program. *Foreign Language Annals, 44*(4), 605–625.

Don, M. R. (2005). An investigation of the fundamental characteristics in quality online Spanish instruction. *CALICO Journal, 22*(2), 285–306.

Dunlap, J. C., & Lowenthal, P. R. (2009). Tweeting the night away: Using Twitter to enhance social presence. *Journal of Information Systems Education, 202,* 129–135.

Ford, S., & Inan, F. (2013). Students' perceived feelings of connectedness in online community college mathematics courses. Proceedings of the international conference of the *Society for Information Technology & Teacher Education.* Chesapeake, VA: Association for the Advancement of Computing in Education (AACE).

Fornara, F., & Lomicka, L. (2019). Using visual social media in language learning to investigate the role of social presence. *CALICO Journal, 36*(3), 184–203.

Garrison, D. R., Anderson, T., & Archer, W. (2000). Critical inquiry in a text-based environment: Computer conferencing in higher education. *The Internet and Higher Education, 2*(2–3), 1–19.

Garrison, D. R., Cleveland-Innes, M., & Fung, T. S. (2010). Exploring causal relationships among teaching, cognitive and social presence: Student perceptions of the community of inquiry framework. *The Internet and Higher Education, 13*(1–2), 31–36.

Glisan, E. W., Adair-Hauck, B., Koda, K., Sandrock, P., & Swender, E. (2003). *ACTFL integrated performance assessment.* Yonkers, NY: American Council on the Teaching of Foreign Languages.

Glisan, E. W., Uribe, D., & Adair-Hauck, B. (2007). Research on integrated performance assessment at the post-secondary level: Student performance across the modes of communication. *The Canadian Modern Language Review, 64*(1), 39–68.

Goertler, S. (2011). Blended and open/online learning: Adapting to a changing world of foreign language teaching. In N. Arnold, & L. Ducate (Eds.), *Present and future promises of CALL: From theory and research to new directions in language teaching* (pp. 471–502). San Marcos, TX: CALICO.

Harker, M., & Koutsantoni, D. (2005). Can it be as effective? Distance versus blended learning in a web-based EAP programme. *ReCALL, 17*(2), 197–216. doi: 10.1017/S095834400500042X

Haythornthwaite, C., Kazmer, M. M., Robins, J., & Shoemaker, S. (2000). Community development among distance learners: Temporal and technological dimensions. *Journal of Computer-Mediated Communication, 6*(1), 0. doi: https://doi.org/10.1111/j.1083-6101.2000.tb00114.x

Herbert, M. (2006). Staying the course: A study in online student satisfaction and retention. *Online Journal of Distance Learning Administration, 9*(4), 0.

Heyman, E. (2010). Overcoming student retention issues in higher education online programs. *Online Journal of Distance Learning Administration, 13*(4), 0. Retrieved from https://www.westga.edu/~distance/ojdla/winter134/heyman134.html

Horne, K. M. (1970). Optimum class size for intensive language instruction. *The Modern Language Journal, 54*(3), 189–195.

Horwitz, E. K., Horwitz, M., & Cope, J. (1986). Foreign language classroom anxiety. *Modern Language Journal, 70*(2), 124–132.

Kanuka, H., & Jugdev, K. (2006). Distance education MBA students: An investigation into the use of an orientation course to address academic and social integration issues. *Open Learning, 21*(2), 153–166.

Kissau, S., & Adams, M. J. (2016). Instructional decision making and IPAs: Assessing the modes of communication. *Foreign Language Annals, 49*(1), 105–123. doi: https://doi.org/10.1111/flan.12184

Krashen, S. (1980). The input hypothesis. In J. Alatis (Ed.), *Current issues in bilingual education* (pp. 175–183). Washington D.C.: Georgetown University Press.

Krashen, S. (1981). *Second language acquisition and second language learning.* Oxford: Pergamon.

Krashen, S. (1982). *Principles and practice in second language acquisition.* Oxford, UK: Pergamon.

Krashen, S. (1985). *The input hypothesis: Issues and implications.* New York, NY: Longman.

Lafford, B. (2006). The effects of study abroad vs. classroom contexts on Spanish SLA: Old assumptions, new insights and future research directions. In C. A. Klee & T. L. Face (Eds), *Selected proceedings of the 7th conference on the acquisition of Spanish and Portuguese as first and second languages* (pp. 1–25). Somerville, MA: Cascadilla.

Liskin-Gasparro, J. E. (1996). Assessment: From content standards to student performance. In R. C. Lafayette (Ed.), *National standards: A catalyst for reform,* (pp. 169–196). Lincolnwood, IL: NTC/Contemporary. (ACTFL Foreign Language Education Series)

Liu, X., Magjuka, R. J., Bonk, C. J., & Lee, S. (2007). Does sense of community matter? An examination of participants' perceptions of building learning communities in online courses. *Quarterly Review of Distance Education, 8*(1), 9–24.

Lombard, M., & Ditton, T. B. (1997). At the heart of it all: The concept of presence. *Journal of Computer-Mediated Communication, 3*(2), 0–0. doi: https://doi.org/10.1111/j.1083-6101.1997.tb00072.x

Lomicka, L., & Lord, G. (2012). A tale of tweets: Analyzing microblogging among language learners. *System, 40*, 48–63. doi: https://doi.org/10.1016/j.system.2011.11.001

Long, M. H. (1985). Input and second language acquisition theory. In S. Gass & C. Madden (Eds.), *Input in second language acquisition* (pp. 377–393). Rowley, MA: Newbury House.

Long, M. H. (1996). The role of the linguistic environment in second language acquisition. In W. Ritchie & T. Bhatia (Eds.), *Handbook of second language acquisition* (pp. 413–468). San Diego, CA: Academic Press.

Lord, G., & Lomicka, L. (2014). Twitter as a tool to promote community among language teachers. *JTATE, 22*(2), 187–212.

Martel, J., & Bailey, K. (2016). Exploring the trajectory of an educational innovation: Instructors' attitudes toward IPA implementation in a postsecondary intensive summer language program. *Foreign Language Annals, 49*(3), 530–543. doi: https://doi.org/10.1111/flan.12210

Moneypenny, D. B., & Aldrich, R. (2016). Online and face-to-face language learning: A comparative analysis of oral proficiency in introductory Spanish. *Journal of Educators Online, 13*(2), 105–133.

Morgan, L. Z. (2000). Class size and second language instruction at the post-secondary level: A survey of the literature and a plea for further research. *Italica, 77*(4), 449–472.

Muñoz, A. P., & Álvarez, M. E. (2010). Washback of an oral assessment system in the EFL classroom. *Language Testing, 27*, 33–49.

Murphy-Judy, K., & Johnshoy, M. (2017). Who's teaching which languages online? A report based on national surveys. *The IALLT Journal, 47*(1), 137–167.

National Council of State Supervisors for Languages, & American Council on the Teaching of Foreign Languages (NCSSFL-ACTFL). (2017). *NCSSFL-ACTFL can-do statements.* Retrieved from https://www.actfl.org/resources/ncssfl-actfl-can-do-statements

National Education Association. (2008). *Class size reduction: A proven reform strategy.* Retrieved from http://www.nea.org/assets/docs/PB08_ClassSize08 .pdf

National Standards Collaborative Board. (2015). *World-readiness standards for learning languages* (4th ed.). Alexandria, VA: Author.

North, B. (2006, March). The common European framework of reference: Development, theoretical and practical issues. Paper presented at the symposium, *A new direction in foreign language education: The potential of the common European framework of reference for languages.* Japan: Osaka University of Foreign Studies.

Orellana, A. (2006). Class size and interaction in online courses. *The Quarterly Review of Distance Education, 7*(3), 229–248.

Peterson, M. (2011). Towards a research agenda for the use of three-dimensional virtual words in language learning. *CALICO Journal, 29*(1), 67–80.

Pichette, F. (2009). Second language anxiety and distance language learning. *Foreign Language Annals, 42*(1), 77–93.

Rourke, L., Anderson, T., Garrison, D. R., & Archer, W. (2001). Assessing social presence in asynchronous, text-based computer conferencing. *Journal of Distance Education, 14*(3), 50–71.

Rovai, A. P. (2002). Development of an instrument to measure classroom community. *The Internet and Higher Education, 5*(3), 197–211.

Russell, V. (2016, May). Promoting online language learners' perceptions of connectedness through pedagogical innovations. Paper presented at the *Computer assisted language instruction consortium (CALICO) conference.* East Lansing, MI: Michigan State University.

Russell, V. (2018). Assessing the effect of pedagogical interventions on success rates and on students' perceptions of connectedness online. In S. Link & J. Li (Eds.), *Assessment across online language education* (pp. 49–70). Sheffield, UK: Equinox. (CALICO Series: Advances in CALL Research and Practice.)

Russell, V., & Curtis, W. (2013). Comparing a large- and small-scale online language class: An examination of teacher and learner perceptions. *The Internet and Higher Education, 6,* 1–13.

Satar, H. M. (2015). Sustaining multimodal language learner interactions online. *CALICO Journal, 32*(3), 480–507. doi: 10.1558/cj.v32i3.26508

Seaman, J. E., Allen, I. E., & Seaman, J. (2018). *Grade increase: Tracking distance education in the United States* (Babson survey research group report), pp. 1–45. Retrieved from http://onlinelearningsurvey.com/reports/ gradeincrease.pdf

Schroeder, R. (2002). Social interaction in virtual environments: Key issues, common themes, and a framework for research. In R. Schroeder (Ed.),

The social life of avatars: Presence and interaction in shared virtual environments (pp. 1–18). London, UK: Springer-Verlag.

Schroeder, R. (2008). Defining virtual worlds and virtual environments. *Journal of Virtual Worlds Research, 1*(1), 2–3.

Shea, P., & Bidjerano, T. (2009). Cognitive presence and online learner engagement: A cluster analysis of the community of inquiry framework. *Journal of Computing in Higher Education, 21*(3), 199–217. doi: 10.1007/s12528-009-9024-5

Shieh, R. S., Gummer, E., & Niess, M. (2008). Perspectives of the instructor and the students. *TechTrends, 52*(6), 61–68.

Shin, N. (2003). Transactional presence as a critical predictor of success in distance learning. *Distance Education, 24*(1), 69–86.

Shohamy, E. (1992). Beyond proficiency testing: A diagnostic feedback testing model for assessing foreign language learning. *Modern Language Journal, 76*, 513–521.

Shohamy, E., Donitsa-Schmidt, S., & Ferman, I. (1996). Test impact revisited: Washback effect over time. *Language Testing, 13*, 298–317.

Shrum, J. L., & Glisan, E. W. (2005). *Teacher's handbook: Contextualized language instruction* (3rd ed.). Boston, MA: Thomson Heinle.

Swain, M. (1985). Communicative competence: Some roles of comprehensible input and comprehensible output in its development. In S. Gass, & C. Madden (Eds.), *Input and second language acquisition* (pp. 235–253). Rowley, MA: Newbury House.

Swain, M. (1993). The output hypothesis: Just speaking and writing aren't enough. *The Canadian Modern Language Review, 50*, 158–164.

Swain, M. (1995). Three functions of output in second language learning. In G. Cook & B. Seidlhofer (Eds.), *Principle and practice in applied linguistics: Studies in honour of H. G. Widdowson* (pp. 125–144). Oxford, UK: Oxford University Press.

Swain, M. (1998). Focus on form through conscious reflection. In C. Doughty, & J. Williams (Eds.), *Focus on form in classroom second language acquisition* (pp. 85–113). Cambridge, UK: Cambridge University Press.

Taft, S. H., Kesten, K., El-Banna, M. M. (2019). One size does not fit all: Toward an evidence-based framework for determining online course enrollment sizes in higher education. *Online Learning, 23*(3), 188–233. doi: 10.24059/olj.v23i3.1534

U.S. Department of State Foreign Service Institute. (n. d.). *Language leaning timelines.* Retrieved from https://www.state.gov/foreign-language-training/

Ushida, E. (2005). The role of students' attitudes and motivation in second language learning in online language courses. *CALICO Journal, 23*(1), 49–78.

VanPatten, B., Trego, D., & Hopkins, W. P. (2015). In-class vs. online testing in university-level language courses: A research report. *Foreign Language Annals, 48*(4), 659–668. doi: https://doi.org/10.1111/flan.12160

Vorobel, O., & Kim, D. (2012). Language teaching at a distance: An overview of research. *CALICO Journal, 29*(3), 548–562.

Wall, D., & Alderson, J. C. (1993). Examining washback: The Sri Lankan impact study. *Language Testing, 10*, 41–69.

Wiggins, G. (1994). Toward more authentic assessment of language performances. In C. Hancock (Ed.), *Teaching, testing, and assessment: Making the connection* (pp. 69–85). Lincolnwood, IL: National Textbook Co.

Wiggins, G. (1998). *Educative assessment.* San Francisco, CA: Jossey-Bass.

World-Class Instructional Design and Assessment (WIDA). (2012). *Amplification of the English language development standards kindergarten–grade 12.* Retrieved from https://wida.wisc.edu/sites/default/files/resource/2012-ELD-Standards.pdf

World-Class Instructional Design and Assessment (WIDA). (2016). *K-12 can do descriptors, key uses edition.* Retrieved from https://wida.wisc.edu/teach/can-do/descriptors

World-Class Instructional Design and Assessment (WIDA). (2018a). *Performance definitions: Listening and reading grades K-12.* Retrieved from https://wida.wisc.edu/sites/default/files/resource/Performance-Definitions-Receptive-Domains.pdf

World-Class Instructional Design and Assessment (WIDA). (2018b). *Performance definitions: Speaking and writing grades K-12.* Retrieved from https://wida.wisc.edu/sites/default/files/resource/Performance-Definitions-Expressive-Domains.pdf

Yamada, M., & Akahori, K. (2007). Social presence in synchronous CMC-based language learning: How does it affect the productive performance and consciousness of learning objectives? *Computer Assisted Language Learning, 20*(1), 37–65. doi: http://dx.doi.org/10.1080/09588220601118503

Yi, H. (2008). The effect of class size reduction on foreign language learning: A case study. *Language and Linguistics Compass, 2*(6), 1089–1108.

Young, D. J. (2008). An empirical investigation of the effects of blended learning on student outcomes in a redesigned intensive Spanish course. *CALICO Journal, 26*(1), 160–181.

Zapata, G. C. (2016). University students' perceptions of Integrated Performance Assessments and the connection between classroom learning and assessment. *Foreign Language Annals, 49*(1), 93–104. doi: https://doi.org/10.1111/flan.12176

Zimmerman, T. D., & Nimon, K. (2017). The Online Student Connectedness Survey: Evidence of initial construct validity. *The International Review of Research in Open and Distributed Learning, 18*(3). doi: https://doi.org/10.19173/irrodl.v18i3.2484

Conclusion

Introduction

In this book, the authors set out to break down the process of designing, developing, and delivering highly effective language courses for online, blended, and flipped learning environments. They also presented valuable resources for online professional development and they pointed readers to a multitude of open educational digital resources that—in most cases—can be downloaded, copied, and redistributed without infringing on copyright laws. The authors also reviewed key strands of research that have implications for online course delivery. Moreover, many practical tips and suggestions are interwoven throughout the book for online course development and delivery. Chapter 1 explained the instructional design process in detail as well as the needs analysis that must precede it. Chapter 2 focused on how to develop online courses using technology tools and applications. It is important to remember that the authors did not advocate the use of any particular tool or application, as these will continue to change and evolve over time; rather, they emphasized the importance of understanding the sound instructional design principles that were presented in Chapters 1 and 2. As technology changes and new tools emerge, language educators who understand the design principles that underpin quality online course development and delivery will be able to adapt new tools and applications to meet the needs of their courses and students. In Chapter 3, the authors explained the tenets of communicative language teaching and provided a number of strategies (with examples) for teaching communicatively online. This chapter also emphasized the importance of using professional standards and building online lessons based upon what students can actually do at their given proficiency level. Examples of online activities that foster interpretive, interpersonal, and presentational communication within a meaningful cultural context were also presented in Chapter 3. Chapter 4 focused on online professional development and open educational resources. The authors also provided information regarding how to connect with a community of online language educators. Connecting with others who teach language online and/or entering into a mentor/mentee relationship are powerful ways to engage in professional development. In Chapter 5, the authors presented research findings on online language teaching and their pedagogical implications. They also gave clear examples of how research can be incorporated into practice. In addition, Chapter 5 included the research on assessment and assessment strategies for effectively measuring learning outcomes in standards-based, communicative language courses. The authors hope that those who read this book will come away with a solid understanding of basic online language course design as well as how to implement an effective, engaging, and efficient online, blended, or flipped language course or program.

Those who deliver instruction online need to be ready to meet the challenges of rapidly changing technologies and instructional contexts. Therefore, the authors suggest that they participate in regular technology training sessions, attend professional development activities that focus on online language pedagogy (e.g., conferences, workshops, webinars), and they should also engage in communities of practice—either at their institutions, online, or both—where they can connect with others who are using educational technologies to teach online, blended, or flipped language classes. Having opportunities to share and interact with other practitioners who deliver instruction online is of paramount importance in our field, especially if the engagement is with those who teach the same language in similar contexts and with learners at similar levels. As professional online language educators, our best resource is each other. At conferences, workshops, and webinars, it is possible to see the creative ways that our peers are using new technologies to engage learners. Moreover, these types of presentations often provide tips to avoid problems and pitfalls when implementing a new technology tool or application.

Successful online language educators must be willing to continually learn as well as to experiment with new technologies. Similar to the effort that it takes to keep up one's language skills, it takes equal effort to stay on top of the latest technologies. When the authors first started teaching language over thirty years ago, the Internet did not exist and classroom technologies consisted of tape recorders, VCRs, and overhead projectors. Many of our young readers will likely be unfamiliar with those outdated technologies! Distance learning consisted of mailing (through snail mail) content, feedback, and exams. It was impossible to imagine our present world thirty years ago; however, those who clung to antiquated technologies and methods were left behind a long time ago. What is clear is that all of us must be lifelong learners who seek out and use new technologies that are able to meet the diverse needs of today's students.

Future Directions

What Is the Future of Online Language Teaching?

By all accounts, it appears that online courses and programs will continue to grow at both the K-12 and postsecondary levels across the globe. Currently, online enrollments in the United States are outpacing traditional, brick-and-mortar enrollments at the postsecondary level (J. E. Seaman, Allen, & J. Seaman, 2018) and they are expanding rapidly at the secondary level for credit recovery, AP course delivery, dual enrollment, and/or for extending the school day (Picciano & J. Seaman, 2010). A recent survey in K-12 online education showed that 21 states currently have virtual public schools with 1,015,760 total enrollments as of early 2020 (Digital Learning Collaborative, 2020, pp. 18–19). This figure does not include private virtual schools or schools that offer blended/hybrid courses; therefore, the number of online enrollments in K-12 education is likely to be even higher. Moreover, the most recently reported growth rate for online enrollments among K-12 students is 6%, with world languages comprising 13% of K-12 enrollments in state virtual schools (Digital Learning Collaborative, 2019, p. 9). Among the largest of the state virtual schools in the United States are the North Carolina Virtual Public School, with over 100,000 enrollments during the 2018–2019 school year—making it the second largest state-led virtual school—and the Florida Virtual School, which reported enrolling over 200,000 K-12 students during the 2018–2019 academic year (with 6,469 K-5 students, 14,160 students in grades 6-8, and 194,876 students in grades 9-12); they also reported graduating 762 full-time online students in 2019, making it the largest state-led virtual school in the United States (Florida Virtual School, 2019, p. 3).

With respect to higher education, more than 6 million postsecondary students in the United States take at least one class online and the growth rate for online enrollments continues to outpace traditional enrollments

(Allen, J. Seaman, Poulin, & Straut, 2016; J. E. Seaman et al., 2018). In fact, online enrollments in higher education have consistently grown over the past fourteen years while enrollments in traditional, face-to-face courses have declined (Allen et al., 2018). Furthermore, increases in online enrollments do not appear to be affected by expansions or contractions in the economy, even though on-campus enrollments are impacted significantly by these factors (Palvia et al., 2018). As many colleges and universities across the United States are facing budget cuts, declining enrollments, and increased pressure to reduce the cost of tuition to make college more affordable, many institutions are developing and offering online courses and programs to attract new students. Graduate-level enrollments in online courses and programs are likely to continue to flourish as we move into the future. Most graduate students are busy, working professionals with families and other life commitments that preclude them from taking classes on a traditional campus. The authors predict that this is a rich area for future grown in online education.

Online learning is also expanding rapidly worldwide, with Open University being a leader among online institutions globally. It currently serves more than 168,000 students in the United Kingdom and in 157 different countries (Open University, 2020). Open University is also one of the oldest distance education institutions, as it celebrated its 50th anniversary in 2019. In India, 1.6 million students are currently engaged in online learning and this number is predicted to grow to 9.6 million by 2021 (Palvia et al., 2018). Similarly, according to Li and Chen (2019), online enrollments in higher education in China have been growing rapidly since the Internet penetration rate surged to 54.3% in 2017; it was only at 1.7% in 2000 (p. 8). At present, 6.45 million higher education students in China are enrolled in online learning (Li & Chen, 2019, p. 9). In Australia and in parts of the developing world, online learning is also growing, but at a slower pace due to a lack of infrastructure and a lack of high bandwidth connectivity in remote locations (Palvia et al., 2018). As technology improves and more users have access to the Internet, increased growth in these countries and regions is likely to occur. Mobile learning may also be a viable solution for locations with poor infrastructure, especially as bandwidths of 6G and beyond become available.

Given the statistics listed above, the outlook for online education in the United States and worldwide is very promising. All indicators point to a need for more language educators who are qualified to deliver instruction online.

How Will Technology Impact Online Language Teaching in the Future?

Future technologies will enable online language educators to create more effective, efficient, and personalized learning experiences for their students. Some of the technologies that will likely play a role in future online course design, development, and delivery include mobile platforms, adaptive learning software (based on data analytics), artificial intelligence (AI), virtual reality (e.g., virtual worlds), augmented reality (e.g., Google Glass), and gamification.

Most of today's online learners want to access their course materials on their mobile phones. While it is now possible to view most content without distortions and pixilation on mobile devices, we have not yet reached the point where online instructors can easily build courses using mobile platforms. As technology improves, this is one area that is likely to make online course development easier—and more portable—for online instructors in the future.

Adaptive learning software may likely make the biggest impact on student learning outcomes in the future, as it will allow instructors to tailor their materials and assessments to meet each student's unique needs and preferred learning styles. Data analytic tools make this type of innovation possible because each student's progress can be tracked, with weaknesses pinpointed in real time. Moreover, adaptive learning software can create tailor-made activities and programs of study to help students practice, learn, and master areas where they are weak. When adaptive learning software is combined with AI, students can receive one-on-one tutoring anyplace/anytime on a large scale. Bernard (2017) reported that AI-based tutoring has already been used by the U.S. Navy with their Education Dominance platform for instructional technology training; the platform functions like a human tutor because it carefully monitors and tracks each student's progress and it tailors the student's assessments accordingly. Adaptive learning software and AI will enable online language educators to better differentiate their instruction in the future, as these technologies will be able to pinpoint learners' exact proficiency levels and proficiency gains in real time. Moreover, these technologies will be able to generate aural and written input materials that are just beyond students' current level for optimal language acquisition to take place (Krashen, 1985). In addition, it is likely that adaptive learning software will replace traditional textbooks in the future (Bernard, 2017).

Virtual meeting rooms and conversation platforms revolutionized online language teaching in the last decade because instructors and students could easily meet and interact synchronously using a web cam, microphone, and speakers. While real-time communication is facilitated through these devices, they can be clunky and using them is less natural than face-to-face interactions. Virtual reality and augmented reality will likely improve virtual meeting spaces in the future to create more personalized and realistic learning environments.

Future technologies may improve online language curricula through gamification, which is defined as applying or introducing the elements of games into non-game contexts such as language courses. According to Oxford Analytica (2016), the primary appeal of gamifying the curriculum revolves around the four freedoms that it creates for learners, which include the freedom to fail (with little consequence), the freedom to experiment (leading to exploration and discovery), the freedom to self-express (or to assume different identities and perspectives), and the freedom from effort (in other words, intensive activity can be followed by periods of inactivity to foster reflection and learning). Some other benefits of gamification include goal setting, social engagement, rapid feedback, collective responsibility, and incremental progression systems (e.g., challenges and quests). Moreover, gamification incorporates visual symbols of achievement (e.g., badges) to keep learners focused on the end goal and not just on the immediate task before them. Entire courses could be built around gamification and virtual and/or augmented reality, which could create powerful online experiences for learners.

Concluding Remarks

The future of online language education appears to be very promising, with enrollments in online courses and programs increasing worldwide. In addition, new technologies will continue to improve instructors' ability to design, develop, and deliver quality online language courses. Data analytics and adaptive learning software are especially promising, as data on learning outcomes from prior courses as well as data that pinpoints each learner's strengths and weaknesses can better inform the instructional design process, which will enable instructors to personalize and tailor their courses for each student.

Some pitfalls to avoid in the future include resisting administrative decisions to enroll large numbers of students in online language classes, where a high level of student-student and student-teacher interaction are needed for successful language learning to take place. In addition, online language educators should abandon discrete-point tests that focus on form in favor of performance-based assessments, such as IPAs, which are a better fit for communicative online language learning environments because students can create digital portfolios to showcase their interpretive, interpersonal, and presentational communication skills. Finally, those who transition from teaching in traditional environments to teaching online should insist upon receiving sufficient professional development in online language pedagogy and in the instructional technologies that they will need to deliver their courses effectively online. Keeping these pitfalls in mind will help ensure success for both online language students and instructors alike.

References

Allen, I. E., Seaman, J., Poulin, R., & Straut, T. T. (2016). *Online report card: Tracking online education in the United States* (Babson Survey Research Group Report), pp. 1–57. Retrieved from http://onlinelearningsurvey.com/reports/onlinereportcard.pdf

Bernard, Z. (2017, December 27). Here's how technology is shaping the future of education. *Business Insider.* Retrieved from https://www.businessinsider.com/how-technology-is-shaping-the-future-of-education-2017-12

Digital Learning Collaborative. (2019). *Snapshot 2019: A review of K–12 online, blended, and digital learning.* Retrieved from https://www.digitallearningcollab.com/snapshot-pubs

Digital Learning Collaborative. (2020). *Snapshot 2020: A review of K–12 online, blended, and digital learning.* Retrieved from https://www.digitallearningcollab.com/snapshot-pubs

Florida Virtual School. (2019). *Florida virtual school district enrollment summary: 2018–19.* Retrieved from https://www.flvs.net/docs/default-source/district/flvs-district-enrollment-summary.pdf?sfvrsn=5c9a7a2a_12

Krashen, S. (1985). *The input hypothesis: Issues and implications.* New York, NY: Longman.

Li, W., & Chen, N. (2019). China. In O. Zawacki-Richterm & A. Qayyum (Eds.), *Open and distance education in Asia, Africa and the Middle East* (Springer Briefs in Education, pp. 7–22). Singapore: Springer.

Open University. (2020). *Facts and figures.* Retrieved from http://www.open.ac.uk/about/main/strategy-and-policies/facts-and-figures

Oxford Analytica. (2016). *Gamification and the future of education.* Retrieved from https://www.worldgovernmentsummit.org/api/publications/document?id=2b0d6ac4-e97c-6578-b2f8-ff0000a7ddb6

Palvia, S., Aeron, P., Gupta, P., Mahapatra, D., Parida, R., Rosner, R., & Sindi, S. (2018). Online education: Worldwide status, challenges, trends, and implications. *Journal of Global Information Technology Management, 21*(4), 233–241. doi:10.1080/1097198X.2018.1542262

Picciano, A. G., & Seaman, J. (2010). *Class connections: High school reform and the role of online learning* (Babson Survey Research Group Report), pp. 1–28. Retrieved from https://www.onlinelearningsurvey.com/reports/class-connections.pdf

Seaman, J. E., Allen, I. E., & Seaman, J. (2018). *Grade increase: Tracking distance education in the United States* (Babson Survey Research Group Report), 1–45. Retrieved from http://onlinelearningsurvey.com/reports/gradeincrease.pdf

Index

accessibility 25, 27, 58–9, 124, 151; for dyslexia 78–9, 105; for visual, hearing, mobility impairment 24, 122, 149, 150; *see also* universal design for learning

ACTFL as association 2, 28, 33, 37, 38, 121, 140, 141, 146, 147, 152–56, 167, 186–87, 203–4, 208, 218, 232, 252, 257; *see also* ACTFL Distance Learning SIG; Can-Do; intercultural reflection tool; Mentoring Program for Online Language Teachers; performance; standards

ACTFL Distance Learning Special Interest Group (DL SIG) 2, 185, 203, 204; *see also* mentoring program

activity 3, 6, 7, 12, 29, 33, 38, 40, 44, 47, 49–50, 54, 55, 62, 76, 77, 78, 80, 82, 84, 85, 87, 89, 90, 92–110 113–15, 118, 119, 123, 134–36, 138, **143**, 155–59, 161–71, 185, 188, 189, 194–96, 199–200, 207, **227**, 229 233–34, 244, **245**, 253, 255–56, 269, 273; open-ended **143**, 159, 161

Adair-Hauck, B. 142, 177, 248, 250, 252–55, 258

Adams, M. J. 253–54

adaptive learning 272–73

ADDIE 4–6, 10–14, 23, 31–2, 60, 62–3, 65, 75, 118, 123

adult education/learners 10, 28, 52, 114 146, 173, 254

affordance(s) 3, 34, 59, 121

Allen, I. E. 133, 209, 213, 214, 270, 271,

American Council on the Teaching of Foreign Languages; *see* ACTFL

analytics 62, 78, 121, 272, 273

Analyze-Design-Develop-Implement-Evaluation design model; *see* ADDIE

Anderson, T. 47, 94, 239

Anxiety; *see* language learning anxiety

Arabic: as language 17, 153, 189, 198, 199–200, 201, 202, 214, **237**; *see also* less commonly taught languages

Archer, W. 47, 239

artificial intelligence (AI) 5, 121, 272

assessment(s) 4, 5, 6, 12, 26, 28, 32, 38–40, 41, 43, 45, 48, 52–61, 62–4, 76–7, 85, 89, 90, 91, 93–4, 110, 111, 114, 115, 116–19, 124, 153, 154, 155, 156, 157, 159, 172–73, 186, 188, 192, **193**, 194, 197, **223**, 224, 228, 230, 233–34, 240, 244, 247–56, 257, 258, 269, 272, 274; formative 12, 43, 63, 14, 116, 118, 153, 172, 247; summative 12, 54, 55, 63, 65; 114, 116, 118, 153, 172, 244, 246, 247, 248, 251; *see also* CEFR; integrated performance assessment; performance-based assessments; WIDA

assignment(s) 12, 26, 32, 40, 41, 45, 59, 76, 80, 91–2, 94, 98, 116, 124, 135, 166, 216, 223–24, 228, 230, 231, 234, 238, 240

asynchronous delivery 17, 22, 27, 38, 43–4, 49, 50, 85, 87, 99, 100, 102, 104, **107–108**, 110, 114, 116, 151, 161, 165, 174, 175, 184, 202, 203, **227**, 229–30

authentic material(s) 42, 46, 106, 114, 115, 116, 137–38, 141, 142, **143**, 162–64, 167–69, 170, 176, 177, **193**, 229, 231, 250, 252, 253, 254, 255, 256

autonomy 4, 9, 26, 27, 40, 76, 78, 101, 121, 123, 124
avatar 48, *96*, 153, 243

Basic Online Language Design and Delivery Collaboratory; *see* BOLDD
Bates, A. 21, 40, 66, 89, 20, 120, 125
behaviorism 12, 158; *see also* grammar
best practices 11, 46, 50, 60, 63, 67, 75, 94, 116, 196, 202, 204, 207, 222, 223, 226, **227**, 231, 238, 239, 256, 257, 259; *see also* effectiveness
Blackboard; *see* learning management system
blended learning; *see* hybrid learning/classroom
blog 82, 105, *107*, 110, 121, 170, 229, 240; microblog 240, 243, 263
Bloom's Taxonomy 33, *42*, 52, 108, *109*
Boettcher, J. 28, 49, 226, **227**, 228 230–40, 246, 257, 259; *see also* Conrad, R. M.
BOLDD 2, 10, 20, 25, 62, 185, 186, 202, 203; survey 21, 29, 31
Bolliger, D. U. 244, **245**, 246, 259; *see also* Inan, F. A.; Online Student Connectedness Survey (OSCS)
Byram, M. 131, 156, 232

Canale, M. 134, 135, 137, 177
Can-Do: descriptors (WIDA) 33, 54, 157, 173, 232, 233; statements (NCSSFL-ACTFL) 33, 38, 40, 43, 46, 54, 55, 58, 65, 93, **94**, 116, 155–57, 158, 172–173, 232, 233
Canvas; *see* learning management system
caption/captioning 59, 112, 143, 149, 150, 162
CEFR 28, 33, 38, 53, 115, 152, 154, 181, 237; *see also* assessment; descriptors; standards
cell phones; *see* mobile devices; smartphone
Center for Advanced Research on Language Acquisition (CARLA) 38, *39*, 43, *55*, *56*, *133*, 169, 192–97, 207, 209, 255; summer institutes 192, 196, 207, 209; technology integration modules 193–96; transitioning to teaching languages online (TTLO) course 196
Center for Applied Second Language Studies (CASLS) 38, 40, 42, 43, 48, 92, *93*, *94*, **94**, 208, 256
Center for Open Educational Resources in Language Learning (COERLL) 145, 197, 207; open educational resources (OER) 48, 106, 115, 145, 197–99, 201; resources for language pedagogy 145, 197, 198, 199–200
Chinese: as language 17, 79, 153, 163, 188, 189, 198, 201, 202, 214, 237; as market 34, 84; *see also* less commonly taught language

classroom; *see* hybrid classroom/learning (includes blended); face-to-face (brick-and-mortar, traditional); online classroom/course
class size 6, 16, 19, 213, 215–18, 256–60, 262–66, 269; CLT; *see* communicative language teaching
commercial provider 14, 17, 48, 59, 106, 114–115, 122, 249
Common European Framework of Reference; *see* CEFR
Communication; *see* mode of communication
Communicative Language Teaching (CLT) 5, 7, 28, 29, 40, 44, 116, 140–44, 172, 175, 176, 177, 180, 182, 268
community college; *see* postsecondary education
Community of Inquiry (COI) 28, 47, 65, 69, 94, *95*, 101, 239, 240, 242, 247, 259
comprehensible input 145, 146, 148, 150, 153, 167, 219, 224
Computer-Assisted Language Instruction Consortium (CALICO) 2, 62, 203–6
Computer-Assisted Language Learning (CALL) 2, 10, 30
Computer Mediated Communication (CMC) 205
connectivism 12, 14
Conrad, R. M. 28, 49, 226, **227**, 228 230–40, 246, 257, 259; *see also* Boettcher, J.
constructionism 12, 14
constructivism 12, 14, 82
content-based: instruction (CBI) 193–94, 209; language instruction 209; language teaching with technology (CoBaLTT) 192–93
content frame; *see* map
conversation: partners 166, 169, 241; platform(s) 166, 220, 221, 248; exchange; *see* virtual exchange
core practices 6, 63, 75, 134, 141–43, 159, 177
corrective feedback 143, 171, 174
Council of Europe (COE) 28, 33, 77, 140, 152, 237
curation 46, *47*, 121, 170, 177
Curtis, W. 215, 216, 257
customized learning 232

D2L Brightspace; *see* learning management system
data analytics; *see* analytics
Davin, K. 253, 254
design: backward 4, 12, 40–3, 52, 65, 89, 92, 116, 143, 144, 202, 233, 251, 256; instructional 9, 10, 11, 13, 21, 28, 50, 52, 57, 144, 186, 187, 226, 238, 268, 273

telecollaboration; *see* virtual exchange
teletandem; *see* virtual exchange
testing: alpha 12, 61, 79, 223, 224; beta 12, 61, 123, 223, 224
textbooks 114, 136, 139, 144, 156, 159, 176, 180, 199, 231, 232, 272; *see also* publisher materials
Today's Front Pages 168, 169
Troyan, F. J. 252, 253, 258
tutoring: as learning service 49, 110, 228; as support service 27, 222, 272

understanding by design (UbD) 41, 66
universal design for learning (UDL) 24, 27, 54, 56, 60, 68, 75, 76, 105, 121, 124
university; *see* postsecondary education
usability 24, 49, 58, 60, 65, 78, 83, 110, 123

VanPatten, B. 159–60, 177, 248 , 257
video 2, 4, 7, 26, 36, 37, 44, 46, 48–50, 52, 55, 57, 59, 76, 80, 82, 85, 86, 88, 91, 95, 95, 96, 102, 105, 106, 110–19, 127, 135, 137, 138, 139, 144, 148–51, 162–66, 169, 176, 178, 199, 200, 220, 221, 225, 229, 231, 232, 236, 240, 241, 249, 252, 253
virtual exchange/telecollaboration/teletandem/ t 31, 49, 103, 108, 110, 128, 177, 194, 195, 209
virtual worlds 122, 205, 240, 242, 243, 265, 272

vocabulary as content 43, 44, 51, 99, 103, 106, 115, 126, 135, 137, 144, 145, 146, 147, 148, 168, 172, 173, 230, 248, 249, 250, 251, 253, 255
voice over internet protocol; *see* VoIP
VoIP **36**, 104

washback effect 248, 255, 256, 257
Web Content Accessibility Guidelines (WCAG) 25, 59, 124
webinar 5, 6, 98, 105, 113, 187, 189, 204, 206, 269
webquest 194, 195
Western Interstate Commission for Higher Education (WICHE) 22
whiteboard 104, 105, 174
WIDA 28, 33, 38, 53, 54, 124, 152, 154, 155, 157, 173, 175, 232, 233, 251; *see also* Can-Do
Wiggins, G. 10, 41, 66, 249
wiki 82, 107, 110, 121, 170, 194, 245
wireframe 22, 234
World-Class Instructional Design and Assessment Consortium, *see* WIDA
writing: as skill 27, 33, 38, 46, 57, 59, 61, 79, 101, 102, 107, 118, 119, 128, 131, 132, 153, 155, 160, 161, 166, 173, 182, 217, 220, 223, 250, 251, 254, 256; social 101, 102; *see also* mode of communication

Zimmerman, T. D. 104, 244, 245